DISMISSING
GOD

Other books by D. Bruce Lockerbie

Billy Sunday
Patriarchs and Prophets
The Macmillan English Series: Books 10 and 12
Success in Writing: Book 5
Major American Authors (general editor)
The Way They Should Go
Purposeful Writing
The Liberating Word: Art and the Mystery of the Gospel
Education of Missionaries' Children
The Apostles' Creed
The Cosmic Center
A Man under Orders
Who Educates Your Child?
Asking Questions: A Classroom Model for Teaching the Bible
The Timeless Moment: Creativity and the Christian Faith
Fatherlove: Learning to Give the Best You've Got
In Peril on the Sea
Thinking and Acting like a Christian
Take Heart (with coauthor Lory Lockerbie)
College: Getting In and Staying In (with coauthor Donald R. Fonseca)
A Passion for Learning: A History of Christian Thought on Education
From Candy Sales to Committed Donors: A Guide to Financing Christian Schools

DISMISSING GOD

Modern Writers' Struggle against Religion

D. Bruce Lockerbie

Baker Books

A Division of Baker Book House Co
Grand Rapids, Michigan 49516

© 1998 by D. Bruce Lockerbie

Published by Baker Books
a division of Baker Book House Company
P.O. Box 6287, Grand Rapids, MI 49516-6287

Printed in the United States of America

Library of Congress Cataloging-in-Publication Data

Lockerbie, D. Bruce
    Dismissing God : modern writers' struggle against religion / D. Bruce Lockerbie.
      p. cm.
    Includes bibliographical references.
    ISBN 0-8010-5804-X (pbk.)
    1. American literature—History and criticism. 2. English literature—20th century—History and criticism. 3. Belief and doubt in literature. 4. Religion in literature. 5. Atheism in literature. 6. God in literature. I. Title.
PS169.B5L63 1998
810.9'382—dc21   98-17390

For current information about all releases from Baker Book House, visit our web site:
    http://www.bakerbooks.com

To deny the reality of god is to deny that there is any final sanction in moral life, a judgment which ultimately allots to each according to his or her deeds. To eliminate the awareness of such a god is to eliminate the police force from human life, the terror that each life will be called before one by whom it will be eternally assessed. . . . [Fear] lies at the origin of religious affirmation because one feels fragility before the terrors of nature or horror before death. But . . . fear lies at the origin of religious denial: atheism is an attempt to remove the threat of eternal judgment.

Michael J. Buckley, *At the Origins of Modern Atheism*

On no clear evidence theologians and philosophers declare God to be omniscient and omnicompetent. Plainly if there were such a God who really wished to reveal Himself to mankind, He would do so in a way that left no doubt.

Robert Gorham Davis, letter to the *New York Times*

Those—dying then,
Knew where they went—
They went to God's Right Hand—
That Hand is amputated now
And God cannot be found—

The abdication of Belief
Makes the Behavior small—
Better an ignis fatuus
Than no illume at all—

Emily Dickinson

For
Vernon C. Grounds
and in memory of Stanley M. Wiersma

Contents

Preface

This book has had a long gestation, spanning more than two decades from conception in its earliest idea to birth by publication.

In 1976, Dr. Vernon C. Grounds, then president of the Conservative Baptist Theological Seminary, Denver, Colorado, invited me to deliver the annual Lectures on Christian Life and Thought. I had been writing articles about literature and reviews of modern fiction for some years; recently one of my books had been published titled *The Liberating Word: Art and the Mystery of the Gospel.* It represented my first serious attempt at developing an aesthetic theory from a Christian perspective.

While puzzling over an appropriate topic for my lectures, a review of *The Liberating Word* came to my attention. Written by Stanley M. Wiersma, poet and professor of English at Calvin College, the review pointed out one of the major weaknesses of my argument in *The Liberating Word:* that the artist is being used for divine purposes. Since all the writers I had selected, Wiersma noted, were themselves confessing Christians, quite naturally they wished their art to praise God. What, then—if anything—had I proved? What of artists who are not believers? Does their gift also come from God and return to him as praise? At the close of his review, Stan Wiersma (who would later become a treasured friend) issued a call for Christian readers of literature and would-be critics to take up a more compelling task, in attempting to grasp the work of writers who do not acknowledge that Jesus of Nazareth is the Word Incarnate—the liberating Word!

Upon reading that challenge, I knew in an instant the topic for my lectures. Now to that same call this book belatedly responds.

Acknowledgments —————

As already indicated, parts of this book began as the 1976 Lectures on Christian Life and Thought, presented at Conservative Baptist Theological Seminary, Denver, Colorado. I thank my friend and mentor, Dr. Vernon C. Grounds, for sponsoring that early effort.

Those and other parts of this book have been the basis for lectures sponsored by the Thomas F. Staley Foundation and delivered at Cornell University, Bennington College, the University of North Carolina at Chapel Hill, Regent College, Wheaton College, Yale University, Cambridge University, and Southern Methodist University.

I am grateful to the many members of these lecture audiences whose probing and thoughtful questions have helped me to rethink and recast my own views before presenting this book to its readers.

Special thanks to Dan Van't Kerkhof formerly of Baker Book House, whose encouragement brought this book to fulfillment.

As on many previous occasions, Phyllis Akins, head of the reference department, Emma Clark Memorial Library, Setauket, New York, gave willingly of her professional time and personal encouragement to help me track down elusive quotations. My daughter Dr. Ellyn Lockerbie Grosh of Wheaton College, and her husband, Dr. Ronald M. Grosh, my colleague in PAIDEIA, Inc., also persevered in the documentation process. To them, my grateful thanks.

And to my wife, Lory, my best friend and critic, who has been with me since the beginning.

Introduction ─────────────

This book presumes the significance of two questions:

1. Why do some human beings—literary artists in particular—feel compelled to challenge belief in the existence of God with such hostility? Why are they so vexed by someone else's choice to place faith in Christianity or in some other religion, as if such a decision were an act of personal effrontery?

2. What can a believing reader—someone for whom such a threat to religious faith is both blasphemous and futile—gain from reading the work of authors who have challenged God for the heavyweight championship of the universe?

"Credo, quia impossibile," said the third-century Christian church father Tertullian. "I believe because it is impossible." For Tertullian, the very immensity of life's most important issues compels faith. Belief in God, in Christ, in the authority of the Bible as Holy Scripture—this is the X-factor that, for Tertullian and others able to believe, resolves the otherwise inscrutable.

But not for everyone. Seventeen centuries after Tertullian, George Bernard Shaw wrote, "It is not disbelief that is dangerous to our society; it is belief."[1] For Shaw, religious belief of any sort is itself villainous, the fuel that ignites passions of religious intolerance and bigotry. His view is supported by a 1992 letter to the editor of the *New York Times,* whose writer comments on the case of novelist Salman Rushdie and the death sentence imposed upon him by Ayatollah Khomeini:

Those in Teheran who condemned Salman Rushdie have been tagged as fanatics, zealots, barbarians. Not so. They are believers, and wherever you find a people who believe, truly believe, you will find a high body count.

Editorial writers on right and left call for a return to religious values. Well, Iran has returned to religious values: intolerance, cruelty, discrimination, hatred, torture, murder, and mayhem. I thank God no one takes religion seriously in America—a land where preachers ride roller coasters, rabbis sleep late, and nuns fly.[2]

The letter quoted above could never have appeared in any newspaper approved for publication by a totalitarian government, whether in Baghdad in 1992 or in Salem in 1692 or Barcelona in 1492; indeed, at one time, it could not have appeared in many alleged modern democracies either. For all their claims of religious tolerance, only a few states, historically, have chosen to permit their citizens the dignity of dissent, an honorable status as both citizens and nonbelievers. Until the latter decades of the twentieth century, most states in the West have preferred to enter into a sham that professes the orthodox purity of its citizens' religious profession in place of an amiable agnosticism or an acceptable atheism that existed in reality.

Of course, the letter writer engages in hyperbole. Contrary to his assertion and the biased media who insist on discrediting legitimate practitioners of religious expression by likening them to fraudulent faith healers, notorious womanizers, pious hucksters, and political opportunists, even in secular America many people seem to take their religion seriously. For instance, to date no American politician—except for Abraham Lincoln—has ever won high office by campaigning as other than a practicing churchman of some sort.

But even so, the letter writer's point should not be lost in his exaggerated rhetoric: Presumably, some correlation between political liberty and religious freedom is axiomatic for most enlightened Westerners. In the modern secular age, freedom of religion also means freedom from religion, if so preferred. Divergent opinions about the validity of belief or unbelief are a treasured characteristic of the most openly democratic and secularized societies, commonly missing from totalitarian governments and ultra-fundamentalist cultures.

Ironically, among the classic explanations for the growth of popular unbelief in Western civilization—in spite of Europe's state churches, England's establishmentarianism, and the Massachusetts Bay Colony's imposed piety—have been the excesses of Torquemada and the Inquisition, the bloodletting between Anglicans and Presbyterians, the witch trials of a paranoid New England theocracy. As a direct result of religious extremism throughout the West, we have witnessed what Malcolm Muggeridge and others call "the end of Christendom." Apostasy has overtaken faith, unbelief has supplanted belief, nonbelievers have overwhelmed believers.

In short, too much religion leads irrevocably to irreligion, a secular reaction against orthodoxy and compulsory or uniformly institutionalized public worship, in time, a revolt against any expression of religious faith, however private. Belief and unbelief in uneasy coexistence are still the expected norm for civilized behavior, which explains why the rules of etiquette continue to proscribe any serious discussion of religion during dinner. Between believers and nonbelievers, a delicate openmindedness—if not to orthodox belief as such, at least to the New Age's spiritual potential—balances itself against the weight of countervaling popular opinion. But that opposition to religious faith increases, especially within the intellectual and political spheres where it has become chic to scoff at "true believers."

In the five hundred years of European influence on this continent, belief has steadily given way to conventional skepticism or outright denial. "I used to consider myself a believer," a brilliant college-preparatory student bound for a selective women's college told me recently.

"Why used to?" I inquired.

"It wasn't intellectually respectable anymore to be a believer," she replied. "There were just too many things I couldn't explain."

The inexplicable—why bad things happen to good people—has always troubled thoughtful persons, as has its converse enigma, why good things happen to bad people! A believer like David the psalmist can resort to divine wisdom and content himself with the maxim, "Do not fret because of evil men or be envious of those who do wrong" (Ps. 37:1). But to the unconvinced—perhaps the person obsessed by the seeming disparity between God's justice and human standards of fairness—a simple refusal to believe,

13

whether you call it unbelief or skepticism or agnosticism, is letting God off too easily.

Beyond the range of unbelief lies the desert of disbelief, comprising a landscape of broken monuments: Imagine Chartres and Notre Dame in ruins, St. John the Divine and the First Baptist Church and Temple Emmanuel desolate; the Torah and the New Testament in shreds; Bach's B Minor Mass and Handel's *Messiah* off-key. Their fallen state designates not merely the collapse of institutionalized Judeo-Christian religion and conventional civil piety through abandonment and disuse but a collapse caused by militant aggression against belief by disbelievers. But the final stage of secularism is not unbelief; not even a mobilized assault on faith called disbelief; it is a frozen tundra in the landscape of the soul in which not even the possibility of active opposition to faith survives.

What brought about the shift from Tertullian to George Bernard Shaw? Why has belief fallen into such disrepair? Why is belief so unpopular in modern culture, so derided by alleged intellectuals on university campuses and by radio and television talk show hosts? More to the point, what is it about belief that so enrages those who choose not to believe? What stirs the animus of certain nonbelievers to become disbelievers, eager to contend against those who profess what the disbeliever denies? What motivates a Ted Turner to forsake his teenage piety and call the Christianity of his youth "a religion for losers"? Why do artists, in particular, seem to need to adopt the stance of a bantam bully picking a fight with an oversized and reluctant deity—a God who would rather embrace than retaliate?

And, finally, what if any value can the believer find in the art of the unbeliever, the nonbeliever, the disbeliever? Does the same "true light that gives light to every man" (John 1:9) shine also in the darkness of disbelief? Or is its potential for enlightened awareness that much greater because denial excludes the validity of any prepackaged answer to life's most pressing issues? Does the real value to a believer, in reading the work of an unbeliever, result from the fact that denial reduces truth to its most absurdly elemental point of beginning—the questions who? and why?—and builds from there?

14

This book makes no claim to answer fully any of these questions. It seeks only to address the fact that, while some writers—Dante, Shakespeare, Milton, Browning, and in our era T. S. Eliot, Graham Greene, Shusako Endo, John Updike—have not been timid about writing from a Christian world-and-life view, other writers have forsaken belief altogether and chosen the vacuum of unbelief; still others, more aggressively, seem obsessed by a warring spirit against belief that compels them to challenge God's supremacy. In a manner of speaking, they seem to have wished to battle God on equal terms. So Emily Dickinson describes an anonymous pugilist who, having worked his way through a roster of lesser opponents,

> then, unjaded, challenged God
> In presence of the Throne.

Alfred Kazin once told me that he had found T. S. Eliot to be a far more interesting writer before Eliot claimed a Christian conversion. "After that," said Kazin, "Eliot knew all the answers." The authors this book examines are, at least, interesting precisely because they have rejected whatever conventional catechism, with its prescribed answers, they previously may have known. In most cases, they have chosen also to abandon even the very questions a believer takes for granted.

As a result, they give a searching perspective on what it means to be—in the words of St. Paul—"without hope and without God" (Eph. 2:12).

My purpose throughout this book, however, is not to judge by approbation or condemnation those writers who, to quote Lawrance Thompson, are engaged in a "quarrel with God." Rather, I choose to look closely at the nature of their quarrel, the way in which it is conducted in the life and art of the writer, and—insofar as may be possible—to discern its outcome.

To accomplish this task genuinely and fairly requires careful reading of a writer's work in its own context. Naturally, in a book such as this, we are able to cite only excerpts; the reader does well, therefore, to keep an open mind until one has reviewed a subject's own text for what it says of itself and its author.

The Ebb Tide of Faith

Matthew Arnold

One evening a few summers ago, my wife and I stayed overnight at the White Cliffs Hotel in Dover, England. We were to take the ferry the next morning across the Channel to Calais. From the window of our hotel room, we could gaze out on Dover Harbor, the sun setting and full moon rising upon the Channel.

Years before, as a schoolboy in Canada, I had sung for the visiting Queen Wilhelmina of the Netherlands "There'll Be Bluebirds over the White Cliffs of Dover." This evening, there were no bluebirds, only gulls, but the imposing chalk cliffs were in full display. Above them loomed the fortress that first repelled an attack by Julius Caesar in 55 B.C. A few feet from our hotel door, across the promenade, stood a monument commemorating the more recent heroism of Dover's citizens in successfully withstanding Nazi bombardment from the French beachhead some eighteen miles across the Channel.

A perfect evening for nostalgia and romance. I took my wife by the hand and in a moment of unconscionable sentimentality, if not a little showmanship, began spouting lines first required for memorization by a high school English teacher—"Dover Beach," of course, by Matthew Arnold:

> The sea is calm tonight,
> The tide is full, the moon lies fair
> Upon the straits;—on the French coast the light
> Gleams and is gone; the cliffs of England stand
> Glimmering and vast, out in the tranquil bay.
> Come to the window, sweet is the night-air!

The poem is justly famous in the catalogue of English poetry. Its sonorities echo onomatopoetically the scene it describes. The gravity of its language; its imitation of the varying waves upon the pebbled beach by means of short lines interspersed by longer and by its subtle and irregular rhyming: All this and more about its rhetoric has given this poem durability in speaking to its generations of readers.

But on that summer evening, I suddenly found myself unwilling to go on with Arnold's poem. It wasn't just that memory might have failed at a critical line; rather, the tone of the poem—its melancholy resignation that Arnold found so fitting to the spiritual malaise of his time—seemed unsuitable to my present mood. Not just because I was on holiday with my own loved one and about to embark on a European grand tour; no, it was more than any emotional incongruity that made me leave off reciting Arnold's "Dover Beach." Instead, it was the fact that I could not accept as true the reasons given for pessimism and despair by the speaker in this poem.

For, when carefully read, the dramatic speaker in "Dover Beach" is offering more than a pleasing rhythmic configuration of language, more than emotion recollected in tranquility. In transcending whatever immediate circumstances prompted this poem, Arnold has given voice to a speaker through whom he offers a highly serious, unquestionably religious, commentary on the human condition. But for all my admiration of the poem as art, I found its analysis of the human predicament and its facile solution alien to my own profession of Christian belief in the lordship of Jesus Christ. But read for yourself:

> The sea is calm tonight,
> The tide is full, the moon lies fair

Upon the straits;—on the French coast the light
Gleams and is gone; the cliffs of England stand,
Glimmering and vast, out in the tranquil bay.
Come to the window, sweet is the night-air!

Only, from the long line of spray
Where the sea meets the moon-blanch'd land,
Listen! you hear the grating roar
Of pebbles which the waves draw back, and fling,
At their return, up the high strand,
Begin, and cease, and then again begin,
With tremulous cadence slow, and bring
The eternal note of sadness in.

Sophocles long ago
Heard it on the Aegean, and it brought
Into his mind the turbid ebb and flow
Of human misery; we
Find also in the sound a thought,
Hearing it by this distant northern sea.

The Sea of Faith
Was once, too, at the full, and round earth's shore
Lay like the folds of a bright girdle furl'd.
But now I only hear
Its melancholy, long, withdrawing roar,
Retreating, to the breath
Of the night-wind, down the vast edges drear
And naked shingles of the world.

Ah, love, let us be true
To one another! for the world, which seems
To lie before us like a land of dreams,
So various, so beautiful, so new,
Hath really neither joy, nor love, nor light,
Nor certitude, nor peace, nor help for pain;
And we are here as on a darkling plain
Swept with confused alarms of struggle and flight,
Where ignorant armies clash by night.[1]

Surely this is a most affecting poem. As an artifice of language, it commands our highest respect for its power to communicate some of the human heart's deepest yearnings. Precisely because these yearnings are recognizably of ultimate concern, they are religious in nature; so their expression in "Dover Beach" must be understood for its religious content, for its serious attention to matters of the spirit.

But even such serious attentiveness may not be enough. T. S. Eliot reminds us, in an essay called "Religion and Literature," that "incumbent upon all Christians is the duty of maintaining consciously certain standards and criteria of criticism over and above those applied by the rest of the world."[2] Rhetorical analysis, literary critique, aesthetic comparison, and moral evaluation are only the beginning; a person of Christian convictions—someone who believes in the efficacy of both words and the Word made flesh—must read further and deeper into a text, using the criteria to which Eliot, among others, refers.

So, in speaking of "a person of Christian convictions," I mean to indicate someone who believes that truth exists absolutely and resides fully in the character of almighty God. To the extent that human beings can perceive such truth, it is perceived only by faith and is revealed both in the person of Jesus of Nazareth and in Holy Scripture, which for orthodox Christians means the canon of the Bible. A Christian also holds that truth conforms with and never contradicts these revelations, which speak of the sovereignty of God in creation; a fallen universe enslaved by sin; redemption provided through a substitutionary atonement achieved by the sinless incarnation, death, burial, and resurrection of Jesus Christ; thereafter, by the personal sanctification of the Holy Spirit's working through the individual believers who constitute the church. From such revelation the Christian believer derives an understanding of human responsibility to God and to our neighbors; an understanding of the acts of God in history, leading to the consummation of this epoch in God's own appointed time; an understanding of the promise and hope of God's everlasting care and concern for a universe lovingly won back to himself.

No Christian literary critic, no careful reader—certainly not Eliot—insists that failure to achieve full marks by these criteria automatically disqualifies a poet or other literary artist from having any value for the Christian reader. A poem should be a poem, not a tract. Art need not be preachy to be of religious significance; indeed, what is preachy—no matter its pious intent—is more often than not less than art. But every poem, every work of art—indeed, every piece of commercial advertising, every tidbit of pop-psych advice on a radio call-in show, every casual and offhanded remark we utter—indicates an attitude toward life, a posture toward the issues that matter most. This attitude or posture can be expressed as one's moral point of view. The Germans have a fancy term for it: They call it *weltanschauung,* meaning "world-and-life view." It is the vantage we adopt from which to see what Emile Cailliet called "the landscape of reality." Our worldview is the platform on which we choose to stand and from which we look out and see the world.

We talk about worldviews informally whenever we compare life to a voyage or a game or a race or a rat race. If life is a voyage, am I the captain of my ship or merely one of the hands on deck taking orders? If life is a voyage, am I sailing on tranquil seas or caught in the middle of a hurricane and threatened with imminent disaster? What is my prevailing worldview? For instance, the Nobel Prize–winning biologist Jacques Monod holds a worldview, declaring that the only option for human beings is to accept "the fundamental postulate that there is no plan, there is no intention to the universe." According to Monod, any sensible person will recognize that "like a gypsy, he lives on the boundary of an alien world. A world that is deaf to his music, just as indifferent to his hopes as it is to his suffering or his crimes."[3]

[The Christian believer also has a worldview—metaphorically speaking, a particular place to stand. The Christian takes that stand at the foot of the cross and at the door of the empty tomb. Paradoxically, both views are necessary to a Christian worldview if it is to be true. From the cross the Christian sees the world with all its values inverted, with vice conquering virtue, with chaos winning out—or so it seems. From the door of the empty tomb, all is changed. Death has been swallowed up in victory! The risen Lord reigns! So, the world-and-life view of the Christian is neither victimized nor pessimistic nor neutral nor even optimistic; the Christian world-and-life view is *hopeful,* focused on hope because of the redemption and resurrection of Jesus Christ.

Now, the Christian reader does not expect the nonbeliever to stand on that same platform and see the world from that same vantage. But by setting standards for the representation of truth, based on its revelation in Jesus Christ and the Scriptures, a believing Christian reader is able to appreciate and respect, on its own terms, the work of those who, Eliot tells us, either "have no belief in a supernatural order" or are even ignorant of the fact that there are still people in the world so "backward" or so "eccentric" as to continue to believe. In fact, Eliot goes on, the Christian reader needs to remain "in a position to extract from [the work of an unbeliever] what good it has to offer us."[4]

What, then, of Matthew Arnold's world-and-life view? What does a thoughtful reading of "Dover Beach" say to believer and unbeliever alike?

The poem describes the human condition, as the speaker views it, from the vantage point of two metaphors: the natural movement of the ocean's tide ("the turbid ebb and flow / Of human misery") and a chaotic battlefield ("a darkling plain / Swept with confused alarms of struggle and flight"). The poem, first, portrays helpless men and women caught by nature's inexorabilities, by the rise and fall of human circumstance, and always subject to the fatalistic expectations of disaster. The fundamental metaphor of this poem—simply put—is that of the withdrawing tide that leaves one high and dry, cut off from the ocean's navigable depths, and therefore incapable of maneuvering one's life to avoid its disastrous shoals.

This is a masterly figure by which to express the poet's view of the world in 1867, when "Dover Beach" was published, but it is not his only description. He changes, in the final quatrain, from a beach at low tide to "a darkling plain" where innocent lovers find themselves embroiled in the charge, retreat, and general confusion of "ignorant armies." This too is a striking image by which to represent the poet's world-and-life view.

But what determines a view of life so somber, so full of "the eternal note of sadness"? Perhaps by looking briefly at the times in which the poem was written, the intellectual and spiritual milieu out of which it speaks, and at the man who wrote it, we may obtain clues to help us answer that question.

In 1867, Matthew Arnold (1822–1888) was in the prime of his extremely active and diverse public life. At age forty-five, he had rooted himself in the national consciousness as the consummate English man of letters. Born into one of the most deservingly respected homes, educated at Winchester and Rugby schools and at Baliol College, Oxford, Matthew Arnold's most lasting teacher had been his own father, Thomas Arnold. That towering personage, almost solely by the force of his character, had revolutionized English schooling in his years as headmaster at Rugby. Through the educational reforms initiated there and eventually adopted by other schools, Thomas Arnold made possible for succeeding generations of schoolboys the opportunity of learning to become gentlemen through the civilizing graces of example, peer pressure, and strong doses of Christian humanism. One has only to read his son's elegy, "Rugby Chapel," published in this same year of 1867, to find how deeply implanted in the poet's mind was the heroic memory of Thomas Arnold, educator and father. In fact, Matthew Arnold carried forward and extended his father's vocation, serving for thirty-five years as school inspector and advocating compulsory and free schooling for the masses.

From his father, Matthew Arnold had also learned to love classical literature; from this love developed a sacramental esteem for art. During the decade he served as professor of poetry at Oxford, Arnold laid down in his lectures the maxims for developing a moral imagination; he imposed upon a generally receptive generation of students those aesthetic criteria that were to make him renowned. He drew heavily upon the philosophies of Epictetus and Marcus Aurelius among the ancients; among his contemporaries, Wordsworth and Emerson, whose death in 1882 prevented by a few months Arnold's meeting him on a visit to America the following year.

Arnold declared culture to be "the study of perfection." For him, poetry was "the criticism of life." His social ideal was expressed as "sweetness and light," personified in "the sweet reasonableness of Jesus."[5] In an age of developing theological liberalism, the voice of Arnold may have ameliorated some of the harsher, less tactful pronouncements of the romantic critics, who disparaged what Arnold most admired: the literary power and influence of the English Bible upon English society.

Yet for all his airy views of "sweetness and light," Matthew Arnold was far from being a cloistered pedant. He knew that the social and technological order were changing before his eyes. Since 1851, he had served as inspector of schools—like William Butler Yeats, in Ireland, some threescore and ten years later. His post carried him throughout the British Isles, to France, Switzerland, Holland, and Germany. Although he was the son of a great public school headmaster—the term *public school* meaning those institutions to which aristocratic and other families of privilege now sent their sons, instead of educating them exclusively at home—Arnold was no educational snob. He saw the need for and advocated the development of state schools, if the middle and working class (which Arnold nonetheless called, respectively, "the Philistines" and "the Populace") were to contribute to a modern democracy.

But most of all, by 1867 Arnold had foreseen the effects upon society of industrialism and so-called scientific progress. He knew that without education in the humanities modern society would fall prey to scientism rampant. In July 1867, he published an essay called "Culture and Its Enemies," later expanded into a book whose title defines the antagonists: culture and anarchy.

The year before had witnessed a unifying of the Old World with the New in the laying of the transatlantic cable. The Paris Exposition of 1867, with its astonishing feats of architecture by Alexandre Gustave Eiffel and others, as well as labor-saving machinery, spelled out the prospects of as-yet undreamed technologies. Socially, the year 1867 also marked the passage of the Reform Act, conferring upon much of England's urban working-class the right to vote. As if in concord with that legislative landmark, the same year also spawned the publication of a work assiduously and passionately written in the reading room of the British Library: *Das Kapital* by Karl Marx.

In this same astonishing year of 1867, Matthew Arnold published his final volume of poems, including "Dover Beach." Its contemporaneity with the events just enumerated, however, and its pervading tone of melancholy were no accident. The culminating cause for Arnold's mood may be found in the effect of two other books published in 1859 and 1863, respectively: Charles Darwin's *Origin of Species* and its celebrated defense, *Man's Place in Nature*, by Thomas Henry Huxley.

To Arnold's questioning mind, the data presented and the argument in its support convinced him that no reasonable person could take a position opposed to Darwin's theory of natural selection. He appears to have revered Darwin, calling him on one occasion "sagacious and admirable." While Arnold may have objected to the stridency with which Huxley advocated Darwin's thought, in most respects Arnold appears willing to concede the argument for an evolutionary origin of life to the man known as "Darwin's bulldog."

Certainly Arnold admitted that conceptions of the universe fatal to the notions held by our forefathers have been forced upon us by physical science. Moreover, in Huxley's intractable opposition to orthodox Christianity—the Christian doctrines of God's creation and redemption of humanity through Jesus Christ—Arnold could find little with which to quarrel. So far as Arnold was concerned, a weakling church had left itself vulnerable to attack because religion—whether the established church or its nonconformist dissenters—had neglected the appeal to reason. So Arnold decried his realization that "our religion has materialized itself in the fact, in the supposed fact; it has attached its emotion to the fact, and now the fact is failing it."[6] As a result, Arnold perceived that there remained "not a creed which is not shaken, not an accredited dogma which is not shown to be questionable, not a received tradition which does not threaten to dissolve."[7]

In so saying, Arnold was reflecting, of course, the damaging influence of theological liberalism upon simple belief whose final recourse is "the Bible tells me so." Throughout the latter nineteenth century, liberalism flourished, spurred on by skeptics, agnostics, and atheists who would make their names as demolition experts of creed, dogma, and received tradition. Did Arnold know at first hand the writings of Friederich Schleiermacher, Albrecht Ritschl, Wilhelm Herrmann, and Adolf Harnack? Perhaps by reputation, if not by reading. Arnold did know the second-century pagan critic Celsus and approved his charge that Christianity from its inception had suffered from "a want of intellectual seriousness." In his preface to *God and the Bible*, Arnold takes up the argument thus:

> The first Christians misunderstood Jesus and had the multitude's appetite for miracles, the multitude's inexact observation and boundless credulity. They it was who supplied the data which Christian theology took from them without question, and has ever since confidently built upon. . . . Many theologians have been very able men, and their reasonings and deductions have been very close and subtle. Still they have always had the defect of going seriously upon data produced and admitted with a want of intellectual seriousness.[8]

It soon becomes apparent that Matthew Arnold was perfectly eligible for membership in the Metaphysical Society, before which audience Thomas Huxley coined the word *agnosticism*. Huxley's own explanation of his word declares that "it is wrong for a man to say that he is certain of the objective truth of any proposition unless he can produce evidence which logically justifies that certainty."[9] To Huxley, God and proof of his existence remain unknowable; and whatever is known—that is, the natural world of sense around us—Huxley contended, issues its own denials of supernaturalism, of miracles, or of revelation to the agnostic mind. Here too, Arnold took his stand with Huxley in rejecting orthodox Christianity on grounds that Christianity relies upon miracles for its validity. A long line of rationalist, empiricist, and materialist thinkers joins Thomas Huxley and Matthew Arnold in their rejection; for each and all claiming agnosticism, the supernatural element of faith is folly.

Yet on one point Arnold opposed Huxley almost to the death. For in Huxley he saw the attempt of dogmatic scientism to expunge from schools and universities the study of humane letters. According to Arnold's systematics, literature was sanctified scripture, the arts a holy temple. From them—from literature, in particular—society obtained those healing powers necessary for harmony and perfection: what Arnold called "the power of conduct, the power of intellect and knowledge, the power of beauty, and the power of social life and manners."[10] These to Arnold were the spiritual graces inherent in the study of *belles lettres.*

In Arnold's view, therefore, Huxley was guilty of little less than blasphemy when he announced that "for the purpose of attaining real culture, an exclusively scientific education is at least as effectual as an exclusively literary education."[11] Already Arnold could warn that "faith in machinery is . . . our besetting danger."[12] He looked with dismay upon

> this strange disease of modern life,
> With its sick hurry, its divided aims.[13]

Far from yielding the day to Huxley and the new scientism he represented, Arnold believed that

> the majority of men will always require humane letters; and so much the more, as they have the more and the greater results of science to relate to the need in man for conduct, and to the need in him for beauty.[14]

"Conduct" and "beauty"—the ideals whereby perfection might be attained—and with perfection, culture, Arnold's version of heaven. But where was one to find the model for ideal conduct and ideal beauty? In the Bible, of course! Arnold could more easily dispense with Homer or Shakespeare than with the English Bible; he was scathingly critical of those who lacked the benefits of biblical knowledge. He considered Roman Catholics to be biblically illiterate, "strangers, or very nearly so, to the Bible." He chided "liberals, who think that religion in general is an obstacle to progress," while themselves remaining "ignorant of the virtue there is in knowing one's Bible."[15]

For in the Bible alone Arnold found his ideal fulfilled: Jesus Christ, the nonpareil. He is "the true greatness of Christianity."

On this theme, Arnold sounds much like the New England evangelist Dwight L. Moody, whose unschooled style he so despised:

> Jesus Christ came to reveal what righteousness really is. . . . Nothing will do except righteousness; and no other conception of righteousness will do, except Jesus Christ's conception of it:—his method and his secret.[16]

How is one to reconcile Arnold's seemingly contradictory stance, clinging to the Bible's description of Jesus of Nazareth while at the same time rejecting the Bible's revelation of his divine authority as Lord? To those acquainted with the writings of liberal theologians or Marxist philosophers, these anomalies begin to sound familiar. One can have it both ways, if one is sufficiently agile of mind. No matter how incompatible Arnold's statements about the doctrines of orthodox Christianity may seem with his praise for the lyricism of the Bible and the exemplary person of Jesus Christ, their resolution is possible. By redefining the terms to suit his prejudices, by excusing a lapse in rationality for emotional overcharge, or by attributing to an ancient writer a less-sophisticated comprehension of natural phenomena, the writer can nonetheless praise the original motives. So, for instance, Ernest Renan, the French apologist for an utterly demythologized Jesus, dismisses the New Testament's resurrection narratives by patronizingly and chauvinistically discrediting the Gospel writers' record of devout women's eyewitness accounts: "Divine power of love! Sacred moments in which the passion of one possessed gave to the world a resuscitated God!"

Caught between admiration for the ideal and disparagement of its claims to historical authenticity, Arnold hopes to extricate himself from an otherwise embarrassing succession of fallacies in reasoning. For a believer like T. S. Eliot, the posture adopted by Arnold and others seems nothing short of parasitical, praising the Bible as literature without also honoring its claim to be the Word of God; Eliot regarded them as "merely admiring it as a monument over the grave of Christianity."[17]

Here, then, we have Matthew Arnold, whom Jacques Barzun calls "the reluctant agnostic," clinging to a memory called Christianity from which he has eviscerated any substantive reality and obliterated its authority as truth. His rationale is summed up in these words from the preface to *God and the Bible:* "Two things about the Christian religion must surely be clear to anybody with eyes in his head. One is, that men cannot do without it; the other, that they cannot do with it, as it is."[18]

In "Dover Beach," perhaps, we have the example of someone's trying to have Christianity under both circumstances at once.

The poem begins with a serenity typical of a nineteenth-century pastorale: the romance of moonlight glimmering upon a bay at full or flood tide; the majesty of nature's handiwork; enduring emblems of national stability and independence; the presence of a loved one with whom to share the scene. Like the sweetness of the night air is the mood of this first stanza: "calm," "fair," "tranquil," a setting utterly placid.

Yet the second stanza changes that mood suddenly, without warning, first intimating, then announcing the presence of a dispirited emotional awareness that anticipates the arrival of ebb tide. Acutely in tune with his natural environment, the poem's narrator hears and feels "the long line of spray," then "the grating roar / Of pebbles" being flung "up the high strand."

Anyone who has ventured upon Dover Beach for sunbathing or bodysurfing knows how harsh its stony surface feels; knows also the power of its undertow. Together, these discomforts and fears combine to alter the mood of the speaker. In this subjective moment, all tranquility seems to vanish as the sea bombards the land with its artillery of stones, cast up by the ebb and flow of the tide. The poem's narrator senses in that pulling tide a rhythm, a tone he identifies as "the eternal note of sadness," reminiscent of an inner spiritual despondency. At the same time, he feels the magnetic force of his classical training, compelling him to find in this physical experience a metaphysical truth to be intellectualized.

He turns in his mind to a classical allusion, to the tragedies of the Greek playwright Sophocles. Twenty years before, in a poem called "To a Friend," Matthew Arnold had named as supporters to his peace of mind Homer, Epictetus, and Sophocles, "who saw life steadily and saw it whole." Now he turns again to the last great dramatist of Greece's golden age, to Sophocles whose long life spanned the fifth century before Christ. Soldier and statesman, he was most acclaimed for his eighteen victories in the Festival of Dionysus, where his trilogy, *Oedipus the King, Oedipus at Colonus,* and *Antigone,* were first performed.

But Sophocles was more than a skilled playwright; he was also a prophet, much in the same tradition as his Hebrew contemporary Malachi—a voice in the secular wilderness, recalling his people to righteousness. Athens in the fifth century B.C. had all but abandoned even the most ceremonial trappings of belief in the mythological gods. In their place, Bernard Knox tells us in *Oedipus at Thebes,* veneration for the city-state itself and for mankind as its builder had replaced worship of the deities of Mount Olympus. Religious skepticism was rife, abetted by the sophists under Protagoras, who wrote in his treatise "On the Gods," "About the gods, I have no means of knowing whether they exist or do not exist or what their form may be." Not surprisingly, in his work "On Truth," Protagoras also declared, "Man is the measure of all things," a phrase whose contemporary equivalent may be read as a bumper sticker, "Man is God" or "Question Authority."

In sophisticated Athens, the search for a rational explanation of the universe apart from the gods had led, as always, from religious apostasy to political anarchy; for as Fyodor Dostoyevsky and Jean-Paul Sartre were to agree some twenty-five hundred years later, if God does not exist, everything is permitted. In the Athens of Sophocles' day, the only deity for whom any credence remained was Tyche or Chance, whom Bernard Knox calls "the principle of chaos" personifying "the absence of causal order in the universe."[19]

Therefore, when in the first play of the Oedipus trilogy Oedipus calls himself "the son of Chance," he has broken the hierarchies of social order; his resulting personal collapse foreshadows the impending doom of Thebes—and, by extension, of Athens also. So Professor Knox sees the fall of Oedipus and Jocasta as symbolic of

> the mental agonies of a generation which abandoned a traditional order of belief with a hopeful vision of an intelligible universe, only

to find itself at last facing an incomprehensible future with a desperation thinly disguised as recklessness.[20]

Surely the similarities to Arnold's era of scientific progress—and to our own age of secular assumptions—must be obvious. But the allusion made by Arnold's speaker is to one of Sophocles' other Theban plays, *Antigone*. Here the bullying Creon has just condemned Oedipus' daughter Antigone to death for her refusal to obey his commands. As she is being led away, the chorus sings:

> Fortunate is the man who has never tasted God's vengeance!
> Where once the anger of heaven has struck, that house is
>   shaken
> For ever: damnation rises behind each child
> Like a wave cresting out of the black northeast,
> When the long darkness under the sea roars up
> And bursts drowning death upon the wind whipped sand.[21]

Arnold's narrator recalls in Sophocles this fatalistic world-and-life view, of one standing upon a windswept beach and watching the thick, dark sea floor's being churned up, as if from the abyss, and hurled ashore by the force of cyclonic winds. In the playwright's analogy, these are the winds of doom sent by the wrath of Zeus to punish human disobedience. His power uproots and engulfs, overwhelming whoever is foolish enough to ignore his divine will or challenge divine authority.

So this image of the ebbing tide leaving behind its murky sediment to invade the land serves both Sophocles and Arnold as a metaphor for "the turbid ebb and flow / Of human misery." More than two millennia later, Arnold's speaker has transported the comparison beyond Sophocles' Aegean Sea, beyond even the literal English Channel, to stand upon the shores of what he calls "the Sea of Faith."

We cannot tell what moves Arnold's thought in this direction; again, the shift is abrupt, implied rather than coherent, almost as if the passion of the poem cannot stay for the niceties of formal transition and continuity. Looking out over the actual waters of the Channel—hearing the beginnings of its actual "grating roar" as the undertow drags with its backwash the fragments of the gravel beach—the speaker envisions another sea ebbing from its strength. Anyone who has lived by the sea knows the barren sight of a beach at low tide. We do not normally choose our vacation spot on the coast of Maine because of the splendors of low tide; we want to see Casco Bay in its fullness. We expect to hear the ocean's breakers pound, not lap like an inland lake. High tide means strength; low tide means the stench of sea weed, the rotting remains of flotsam and jetsam.

In three brief lines, Matthew Arnold reveals his reluctance toward unbelief, his hesitancy to let slip away the flood tide of faith. Can there be any mistaking the forlorn tone, "the eternal note of sadness," when he says,

> The Sea of Faith
> Was once, too, at the full, and round earth's shore
> Lay like the folds of a bright girdle furl'd.

For Arnold, the alternative to faith is clearly delineated in the gloomy language of the next five lines:

> But now I only hear
> Its melancholy, long, withdrawing roar,
> Retreating, to the breath
> Of the night-wind, down the vast edges drear
> And naked shingles of the world.

When faith no longer swells, the only condition remaining is the melancholy sight of an exposed shoal, the dreary emptiness of a life left high and dry. This wretchedness, he seems to be saying, is the logical outgrowth of alienation from God. And how is such alienation brought about? By outgrowing an infantile faith too simple to navigate the shallows of real life in a scientific, post-religious age.

For consolation, Arnold's narrator must turn to human fidelity. The natural scene will change; the spiritual climate and religious landscape will be reshaped by forces stronger than mere piety can resist, dictated by the winds of Chance, Doom, Fate, or whichever deity one chooses to regard. But to the romantic liberal, one dream remains constant. In spite of the moral vacuum in which he speaks—the chilling absence of joy, love, light, certitude, peace, and even human compassion—the enraptured idealist can still believe in that most mutable, most transient virtue—human fidelity. Even though caught, as it were, in the middle of a battlefield, between opposing armies who have long since lost interest in their cause and fight only out of animalistic blood lust, the idealistic narrator can still cry out,

> Ah, love, let us be true
> To one another!

It may be a noble intention, faithful to Arnold's own sincerity of mind and character, but does Arnold's own world-and-life view stand the test? Given the circumstances he describes—either of the principal analogies of ebbing tide or aimless armies will do—the poet offers no basis for hope in the efficacy of either love or faithfulness to one another. For is it not axiomatic that, when faith declines, when the rocks show their rough edges, mere idealism evaporates into cynicism?

Thus, it would seem, Arnold's poem ends in the futility of a romantic pipe dream, for love and truth are absolutes. Without the presence of light, certitude, and the joy they bring, any promise of love is vain; the likelihood of finding truth, negligible. Yet Matthew Arnold chooses, however reluctantly, to take his stand isolated on the shifting sands of life, choosing the low tide of skepticism, his narrator and his unknown beloved gripped by an undertow of desperation no meliorism may deny.

The Abdication of Belief

Emily Dickinson

Sometime in the early 1880s, a woman more than fifty years of age sat in her father's house in Amherst, Massachusetts, musing on death. She was well acquainted with its inevitability: No one could escape. Her father, much feared and much beloved, had died almost ten years before; more recently, her mother had also died. Within the past few months others had fallen, great and small. President James A. Garfield had been assassinated; the novelist George Eliot and the dominant figure in American letters, Ralph Waldo Emerson, both admired, had also died. Among her personal acquaintances she numbered one of whom she had written, "My closest earthly friend died in April."

All this dying and its grief had taken a toll upon her peace of mind, especially as she must have anticipated her own death, not more than four years hence. In particular, she considered the several attitudes with which her loved ones had faced death, the varying spiritual states in which they had died. From these thoughts Emily Dickinson framed a series of images in her mind and wrote this poem:

> Those—dying then,
> Knew where they went—

They went to God's Right Hand—
That Hand is amputated now
And God cannot be found—

The abdication of Belief
Makes the Behavior small—
Better an ignis fatuus
Than no illume at all—[1]

Dickinson's poem raises issues of faith and doubt, belief and disbelief, that require thoughtful review. Simple at a glance, this poem has levels of ambiguity that make it, like mercury, elusive. For instance, the tone of the speaker is anything but certain: Is the tone patronizing to the saints of old in their religious delusion, or does the speaker matter-of-factly declare that, unlike us, "Those—dying then" really knew their destination in the afterlife? What of that word *amputated*? Does it carry mere shock value, or is it intended to describe the violent manner in which God has been rejected? Is the reason that "God cannot be found" his being, by nature, a *deus absconditus,* a hidden God? Or has the fact of God's dismemberment driven him from view?

Whatever the answers to these questions, the contrast between faith *then* and the absence of faith *now* seems accounted for by the evocative word *abdication*. Almost any middle-aged or older English-speaking or European person—especially those with national attachment to the British monarchy—responds to the word *abdication* with passion. Its specific connotations, almost certainly, point to Edward VIII's dramatic decision, announced on December 11, 1936, to surrender the crown of Great Britain and the Empire in order to claim as his wife the woman he loved. His act of abdication—a king's giving up his rights as sovereign in favor of his beloved—represented then, as it still does today, the most romantic story of our time.

But beyond the personal story of the Duke and Duchess of Windsor lie larger implications. Inherent in the meaning of *abdication* may also be negative connotations of forsaken priorities and abandoned responsibilities. To return to the case in point, King Edward VIII made his choice between the demands of royal duty and his desire to marry Mrs. Wallis Warfield Simpson, a divorced American woman whom he could not raise to become his queen. Given his options, he could choose either fulfillment of national and imperial trust or the gratifying of personal pleasure. To satisfy the latter, it was necessary for the king to abdicate the former.

Here a semantic distinction becomes clear: One never abdicates from a lower position to assume a higher. The act of abdication always results in demotion in rank; but because abdication purports to be a willing renunciation of one's present rights and condition, it must be assumed that the person choosing to abdicate does so because he prefers the lower state to the higher.

Thus the abdication of Edward VIII seems to illustrate well Dickinson's comment on the consequences of demitting one's faith in God:

> The abdication of Belief
> Makes the Behavior small—

Just as a king reduces his realm to a suite in the Waldorf Towers and his titles to an honorific yet essentially meaningless duchy, so too with anyone who forsakes belief in God. He constricts his life, limits his range of experience, narrows his horizons. Say it any way you wish: Abdication means loss.

That Emily Dickinson should write so vividly about the consequences of abandoning belief in the Christian gospel should not surprise. Her life was her own example. Born on December 10, 1830, into a conventionally pious home, she grew up loving and fearing her father, the Honorable Edward Dickinson, one of Amherst's leading citizens. Lawyer, treasurer of Amherst College, United States congressman, he led his family in evening prayers long before he made his public confession of faith in Jesus Christ at age forty-seven.

Emily Dickinson's mother was also at least a nominal Christian. Emily's sister Lavinia, converted during the famous 1850 revival in Amherst, wrote to their brother Austin, "How beautiful if we three could all believe in Christ, how much higher object should we have in living!"[2] For his part, Austin too professed his faith six years later, joining the First Congregational Church of

Amherst, which for years the Dickinson family had all been attending regularly.

But early on, Emily Dickinson expressed her typical independence from mere conventional religiosity. According to one biographer, Richard B. Sewall, her mother reported that at age six Emily seemed "quite inclined to question the authority of everything; the Bible she says does not *feel* as if it was true."[3] This childish tinge of rebellion turned to skepticism, which, from time to time, magnified or lessened in intensity yet remained throughout her life with only one exceptional interim.

In 1846, Dickinson's letters to her most intimate friend, Abiah Root, spoke with great compassion of her tears at the news of Abiah's readiness to give her life to Christ. Then Emily confided to her friend that, sometime before, she too had professed her faith in Christ: "I felt I had found my savior," she wrote. "I never enjoyed such perfect peace and happiness." What happened then? No scholarship has disclosed specifically how much earlier Dickinson had known this "perfect peace and happiness"—presumably between the age of six and her then-fifteen years. Apparently, like the seed sown upon rocky soil, the experience of joy in salvation did not find sufficient nurture to survive. The feeling of "perfect peace and happiness" did not last. "I soon forgot my morning prayer or else it was irksome to me," she wrote. "One by one my old habits returned and I cared less for religion than ever." Yet, once having tasted the bliss of forgiveness, a lingering nostalgia remains: "I feel that I shall never be happy without I love Christ."[4]

This confession—one remembers—is not the remorse of a hardened atheist nor even the philosophical skepticism of an agnostic; rather, it is the frankness of a sensitive adolescent, so subject to emotionalism that she did not even dare to attend the evangelistic meetings at which so many of her friends were being converted. She could not engage in the hypocrisy of an emotionally derived profession of faith that is not genuine; she knew herself too well to risk exposing herself to that danger. "Perhaps you will not beleive [sic] it Dear A.," she wrote to Abiah Root, "but I attended none of the meetings last winter. I felt that I was so easily excited that I might again be deceived and I dared not trust myself."[5]

For Dickinson always, the *feeling* must be right. By her own definition of poetry, given to one of her few literary advisers, Thomas Wentworth Higginson, one can see how deeply she relied on emotional reaction to determine the truth of literature.

> If I read a book and it makes my whole body so cold no fire ever can warm me, I know *that* is poetry. If I feel physically as if the top of my head were taken off, I know *that* is poetry. These are the only way I know. Is there any other way?[6]

Knowing herself too easily swayed by feelings, she shut herself off from circumstances she feared might provoke in her too excited a response. By her own admission, there were times in Amherst or away at school in South Hadley when she felt herself to be in a distinct minority of unbelievers. "Christ is calling everyone here," she wrote in the spring of 1850, "all my companions have answered, and I am standing alone in rebellion."[7] It was a wretched condition, she freely acknowledged; still, it seemed inexplicably impossible for her to cross over from her unbelief and claim the joy and forgiveness she sought. A few months later she wrote, "I wish I were somebody else—I would pray the prayer of the 'Pharisee,' but I am a poor little 'Publican.' 'Son of David,' look down on me!"[8]

Clearly, she knew herself to be a sinner in need of God's mercy, but for whatever reasons, the Pharisee's pride in her would not allow her to commit herself utterly to God's grace. Instead, she blames the fact that anyone may be "lost" on the medium through which the message of the gospel is conveyed. Too often, for Emily Dickinson's liking, Christian doctrine came to her in tones of dire threats and terror. Its power to win converts through love was often subverted by appeals to that which might frighten men and women into turning to God.

When Dickinson was twenty-four years old, she wrote of such a sermon and the preacher's apparent delight in the effect his scare tactics had upon his congregation: "The subject of perdition seemed to please him, somehow." On other occasions, the gospel story, as it was represented to her, consisted of

> Much Gesture, from the Pulpit—
> Strong Hallelujahs roll—

Yet emotionalism was not itself a proper vehicle for the Good News; nor could all the shouts from the "Amen Corner" quiet her doubts or answer her questions:

> Narcotics cannot still the Tooth
> That nibbles at the soul—[9]

What was the religious and moral environment in which Emily Dickinson wrote her cryptic poems and letters? Revivalistic fervor was sweeping through the Connecticut River valley towns in the mid-nineteenth century. A young person needed sturdy convictions to ward off the call to religious conversion. Yet, in spite of powerful influences on her—at home, at church and school, and among her friends—Dickinson continued her resistance. She faithfully attended Amherst's First Congregational Church until she was at least thirty years old. There she came under the teaching and preaching of presumably godly pastors, the Reverend Aaron M. Colton and the Reverend Edwin S. Dwight, whose sermons made a lasting impression on her.

With her poet's ear for language, the rhetoric of her pastors and other preachers had its imprint on her own use of language, just as the hymns she sang affected the metrics of her verse. She referred to sermons in her letters and sometimes in her poems. By her own account, however, the sermons that most fascinated her were those tinged by the subject of despairing failure to believe. In 1854, while she was still a church adherent, she wrote to her eventual sister-in-law Susan Gilbert concerning two of Dwight's "precious" sermons. "One about unbelief," she wrote, "and another Esau. Sermons on unbelief did ever attract me."[10]

Twenty years later, she wrote in another letter,

The loveliest sermon I ever heard was the disappointment of Jesus in Judas. It was told like a mortal story of intimate young men. I suppose no surprise we can ever have will be so sick as that. The last "I never knew you" may resemble it.[11]

But while certain sermons perversely appealed to her imagination, others apparently served to deflect her from the path of faith. In at least one instance, the style and content of a preacher's sermon seemed so contradictory, she excoriated him in this poem:

> He preached upon "Breadth" till it argued him narrow—
> The Broad are too broad to define
> And of "Truth" until it proclaimed him a liar—
> The Truth never flaunted a Sign—
>
> Simplicity fled from his counterfeit presence
> As Gold the Pyrites would shun—
> What confusion would cover the innocent Jesus
> To meet so enabled a Man![12]

Her refusal to believe, however, seems not to have been based solely upon this or any other examples of alleged hypocrisy among professing Christians. Rather, the source of her defiance may well have been what her mother had long before identified as her natural inclination "to question the authority of everything." Christian faith for Emily Dickinson was not so much a problem of belief as it was a problem of submission to the sovereign authority of God and the lordship of Jesus Christ.

Nonetheless, her doubtings neither eased her mind nor delivered her from a state of spiritual uncertainty. Instead, she lingered in irresolution, unable to decide between full commitment to the Jesus whom she admired or total dismissal of the claims of Christ in favor of an Emersonian self-reliance. For her it was to be a lifelong struggle.

Nowhere is this struggle more obvious than in her letters written during her school years. Throughout the 1840s and 1850s, Amherst was the center of periodic spiritual reawakenings, such as the revival in December 1845, whose meetings Dickinson steadfastly refused to attend. In the spring of 1846, another renewal of revivalism sprang up in Amherst. This time Dickinson wrote,

> I know that I ought now to give myself to God and spend the spring-time of life in his service for it seems to me a mockery to spend life's summer and autumn in the service of Mammon and when the world no longer charms us . . . to yield our hearts because we are afraid to do otherwise and give to God the miserable recompense of a sick bed for all his kindness to us.[13]

Surely she had heard this very appeal from evangelists calling for sinners not to cheat God of the best years of their lives by waiting for a deathbed conversion. But while Dickinson reasoned well, she paid no heed to her own best wisdom. Six months later, she broached "the all important subject" in a letter to her friend Abiah Root, who by this time had become a believer.

> I am not unconcerned Dear A. upon the all important subject, to which you have so frequently and so affectionately called my attention in your letters. But I feel that I have not yet made my peace with God. I am still a stranger—to the delightful emotions which fill your heart. I have perfect confidence in God & his promises and yet I know not why, I feel that the world holds a predominant place in my affections. I do not feel that I could give up all for Christ, were I called to die. Pray for me Dear A. that I may yet enter into the kingdom, that there may be room left for me in the shining courts above.[14]

A year after writing this letter, in September 1847, Emily Dickinson was sent to a boarding school—Mount Holyoke Female Seminary, now Mount Holyoke College—in nearby South Hadley. There she met a remarkable woman, the founding principal of the school, Mary Lyon. In addition to being an educator concerned for her pupils' intellectual growth, Mary Lyon was also an earnest Christian, concerned about her girls' spiritual needs. She addressed the school in chapel talks that were, in fact, evangelistic sermons; she taught the chemistry class in such a way as to demonstrate the wonder of God's handiwork in creation. She was committed to developing in her graduates a missionary vision of the needy world lost without faith in Jesus Christ.

Moreover, Mary Lyon met weekly with three groups of students whom she classified by their profession of faith or lack of it into "established Christians," those who had "expressed hope" of coming to belief, and those "without hope." In April 1848, Mary Lyon told a correspondent that her student body of just over two hundred girls included "about thirty without hope." Emily Dickinson was one of these. Her cousin and roommate Emily Norcross wrote after four months of the school term,

> Emily Dickinson appears no different. I hoped I might have good news to write with regard to her. She says she has no particular objection to becoming a Christian and she says she feels bad when she hears of one and another of her friends who are expressing a hope but still she feels no more interest.[15]

During her time at Mount Holyoke, Dickinson must have come very close to surrendering her will to God; certainly, she was given every encouragement. Still, she resisted until, at last, she wrote in the final months of her time at Mount Holyoke,

> I tremble when I think how soon the weeks and days of this term will all have been spent, and my fate will be sealed, perhaps. I have neglected the *one thing needful* when all were obtaining it, and I may never, never again pass through such a season as was granted us last winter.[16]

Her reference to "last winter" may be to a special meeting called by Mary Lyon on January 17, 1848, to summon the still-uncommitted to a point of decision. According to another teacher present, "Emily Dickinson was among the number." For her text, the principal of Mount Holyoke Female Seminary quoted Joshua's challenge to Israel, "Choose you this day whom ye will serve; . . . but as for me and my house, we will serve the LORD" (Josh. 24:15 KJV). Evidently, Dickinson did not side with Joshua. Thus she goes on in her letter to speak of the consequences of that decision:

I am not happy, and I regret that last term, when that golden opportunity was mine, that I did not give up and become a Christian. It is not now too late, so my friends tell me, so my offended conscience whispers, but it is hard for me to give up the world.[17]

A subsequent letter written in January 1850 to her friend Jane Humphrey reveals a far different tone—no longer sorrowful but marked by irony—as she describes her preference for "the world." She confesses as "perfectly hateful to me" any

opportunity rare for cultivating meekness—and patience—and submission—and for turning my back to this very sinful, and wicked world. Somehow or other I incline to other things—and Satan covers them up with flowers, and I reach out to pick them. The path of duty looks very ugly indeed—and the place where I want to go more amiable—a great deal—it is so much easier to do wrong than right—so much pleasanter to be evil than good, I don't wonder that good angels weep—and bad ones sing songs.[18]

Thereafter, Dickinson regarded her alienation from God as a separation between estranged lovers for whom the old passions remain strong. She spoke in quips and jibes and witticisms, her wry humor becoming a typical cover for the seriousness with which she endured the broken relationship. In another letter she wrote, "On subjects of which we know nothing, . . . we both believe and disbelieve a hundred times an Hour, which keeps Believing nimble."[19] Here Dickinson shows her hair-trigger religious temperament, subject to the slightest pressure, resulting in a "nimble" if not capricious set of values.

But to be more theologically precise, Dickinson was an *un*believer rather than a *dis*believer. She did not militantly oppose the gospel as untrue and unworthy of faith; she simply did not choose to commit herself to belief. She was neither an atheist nor an agnostic, for she never denied either the existence of God or the human capacity to know God as ultimate reality. As we have seen, too many of her letters and 1,775 poems are given over to affirmations of God's presence and power for her unending spiritual quest to be ignored. In this respect, her quandary resembles that of her contemporary, Fyodor Dostoyevsky, who wrote in an 1854 letter, "You cannot imagine the terrible torment the desire to believe has caused and still causes me, for it is a desire that grows all the stronger in my heart the more arguments I have against it."[20]

Yet, after her childhood profession of faith and the lapse that followed, Dickinson never again professed to believe. In an early letter to Thomas Wentworth Higginson, she described her family: "They are all religious—except me—and address an Eclipse, every morning—whom they call their 'Father.'"[21] In a neighbor's household, apparently less austere in its outward piety—the home of Dr. and Mrs. Josiah Holland—Dickinson found a different kind of relationship with God. Almost thirty years later, she recalled in a letter to Mrs. Holland her first impressions of that home:

> I shall never forget the Doctor's prayers, my first morning with you—so simple, so believing. *That* God must be a friend—*that* was a different God—and I almost felt warmer myself, in the midst of a tie so sunshiny.[22]

Why did Dickinson never come to know for herself the God she recognized through the experience of others? Why did God continue to be "an Eclipse," an awesome power she once described as "somewhat of a recluse"? What puzzled her most deeply was God's apparent hiddenness. Around 1862—half in play, half in quest—she wrote,

> I know that He exists.
> Somewhere—in Silence—
> He has hid his rare life
> From our gross eyes.
>
> 'Tis an instant's play.
> 'Tis a fond Ambush—
> Just to make Bliss
> Earn her own surprise!
>
> But—should the play
> Prove piercing earnest—

Should the glee—glaze—
In Death's—stiff—stare—

Would not the fun
Look too expensive!
Would not the jest—
Have crawled too far![23]

Even while writing this poem, Dickinson must have known Christian orthodoxy's tenet, that in the cosmic game of hide-and-seek, God has left—in the person of Jesus of Nazareth—an unmistakable clue to his whereabouts and identity. Still, she remains the perpetual doubter, an inquirer for whom the answer given is never sufficient, for whom one question must always lead to another. In the best sense of the word, she was a skeptic, which in its Greek derivation means "thoughtful."

Her own skepticism reminded her of Thomas, the doubting apostle. In a poem of the same period, she begins with an exhortation she might have heard in the late twentieth century from any modern exponent of "possibility thinking" or other healthy-minded optimism: "Trust in the Unexpected—" She follows her maxim with examples of those who have been willing to risk everything because of their faith in the unknown: the famous pirate, Captain William Kidd, and Columbus, for instance. Then in the final stanza she writes,

The Same—afflicted Thomas—
When Deity assured
'Twas better—the perceiving not—
Provided it believed—[24]

To comprehend this poem, we need to see how its verbs affect the speaker's tone. Captain Kidd has been "persuaded of the Buried Gold" and Columbus "allured" by "an Apparition." These verbs, when read in context with "afflicted," in the stanza quoted above, tilt toward a negative opinion of what orthodox Christians might call "walking by faith, not sight." If Thomas is "afflicted," it means that he is troubled or distressed by the need to "Trust in

45

the Unexpected." From reading John 20:24–29, we know the accuracy of Dickinson's verb, for on the evening of the resurrection, Thomas was absent when the risen Lord appeared to the rest of the apostles. Later, when Thomas heard the news, he was dismayed by what he considered the gullibility and wishful thinking of those who claimed to have seen Jesus alive again.

Being a pragmatic realist, Thomas proposed a test before he would believe: He would jab his finger in the wounded hand, thrust his fist into the gaping side. In short, he would rely solely on empirical evidence to see that the alleged risen body is the same one he last saw hanging in crucifixion, then placed in a sepulchre.

But Thomas is also "afflicted" by the living proof presenting itself before him a week later, calling him to perform his experiment, challenging him to "be not faithless, but believing." At this point, Thomas does what Dickinson had so far refused to do: He throws himself down, prostrate in submission to the authority of Jesus Christ, and calls him "My Lord and my God" (John 20:28). Then comes the point of the poem, because Thomas is also "afflicted" by a mild reprimand from Jesus: "Because you have seen me, you have believed; blessed are those who have not seen and yet have believed" (John 20:29).

Presumably, Jesus refers here to two groups of believers. First, there may well have been some who, in the week since the resurrection, had heard from eyewitnesses and had believed without ever having seen the living Lord themselves. Second, in the two millenia since the resurrection, there have been millions who have never seen with physical eyes and yet have believed. To all these believers Jesus gives his blessing, the import of which—as the poet states—is to reward those who believe sight unseen:

> 'Twas better—the perceiving not—
> Provided it believed—

So, where does that leave Thomas? Or Emily Dickinson? Forgiven his skepticism, even his active disbelief—for what could have been more aggressively disbelieving than the ghoulish threat to desecrate a corpse?—Thomas was nonetheless "afflicted" with knowing that there were, and would continue to be, those whose faith exceeded his own. This too was Dickinson's affliction, by which she deprived herself of the grace implied in Thomas' humble acknowledgment, "My Lord and my God." Instead, Dickinson settled for a quip: "Thomas' faith in anatomy was stronger than his faith in faith."

In the early 1860s, Dickinson experienced a great surge in her writing, apparently composing at the rate of a poem a day. As earlier, she continued to vaccilate between a seeming eagerness to believe and deep-seated unbelief. Although her withdrawal to the confines of her father's house now kept her from attending church, she clung to some elements of religious practice, while rejecting others. These lines illustrate her ambivalence.

> Some keep the Sabbath going to Church—
> I keep it, staying at Home—
> . . . .
>
> Of course—I prayed—
> And did God Care?
> . . . .
>
> At least—to pray—is left—is left—
> Oh Jesus—in the Air—
> I know not which thy chamber is—
> I'm knocking—everywhere—
>
> Thou settest Earthquake in the South—
> And Maelstrom, in the Sea—
> Say, Jesus Christ of Nazareth—
> Hast thou no Arm for Me?[25]

Her theology was confused by her inability to commit or utterly reject. But as her own life moved toward its close, one topic preoccupied her: the hope of life everlasting. The constancy of her inquiries into the eternal whereabouts or prospects of her dead or dying friends and relatives prompted her to write to the Reverend Washington Gladden, himself a poet and author of such hymns as "O Master, Let Me Walk with Thee." Her letter asked,

"Is immortality true?" On May 27, 1882, Gladden replied, assuring her that "it is true—the only reality—almost; a thousand times truer than mortality, which is but a semblance after all."[26] To reassure herself, Dickinson apparently read St. Paul's discourse on the resurrection and his rhetorical questions in 1 Corinthians 15:35, which she quoted in a poem rushing to confirm her hope in an ecstasy of confidence.

> "And with what body do they come?"—
> Then they do come—Rejoice!
> What Door—What Hour—Run—run—My Soul!
> Illuminate the House!
>
> "Body!" Then real—a Face and Eyes—
> To know that it is them!—
> Paul knew the Man that knew the News—
> He passed through Bethlehem—[27]

For Dickinson, Bethlehem is always an important location: the focal point of the incarnation, the intersection of time and eternity. Born in Bethlehem, Jesus is "the Man that knew the News" about everlasting life and how to attain it. The apostle Paul, whose text excited the poet's ecstatic utterance, had passed along to his own readers the truth he had received in revelation, "that Christ died for our sins according to the Scriptures, that he was buried, that he was raised on the third day according to the Scriptures" (1 Cor. 15:3–4).

Thus we come full circle, for may not this affirmation be the reason for the hope inspiring "Those—dying then"? St. Paul and all early Christians possessed a sure knowledge of their eternal destiny. They too "knew the Man that knew the News"; thus, they also

> Knew where they went—
> They went to God's Right Hand—

Somehow, the certainty of Christian hope known *then* had changed to emptiness, hopelessness, and despairing resignation. Whatever era may be signified by now, it is marked by faith turned to doubt, belief soured by unbelief, childlike trust shattered by disbelief. The hiddenness of God has been replaced by the dismembering of God; the amputation has resulted in the patient's death.

Yet, while Dickinson asserts what has become accepted dogma in nihilism, she is too honest to pretend to agree with those who claim that our only freedom as human beings comes at the price of admitting that we are lost, joyously abandoned to survive on our own. Dickinson knows otherwise because she has lived in that lostness, that abandonment self-imposed, and found it to be slavery rather than freedom. She knows the reality and consequences of her choice to demit her early faith; she knows that her life has been constricted ever since by unresolved doubt. Abdicating her belief, she has minimized the scope of her soul's experience.

An alternative to outright unbelief, however, may be retained. True, it falls short of commitment, but it is better than nothing:

> Better an ignis fatuus
> Than no illume at all—

An *ignis fatuus*—literally a "foolish fire"—is that natural phenomenon sometimes seen as a glow of light over a marsh. It appears to be caused by combustion of gases from decaying organic matter. Whatever its source or substance, it is not a genuine light; yet it shines in the dark!

One does not presume to know exactly what Emily Dickinson meant by these enigmatic lines. In context, however, they seem to suggest that loss of faith means not only diminished scope but also diminished light. "God is light," says the apostle John, "in him there is no darkness at all" (1 John 1:5). To reject belief in God—to sever "God's Right Hand" and cut off all the benefits of knowing God—is to choose darkness rather than light.

Perhaps the poet is acknowledging that in this darkness of unbelief, hope in Jesus Christ and the promise of his resurrection is little more than a false light; yet even this delusion is a better light than none at all—especially in the face of death and its impending unknown. Or, perhaps, the poem suggests a grudging resignation, an unwilling concession to take the safe course of belief—

for all its evident folly!—just in case "Those—dying then" turn out to have been correct. Or, perhaps, the poem indicates—ironically, even paradoxically—that the seemingly foolish act of belief is really something quite different from what today's sophisticated unbeliever—today's militant disbeliever—supposes: that, indeed, belief is nothing less than trusting in the light of the world.

To the end of her life, on May 15, 1886, Emily Dickinson remained equivocal about her relationship with God, sometimes belligerent and rejecting, sometimes almost plaintively appealing for grace, as in this dialogue poem:

> "Unto Me?" I do not know you—
> Where may be your House?
>
> "I am Jesus—Late of Judea—
> Now—of Paradise"—
>
> Wagons—have you—to convey me?
> It is far from Thence—
>
> "Arms of Mine—sufficient Phaeton—
> Trust Omnipotence"—
>
> I am spotted—"I am Pardon"—
> I am small—"The Least
> Is esteemed in Heaven the Chiefest—
> Occupy my House"—[28]

To what extent Dickinson found herself willing, at last, to "Trust Omnipotence," one cannot say. Her final written message, a deathbed note to cousins, announces that she has been "called home." Is it not apparent, therefore, that Dickinson never completely closed herself off from the possibility of grace? In spite of skepticism and doubt, she took what consolation she could from promises whose very mercy exceeded her intent, lighting her way and nourishing her soul—almost in spite of herself.

The Self as American Messiah

Walt Whitman and Ralph Waldo Emerson

All poetry is religious. By this reiteration we mean that anyone who expends intellectual and emotional energy in the formation of words into imagery and musicality by means of verbal harmonics indicates an elevated seriousness of purpose that is one definition of *religious.* But having granted, at least, seriousness of intent to all poets, one may go on to say that Walt Whitman was the high priest of poetic religiosity. The deity he worshiped was himself. From the early sections of "Song of Myself" through the late scribblings of a paralyzed, almost forgotten old man abound songs and hymns and spiritual songs in praise of syncretism's only god—a deity worthy of the amalgam of all formal creeds and faiths into one, an American messiah.

William Wordsworth's phrase is true: "The Child is father of the Man." In Whitman's case, neither his self-deification nor the art that expressed it sprang from some vacuum or void. In the words of Ralph Waldo Emerson's famous letter of congratulations, written in 1855 upon Emerson's first reading of *Leaves of Grass,* Whitman's development into an American messiah must have "had a long foreground somewhere."[1]

That foreground included Whitman's exposure to the doctrines of John Calvin and other reformers, as well as the Quaker teachings of John Woolman, George Fox, and Elijah Hicks, which Whitman learned both at home and in churches he attended. While Whitman grew into heterodoxy, too little has been made of the fact that in his youth Whitman knew at least the framework of Christian orthodoxy.

Born near Huntington on Long Island, New York, in 1819, the boy Whitman moved with his parents to Brooklyn. There, under his mother's influence, he attended several Sunday schools, including those at both the Dutch Reformed Church and St. Ann's Episcopal Church. Louisa Whitman seems to have been eclectic in her multi-denominationalism; brought up in a devout Quaker family herself, she and her nine children—two of whom were mentally handicapped—attended various Brooklyn churches, and she chose a Baptist minister to officiate at her husband Walter's funeral in 1855. For his part, the elder Whitman was never aligned with any church; he may have been a freethinker, like his hero, Tom Paine. Still, he allowed his wife her religious practices, although there were no religious observances of any kind in the home. The only known religious influence was the Quaker schismatic Elijah Hicks, a personal friend; on one occasion the senior Whitman took his family to hear Hicks preach.

After only five or six years of formal schooling, at age thirteen, Walt Whitman went to work. His employers William Hartshorne and Alden J. Spooner encouraged the boy to attend the Presbyterian church with them. Years later, in the poem "A Child's Amaze," Whitman recalls,

> Silent and amazed even when a little boy
> I remember I heard the preacher every Sunday put God in his
>   statements,
> As contending against some being or influence.[2]

Whitman made use of his churchgoing to dramatize his vignettes or catalogues of American experience. For instance, he witnessed an old-time Methodist revival at a chapel where public display of repentance and "second-blessing" were common. In spite of the hyperemotionalism of such events, Whitman wrote, in "Song of Myself,"

> Pleas'd with the earnest words of the sweating Methodist
>   preacher, impress'd seriously at the camp-meeting.[3]

In at least one instance, Whitman also used his church attendance to spark a poem, "The Rounded Catalogue Divine Complete," whose headnote reads,

> (Sunday _____ ___ ____. Went this forenoon to church. A college
> professor, Rev. Dr. _____, gave us a fine sermon, during which I
> caught the above words; but the minister included in his "rounded
> catalogue" letter and spirit, only the esthetic things, and entirely
> ignored what I name in the following:)
>
> The devilish and the dark, the dying and diseas'd,
> The countless (nineteen-twentieths) low and evil, crude and
>   savage,
> The crazed prisoners in jail, the horrible, rank, malignant,
> Venom and filth, serpents, the ravenous sharks, liars, the dis
>   solute;
> (What is the part the wicked and the loathsome bear within
>   earth's orbic scheme?)
> Newts, crawling things in slime and mud, poisons,
> The barren soil, the evil men, the slag and hideous rot.[4]

Elsewhere in "Song of Myself," he compressed several aspects of common worship into a few lines:

> To the mass kneeling or the puritan's prayer rising, or sitting
>   patiently in a pew,
> Ranting and frothing in my insane crisis, or waiting dead-like till
>   my spirit arouses me . . .[5]

All these manifestations of piety Walt Whitman had witnessed himself in the many religious services he attended.

For a period in his late teenage years, Whitman taught school on Long Island. In Smithtown, he attended the only church in the village, a Presbyterian church at the intersection of Jericho Turnpike and North Country Road. He was also a member of the village's debating society and took part in public speaking events. Whitman appears to have been vain about his oratorical skills, especially his powers of declamation. Among his favorite recitations were passages from the Bible; in fact, Whitman describes his walking along the beach at Coney Island, declaiming texts from the Scriptures, as well as from Shakespeare and Homer.

An acquaintance, John Taylor Trowbridge, wrote of Whitman, "The book he knew best was the Bible, the prophetical parts of which stirred in him a desire to be the bard or prophet of his own time and country."[6] We shall return to this telling observation later; for now, it is sufficient to note that, for all his familiarity with Christianity, Whitman never professed to be a believing Christian. He was much more attuned to the heterodoxy of Emerson, whom he regarded as his mentor in absentia.

Ralph Waldo Emerson was the son of a Congregational pastor of Boston's First Church, which by Emerson's birth in 1803 had fallen into Unitarian apostasy. Emerson followed his father into the pastorate, graduating from Harvard and its divinity school. He was ordained and appointed to Boston's Second Church in 1829. But from the outset, Emerson was uncomfortable with the "rational Christianity" in which he had been brought up; with increasing certainty, Emerson turned inward to find his own wisdom.

His journals as a young pastor are revealing:

> To reflect is to receive truth immediately from God without any medium. That is living faith. . . . It is by yourself without ambassador that God speaks to you. . . .

> I have sometimes thought that, in order to be a good minister, it was necessary to leave the ministry. The profession is antiquated. In an altered age, we worship in the dead forms of our forefathers.

> Were not a Socratic paganism better than an effete, superannuated Christianity? . . .

Instead of making Christianity a vehicle of truth, you make truth only a horse for Christianity. It is a very operose way of making people good. You must be humble because Christ says, "Be humble."

"But why must I obey Christ?" "Because God sent him." But how do I know God sent him? Because your own heart teaches the same thing he taught. Why then shall I not go to my own heart at first? . . .

> That which myself delights in shall be Good,
> That which I do not want, indifferent;
> That which I hate is Bad. That's flat.[7]

By October 1832, Emerson realized that even the liberal Unitarian sect was too constricting for him. He resigned his pulpit over an issue of principle: He could not continue to officiate at the regularly scheduled celebrations of Holy Communion as ordinances of the church required; therefore, he demitted the ministry and left the Unitarian fold to heed that risky vocation as a man of letters. Over the next fifty years, Emerson devoted himself to expostulating a new liturgy for an old faith, a churchless church whose creedless creed was as diverse as his 1836 essay "Nature" suggested, whose only dogma was the self-reliance for which Emerson called.

Along the way he managed to offend most of his former Unitarian colleagues, particularly by his outrageous address to the Harvard Divinity School's graduating class of 1838. The year before, Emerson had addressed the Phi Beta Kappa Society at Harvard College in what we would call a convocation to open the academic year. His address on that occasion, "The American Scholar," continued to build on the foundation of individualistic insight he had laid in his pastoral journals. He called for an end to America's "day of dependence, our long apprenticeship to the learning of other lands." For this to happen, Emerson asserted, Americans must come to experience directly a relationship with knowledge through nature rather than indirectly through books and the past. "Meek young men grow up in libraries," Emerson declared, believing it their duty to accept the views which Cicero, which Locke, which Bacon, have given; forgetful that Cicero, Locke, and Bacon were only young men in libraries when they wrote these books.[8]

From such an assertion it follows that a young man must also find his own opinions:

Let him not quit his belief that a popgun is a popgun, though the ancient and honorable of the earth affirm it to be the crack of doom. . . . In self-trust all the virtues are comprehended. Free should the scholar be,—free and brave.[9]

When Emerson rose to his peroration, in the best tradition of Unitarian homiletics, he called for "the American Scholar" to take his rightful place, no longer a listener "to the courtly muses of Europe," but as his own "Man Thinking."

We will walk on our own feet; we will work with our own hands; we will speak our own minds. The study of letters shall no longer be a name for pity, for doubt, and for sensual indulgence. . . . A nation of men will for the first time exist, because each believes himself inspired by the Divine Soul which also inspires all men.[10]

The response to "The American Scholar" heralded Emerson's speech as an intellectual Declaration of Independence, not merely from European and British hegemony but from any other authoritarian control. So the governors of Harvard Divinity School may well have been nervous when its budding young preachers invited as speaker an alumnus who had already turned in his own ordination credentials. These established Unitarian clergy—lapsed Congregationalist ministers, non-Trinitarians all—knew heresy when they heard it. But no one—not Andrews Norton, the Divinity School president, nor Theodore Parker, the most eminent Unitarian divine of that day—was prepared for the heresy Emerson would utter on July 15, 1838.

Emerson began mildly enough, then turned upon the education he himself had received and the church that had nurtured him. For a dozen years he had been pointing toward this moment;

just a week earlier, his journal entry for July 8 had included a threat to "take away titles even of false honor from Jesus."[11] Now the scope of his attack became apparent. First, Emerson disparaged what he called "a decaying church and a wasting unbelief," blaming the very teaching the Unitarians and Harvard Divinity School had to offer. Next, Emerson took aim at two elements of doctrine: the unique personhood of Jesus and special revelation as a past event.

Emerson decried the "noxious exaggeration about the person of Jesus" because, he declared, "the soul knows no persons." He objected to the fact that the name of Jesus has been "petrified into official titles." Along with an undeserved special status, Emerson argued, to Jesus had been attributed miracles: "To aim to convert a man by miracles is a profanation of the soul." At this, Andrews Norton gasped.

But there was more to come from Emerson. "The second great defect," he announced, is that "men have come to speak of the revelation as somewhat long ago given and done, as if God were dead." To Emerson, "the need was never greater of a new revelation than now." To bring about such a revelation, Emerson advocated salvaging only two elements of institutional Christian practice, which he named as "inestimable advantages Christianity has given us": the Sabbath, by which he meant Sunday observance, and "the institution of preaching." Here Emerson offered what must still be considered some of the wisest counsel on homiletics ever written: "The true preacher can be known by this, that he deals out to the people his life—life passed through the fire of thought."

Then he concluded with a brief dismissing of the Scriptures as having "no epical integrity." Instead, Emerson awaited the arrival in the West of "the new Teacher," whose words would take the place of the ancient and outmoded oracles whose beauty had "ravished the souls of those Eastern men."

The Unitarian establishment reacted as if its own heresy had not spawned further heresy. The American historian Perry Miller calls their reaction "inspired by nothing less than pure rage." Andrews Norton editorialized against Emerson, and a former colleague at Boston's Second Church, Henry Ware Jr., preached a sermon of rebuttal, affirming the special personhood of Jesus. For all purposes, Emerson had been rebuffed and cut off from his roots.

But if, thereafter, Emerson became *persona non grata* among Boston's Unitarian brahmins, he also attracted the loyalty of every other young nonconformist and solipsist who came upon his essays. "Self-Reliance," published in 1841, became a stump speech for "rugged individualism." The gauntlet of intellectual and spiritual rebellion against convention had been thrown down; the banner of individual and selective truth had been raised. A dozen decades later, its motto would be restated as "Do your own thing."

> To believe your own thought, to believe that what is true for you in your private heart is true for all men,—that is genius. Speak your latent conviction, and it shall be the universal sense . . .

> Trust thyself: every heart vibrates to that iron string. . . .

> Whoso would be a man must be a nonconformist. . . . Nothing is at last sacred but the integrity of your own mind.

> Suppose you should contradict yourself; what then? . . . A foolish consistency is the hobgoblin of little minds. . . . Speak what you think now in hard words and tomorrow speak what tomorrow thinks in hard words again, though it contradict every thing you said today.

> . . . To be great is to be misunderstood.[12]

A more esoteric essay, "The Poet," published in 1843, defined the role of poet as that of "a sovereign and stands on the center . . . emperor in his own right."[13] The poet is above social critique and can rightly claim an "intellect inebriated by nectar." This, to Emerson, explained why "bards love wine, mead, narcotics, coffee, tea, opium, the fumes of sandalwood and tobacco, or whatever other procurers of animal exhilaration." Pot for Poets? One can almost imagine the former cleric-turned-philosopher on a picket line with Allan Ginsberg, advocating the decriminalization of marijuana!

"I look in vain for the poet whom I describe," Emerson lamented; but he was certain that somewhere an artist would feel the impulse to say, "By God it is in me and must go forth of me."

Having made this commitment, the poet would be granted this reward: "That the ideal shall be real to thee, and the impressions of the actual world shall fall like summer rain, copious. . . ."[14]

Certainly Emerson's message stirred the soul of one young, aspiring poet, a journalist and editor of the *Brooklyn Daily Eagle*. "I was simmering, simmering, simmering," wrote Walt Whitman, "and Emerson brought me to a boil." The kettle that boiled over contained a collection of writings the likes of which the world had never seen before. In the summer of 1855, *Leaves of Grass* was published, a slim volume without any more identification of its author than a frontispiece lithograph portrait showing a young man in a white blouse-like shirt open at the neck; on his head a broad-brimmed hat set at a cocky angle. Buried in one of the long, rambling, unorthodox poems was this single reference: "I, Walt Whitman, a cosmos, one of the roughs . . ."[15]

In a burst of self-promotion, the poet sent a copy of his book to his hero, the quiet and refined Emerson, who replied with a letter that sent Whitman soaring. "I am not blind to the worth of the wonderful gift of 'Leaves of Grass,'" wrote Emerson.

> I find it the most extraordinary piece of wit and wisdom that America has yet contributed. I am very happy in reading it, as great power makes us happy. . . . I give you joy of your free and brave thought. I have great joy in it. I find incomparable things said incomparably well, as they must be. . . . I greet you at the beginning of a great career. . . .[16]

So elated was Whitman that he blundered in the two worst ways possible to offend Emerson's tender sensibilities. First, when he published a second edition of *Leaves of Grass* the following year, he chose—without first obtaining Emerson's permission—to quote Emerson on the spine of the 1856 volume: "I greet you at the beginning of a great career. R. W. Emerson." Using the blurb itself would not have been so unforgivable had not Whitman also chosen to include, in this second edition, some of the most auto- and homoerotic poems Americans had ever read. Emerson was aghast at the double insult and never forgave Whitman for so compromising him.

But as Emerson had predicted, Whitman's "great career" was underway. A total of nine editions of *Leaves of Grass* appeared, each somewhat different from its predecessor, organically growing like its central metaphor and carrying with it a representation of how the poet's soul was also developing and transforming with the years.

In particular, Whitman more and more adopted for himself the impression at first suggested by others that he was a Christ-figure—if not, in fact, the Christ himself. According to the scholar Gay Wilson Allen, by the time Whitman's close-cropped beard had grown to flowing proportions, friends "did not blush at suggesting a parallel with the Messiah Carpenter of Galilee."[17] Whitman did nothing to dissuade them.

The growth of a messianic complex in Whitman heightened during the Civil War and his period of volunteer service as a "wound dresser" to injured soldiers in Washington, D.C., hospitals. In Whitman's own account, he tells of the activities and amusements he carried on to entertain the wounded: reciting declamatory pieces, juggling oranges, playing twenty questions, and expounding texts from the Bible. Van Wyck Brooks expresses his wonderment when he writes of "the distinction between Whitman and all other American men of letters of his time."

> Could Emerson have recited "declamatory pieces," even if it was at the right moment the one thing to do? Could [William Cullen] Bryant have led a game of twenty questions? Could Edgar Allan Poe have expounded the Bible?[18]

The answer to these rhetorical questions is, presumably, a comical "Of course not!" But beyond Whitman's versatility in bedside care for the wounded, there remains what Allen refers to as Whitman's creation of a persona, a self, to match the narrator of his poems. As Allen writes, Whitman "had honestly cultivated his own personality in order to create great poems; he could not believe in them without believing in himself."[19]

What, then, did Whitman believe? No easy answer exists, for Whitman himself was content to echo Emerson's call to unapologetic capriciousness:

> Do I contradict myself?
> Very well then I contradict myself,
> (I am large, I contain multitudes.)[20]

While systematic theology was not a virtue Whitman prized, some patterns of belief can be traced through Whitman's poetry.

In the rituals of organized religion, Whitman saw evidence of the human being's primary search for meaning; but he reversed the usual order so that the searcher became the subject of the search. That search culminated not in formal rites of worship but in idiosyncratic impulses and acts of devotion. The object of that devotion was the whole human race—ultimately, by extrapolation, oneself.

Whitman acquired his self-sanctifying consciousness by a process of discarding those tenets of orthodoxy with which he felt no compatibility, then attaching to himself those that fit his own preferences. In "Song of Myself," after cataloguing a roster of deities—Jehovah, Kronos, Zeus, Hercules, Osiris, Isis, Belus, Brahma, Buddha, Allah—along with "the crucifix engraved, / With Odin and the hideous-faced Mexitli and every idol and image," Whitman sums up his syncretism and ecumenicity in these telling lines:

> Taking them all for what they are worth and not a cent more,
> Admitting they were alive and did the work of their days.[21]

To Whitman, religion was a map, a chart for "the Divine Ship, the World," in which "all peoples of the globe sail together." Or religion might be considered the keystone or steadying principle, as Whitman expressed in a short poem whose title serves as its initial statement: "The Calming Thought of All,"

> That coursing on, whate'er men's speculations,
> Amid the changing schools, theologies, philosophies,
> Amid the brawling presentations new and old,
> The round earth's silent vital laws, facts, modes continue.[22]

Whatever religion was or was not, Whitman would not insist on anyone else's conforming to his opinions. "I have no chair, no church, no philosophy,"[23] he writes.

For instance, in one breath Whitman—like Emerson—seemed to put no stock in any biblical claims of exclusivity regarding the divinity of Jesus of Nazareth; in the next, Whitman could compose such lines as these:

> Accepting the Gospels, accepting him that was crucified,
> Knowing assuredly that he is divine.[24]

He could compile a catalogue of world religions, declaring that "the religion of Christ is incomparably superior to all other religions." Then, without missing a beat, he could utter these self-adoring lines:

> Divine am I inside and out, and I make holy whatever I touch or
>   am touched from,
> The scent of these arm-pits aroma finer than prayer,
> This head more than churches, bibles, and all the creeds.[25]

At its core, Whitman's religion was a blend of pantheism—the deification of nature—and solipsism—the deification of self. To Whitman, this deification was sometimes overt, sometimes masked by metaphor. His favorite mask was the persona of a Christ-figure, perhaps even a messianic obsession. In "Song of Myself," for instance, Whitman presents a tableau of common people at work or at play; each is performing a task in keeping with vocation or avocation. In this context, a woman appears:

> The prostitute draggles her shawl, her bonnet bobs on her tipsy
>   and pimpled neck,
> The crowd laughs at her blackguard oaths, the men jeer and
>   wink to each other,
> (Miserable! I do not laugh at your oaths nor jeer you).[26]

How like the pericope of John 8:1–11, the story of the adulteress brought before Jesus. His question, "Where are your accusers?" leads to her awareness that they have all departed without so much as a condemning word. So Jesus offers his comforting admonition: "Neither do I condemn you. Go and sin no more." Can there be any doubt that Whitman compares his own humanitarian concern for the sinner to that of Jesus?

In another section of "Song of Myself," the poet declares,

> This is the meal equally set, . . .
> It is for the wicked just the same as the righteous, I make
> appointments with all,
> I will not have a single person slighted or left away,
> The kept-woman, sponger, thief, are hereby invited;
> There shall be no difference between them and the rest.[27]

Here he echoes a passage from Matthew 9:10–13, which shows Jesus at dinner with a mixed company of tax collectors and other notorious sinners.

> When the Pharisees saw this, they asked his disciples, "Why does your teacher eat with tax collectors and 'sinners'?"
> On hearing this, Jesus said, "It is not the healthy who need a doctor, but the sick. But go and learn what this means: 'I desire mercy, not sacrifice.' For I have not come to call the righteous, but sinners."

This same spirit of identification with sinners marks Whitman, who calls himself "brother of rejected persons—brother of slaves, felons, idiots, and of insane and diseased persons."[28] In fact, Whitman reveled in his reputation as a Bohemian who frequented Pfaff's, a notorious restaurant, where he associated with known political and artistic nonconformists. The implications, then, are clear: Like Jesus of Nazareth, says the poet, all are welcome to sit with me at my table.

Whitman was not content, however, merely to associate with outcasts; he must also identify himself as the Christ himself. To see, to observe, to record, to cry out against the calamities and injustices of life did not satisfy Whitman. He must attempt to enter into the experience of others: "I am the man, I suffer'd, I was there."[29] Leslie A. Fiedler comments: "The images of pain by which he asked to be possessed are too much for him. 'Enough! enough! enough!' he pleads. 'Stand back!' This time, however, he is not delivered from suffering and doubt until he sees himself first as the crucified Christ, then as Christ resurrected."[30]

> That I could forget the mockers and insults!
> That I could forget the trickling tears and the blows of the bludgeons and hammers!
> That I could look with a separate look on my own crucifixion and bloody crowning!
> I remember now,
> I resume the overstaid fraction,
> The grave of rock multiplies what has been confided to it, or to any graves,
> Corpses rise, gashes heal, fastenings roll from me.
> I troop forth replenish'd with supreme power, one of an average unending procession.[31]

Reinvigorated and restored to confidence, Whitman as the resurrected Messiah addresses his disciples, his pupils, and encourages their inquiries of him:

> Eleves, I salute you! come forward!
> Continue your annotations, continue your questionings.[32]

In the resurrection of Jesus Christ, Whitman has found the ideal figure for his own cosmic image of the ultimate survivor, the man whom even death cannot conquer.

But Whitman moves beyond his apparent psychotic identification of himself as Jesus Christ to a syncretism in which he and Jesus stand together as models of brotherhood, the ideal of all religions. Whitman's preferred word is *adhesiveness,* a term borrowed from phrenology. This occult study of the shape and contours of one's cranium was popular in Whitman's day and appears to have fascinated him.

Two of Whitman's poems, "A Sight in Camp" and "Passage to India," will serve to illustrate. When the Civil War broke upon the Union in April 1861, Whitman was dismayed. But he found no active role until the following year when his brother George, a lieutenant, was reported to have been wounded in battle. Whitman went to Virginia to find his brother and returned with him to the hospital in Washington, D.C. There Whitman was appalled by the conditions he saw, the results of a devastating war. Whitman chose to stay on as a volunteer, working as a clerk to support himself but giving much of his time to visiting the wounded and offering them comfort and assistance as he was able.

Out of this experience came one of his finest collections of poems, "Drum-Taps," a vivid portrayal of the horrors of war, which Whitman included in the 1865 edition of *Leaves of Grass*. One of these poems is "A Sight in Camp."

A sight in camp in the daybreak gray and dim,
As from my tent I emerge so early sleepless,
As slow I walk in the cool fresh air the path near by the hospital
     tent,
Three forms I see on stretchers lying, brought out there
     untended lying,
Over each the blanket spread, ample brownish woolen blanket,
Gray and heavy blanket, folding, covering all.

Curious I halt and silent stand,
Then with light fingers I from the face of the nearest the first just
     lift the blanket;
Who are you elderly man so gaunt and grim, with well-gray'd
     hair, and flesh all sunken about the eyes?
Who are you my dear comrade?

Then to the second I step—and who are you my child and
     darling?
Who are you sweet boy with cheeks yet blooming?

Then to the third—a face nor child nor old, very calm, as of
     beautiful yellow-white ivory;

> Young man I think I know you—I think this face is the face of
>   the Christ himself,
> Dead and divine and brother of all, and here again he lies.[33]

An eerie tenderness pervades this poem; a photographic real-ity as of a Matthew Brady close-up from a Virginia battlefield. The three corpses have been brought through the predawn gloom and placed before the hospital tent for quick burial. The poem's narrator—presumably, as always, Whitman himself—removes from each face the blanket. Of the first two—an older man and a youth—he asks, "Who are you?" But coming to the third stretcher and looking at its victim, he has no need to inquire: "Young man I think I know you." The narrator identifies the face of the Christ in the serene and placid death mask countenance of the dead soldier. As if once more interred in the Arimathean's tomb, this body has been sacrificed for the sins of the world. So too, of course, has each of the others; so too are they divine and the brothers of us all. The point is to recognize the meaning of Christ's atoning death and its application to universal brother-hood as adhesiveness.

The possibility of attaining such brotherhood Whitman cele-brated in "Passage to India," first published in 1871 as an adden-dum to the fifth edition of *Leaves of Grass*. "Passage to India" glo-ries in the new technology that brings distant continents together and diminishes barriers to communication.

> Our modern wonders, (the antique ponderous Seven outvied,)
> In the Old World the east the Suez canal,
> The New by its mighty railroad spann'd,
> The seas inlaid with eloquent gentle wires . . .[34]

To be sure, the opening of the canal brought West and East closer together; the transcontinental railroad and the Atlantic cable cut travel and communication immeasurably. But even these remark-able developments pale before the real theme of the poem, which is Whitman's challenge to his readers to transcend such physical and commercial attainments in order to set sail upon "the seas of God."

Whitman first invokes the past: "For what is the present after all but a growth out of the past?" He subjugates "proud truths of the world" and "facts of modern science" to "myths and fables . . . / The far-darting beams of the spirit, the unloos'd dreams, / The deep diving bibles and legends, / The daring plots of the poets, the elder religions." In them, Whitman discerns "God's purpose from the first," namely,

> The earth to be spann'd, connected by network,
> The races, neighbors, to marry and be given in marriage,
> The oceans to be cross'd, the distant brought near,
> The lands to be welded together.

Thus Whitman offers a foretaste of contemporary globalism—oneness in terms geographic, racial, and social—to be brought about by blending technology with spirituality, an adhesiveness derived from human skill dedicated to religious purpose:

> A worship new I sing,
> You captains, voyagers, explorers, yours,
> You engineers, you architects, machinists, yours,
> You, not for trade or transportation only,
> But in God's name, and for thy sake O soul.

This worship is not orthodox religion but scientism, a worship of the potential achievements of technology; and its priest is not some theologian nor even some experimentalist. Rather, it comes as no surprise to learn that the same worthy poet who is the persona of *Leaves of Grass* is the new messiah.

> After the seas are all cross'd (as they seem already cross'd,)
> After the great captains and engineers have accomplish'd their
>   work,
> After the noble inventors, after the scientists, the chemist, the
>   geologist, ethnologist,
> Finally shall come the poet worthy that name,
> The true son of God shall come singing his songs.[35]

In his "Divinity School Address," Emerson had referred to the message of Jesus as "this high chant from the poet's lips." Again, in "The Poet," which became Whitman's inspiration, Emerson had devised a parallel Trinity, in which the Son is the poet, "the sayer, the namer, and represents beauty."[36] R. W. B. Lewis, in *The American Adam*, comments that "such a conviction contributed greatly to Whitman's ever enlarging idea of the poet as the vicar of God, as the son of God—as God himself."[37] For Whitman, therefore, the arrival of "the poet . . . the true son of God" ushers in the fulfillment of life's meaning.

> All these hearts as of fretted children shall be sooth'd,
> All affection shall be fully responded to, the secret shall be told,
> All these separations and gaps shall be taken up and hook'd and
>   link'd together,
> The whole earth, this cold, impassive, voiceless earth, shall be
>   completely justified . . .[38]

St. Paul, addressing the Christians in Rome, could not have said it any more poetically. But Whitman has more to add in his hymn of joyful anticipation:

> Trinitas divine shall be gloriously accomplish'd and compacted
>   by the true son of God, the poet, . . .
> Nature and Man shall be disjoin'd and diffused no more,
> The true son of God shall absolutely fuse them.[39]

First adhesiveness, then fusion, then brotherhood. Launched on such a cosmic voyage, the poet contemplates his journey's end:

> Reckoning ahead O soul, when thou, the time achiev'd,
> The seas all cross'd, weather'd the capes, the voyage done,
> Surrounded, copest, frontest God, yieldest, the aim attain'd,
> As fill'd with friendship, love complete, the Elder Brother found,
> The Younger melts in fondness in his arms.[40]

We never learn precisely who the Elder Brother is or, for that matter, the Younger. We are left only with allusions to such relationships, and Whitman expects us to use our own imagining to complete the portrait.

In any case, Whitman's spiritual journey is complete—but only on his own terms. In a tone of religiosity, Whitman's voice is almost contemptuous of creedal orthodoxy. For instance, utterly self-satisfied, he will have no part of repentance:

> (Let others deprecate, let others weep for sin, remorse,
>   humiliation,)
> O soul, thou pleasest me, I thee.[41]

But he adds, "Ah more than any priest O soul we too believe in God." Still, hedging a little, Whitman concedes that "with the mystery of God we dare not dally."

A few lines later, echoing Emerson, he writes, "Have we not darken'd and dazed ourselves with books long enough?"[42] The implication is clear: Freed from the shackles of creed and conventional religion, Whitman can command his own system of belief. This he seeks to do in a climactic paean to self-reliance:

> Sail forth—steer for the deep waters only,
> Reckless O soul, exploring, I with thee, and thou with me,
> For we are bound where mariner has not yet dared to go,
> And we will risk the ship, ourselves and all.[43]

For Whitman—as for Emerson before him—the risk seemed well worth the taking. For, as Whitman wrote in "Song of Myself,"

> My rendezvous is appointed, it is certain,
> The Lord will be there and wait till I come on perfect terms,
> The great Camerado, the lover true for whom I pine will be
>   there.[44]

Confident in himself, Walt Whitman's eternal destiny seemed sure, no matter how unorthodox the charts and course he had followed.

Uncomfortable Unbelief

Nathaniel Hawthorne and Herman Melville

In the summer of 1850, a New York publisher named Evert Duyckinck, vacationing at the home of one of his authors, contrived to
introduce his host to another American novelist. Although both
writers had summer homes nearby in the Berkshire mountains
of western Massachusetts, they had never met. Like the Hamp-
tons on Long Island or Malibu by the Pacific today, the commu-
nities of Pittsfield, Lenox, and Stockbridge were popular summer
locations for the literati of Boston and New York in the mid-nineteenth century. Henry Wadsworth Longfellow, Oliver Wendell
Holmes, and William Cullen Bryant also had homes there. Setting up a meeting between two writers—one a New Englander,
the other a New Yorker—would not be difficult.

Duyckinck's intention carried with it some elements of a practical joke. As editor of the periodical *Literary World,* Duyckinck had
commissioned his host to prepare a review of the other writer's
stories. In the custom of the time, the review would be published
anonymously; so if Duyckinck's scheme worked, the reviewer
would meet the unwitting subject of his review without that
author's ever knowing he was under such scrutiny.

On the surface, the two men would seem to have little in common. One was quiet and introspective; the other gregarious, sometimes even crude. One had scarcely ever left the confines of New England; the other had traveled the world on whaling vessels and navy frigates. Still, Duyckinck hoped that Nathaniel Hawthorne and Herman Melville might find some bond in common. Having already written three volumes of stories, Hawthorne had just published *The Scarlet Letter* to favorable notices; Melville was the author of two popular romances about the South Sea islands, *Typee* and *Omoo*. Melville had teased his readers with erotic hints of a Polynesian nymph named Fayaway, but as his publisher, Duyckinck perceived that something deeper, something more substantial, lay within the soul of the brash, young Melville.

On an early August day, as he later informed his wife, Margaret, in a letter, Duyckinck led a party to the home of Oliver Wendell Holmes in Stockbridge, where Melville was introduced to Hawthorne. From there they trekked up Monument Mountain, where a sumptuous picnic dinner, lasting three hours, ensued. Another hike through a mountain pass followed that meal; then, upon returning to the Holmes's house, more conversation and "at 10 o'clock the railway home, a short walk under the stars and we turned in at this Melville house."[1]

Hawthorne had said little during the course of that day, but Duyckinck told his wife that he anticipated "another day for a visit to Hawthorne." Three days later, the visit occurred. Sophia Peabody Hawthorne, writing to her sister Elizabeth, described each of her husband's guests, saying of Melville, "Mr. Typee is interesting in his aspect—quite—I see Fayaway in his face."[2] Hawthorne had champagne to serve, and according to Duyckinck's account to his wife, "It all went off in excellent style."[3] Just as Duyckinck had hoped, a relationship had been forged between two men of like mind and heart.

A few days later, Duyckinck returned to New York, carrying with him Melville's review of Hawthorne's collection of stories, *Mosses from an Old Manse*, which Melville had titled *Hawthorne and His Mosses*, to be published in two installments, the first within days. Melville was reasonably pleased by the published article, but Hawthorne's wife, Sophia, was downright ecstatic over the anonymous review. "Do not wait an hour," she wrote to her mother, "to procure the two last numbers of 'The Literary World,' and read a new criticism on Mr. Hawthorne. At last some one speaks the right word of him," she said proudly. Having no notion that the reviewer was known to her, she wrote in jubilation to Duyckinck, "Who can he be, so fearless, so rich in heart, of such fine intuition? Is his name altogether hidden?" Her very next sentence completed Duyckink's amusement: "We have been very much interested in Mr Melville's books."[4]

Within a few weeks, Duyckinck's device had come unraveled; but the friendship born out of a third party's trick had already cemented itself. For in those initial meetings—and in the social visits that followed—these two men had discovered that they were indeed kindred spirits. What bound them was not ancestry nor avocation; certainly not the fact that each had written novels—writers are notoriously suspicious and resentful of each other, as if one's stumbling upon an apt phrase or glorious metaphor forever robs the other. No, the tie that drew Hawthorne and Melville together was, in Melville's phrase, their common worldview, however differently expressed. This worldview centered upon an apprehension of what Melville called "the blackness of darkness," the mystery of existence in a world shaped by the seeming remoteness of God.

Less voluble than Melville, Hawthorne did not disclose much about his own religious beliefs, but he wrote extensively from a heritage that had begun ignobly and never fully recovered its faith. The cloud over Nathaniel Hawthorne—he added the *w* to his family name—was his filial connection to the greatest incident of religious madness and injustice ever perpetrated in America, the Salem witch trials of 1692. One of his ancestors, John Hathorne, had been a member of the tribunal in Salem, which heard charges of witchcraft made by hysterical young girls against a slave woman Tituba and hundreds of other men and women. Twenty of them were sentenced to be executed, including Martha Carrier, about whom Cotton Mather wrote, "The Rampant Hag, Martha Carrier, was the Person of whom the Confessions of the Witches, and of her own Children among the rest, agreed, That the Devil had promised her, she should be Queen of Hell."[5]

One of Judge Hathorne's colleagues on the Salem tribunal, Samuel Sewall, had kept a diary during and following the trials. A few of his entries recapture the setting:

April 11, 1692 Went to Salem, where, in the Meeting-house, the persons accused of Witchcraft were examined; was a very great Assembly; 'twas awful to see how the afflicted persons were agitated. Mr. Noyes pray'd at the beginning, and Mr. Higginson concluded.

August 19, 1692 This day George Burrough, John Willard, Jn Procter, Martha Carrier and George Jacobs were executed at Salem, a very great number of Spectators being present. Mr. Cotton Mather was there, Mr. Sims, Hale, Noyes, Chiever, &c. All of them said they were innocent, Carrier and all. Mr. Mather says they all died by a Righteous Sentence. Mr. Burrough by his Speech, Prayer, protestation of his Innocence, did much move unthinking persons, which occasions their speaking harshly concerning his being executed.

September 21, 1692 A petition is sent to Town in behalf of Dorcas Hoar, who now confesses: Accordingly an order is sent to the Sherrif to forbear her Execution, notwithstanding her being in the Warrant to die tomorrow. This is the first condemned person who has confess'd.[6]

From the outset of his participation in the Salem trials, Samuel Sewall had been troubled in his spirit. On April 20, a few days after the trials had begun, he was prompted to record, "Being pressed with the sense of my doing much harm and little good, . . . I kept a Fast to pray that God would not take away but uphold me by his free Spirit."[7]

By October 15, Sewall and another member of the tribunal, Thomas Danforth, were holding discussions as to how to bring their proceedings to an end. Governor William Phipps, by whose order the trials had commenced, now ordered the trials suspended; on October 26, 1692, Sewall wrote, "A Bill is sent in about calling a Fast, and Convocation of Ministers, that may be led in the right way as to the Witchcrafts."[8] That special assembly convened, as Sewall noted:

November 22, 1692 I pray'd that God would . . . choose and assist our Judges, &c., and save New England as to Enemies and Witchcrafts, and vindicate the late Judges, consisting with his Justice and Holiness, &c., with Fasting.[9]

The craze subsided but not the fear of God's judgment upon the unjust judges. Almost five years after the witch trials began, Sewall wrote in his journal:

January 14, 1697 Copy of the Bill I put up on the Fast day; giving it to Mr. Willard as he pass'd by, and standing up at the reading of it, and bowing when finished; in the Afternoon. Samuel Sewall, sensible of the reiterated strokes of God upon himself and family; and being sensible, that as to the Guilt contracted upon the opening of the late Commission . . . at Salem (to which the order for this Day relates) he is, upon many accounts, more concerned than any that he knows of, Desires to take the Blame and shame of it, Asking pardon of men, And especially desiring prayers that God, who has an Unlimited Authority, would pardon that sin and all other his sins; personal and Relative: And according to his infinite Benignity, and Sovereignty, Not Visit the sin of him, or of any other, upon himself or any of his nor upon the Land: But that He would powerfully defend him against all Temptations to Sin, for the future; and vouchsafe him the efficacious, saving Conduct of his Word and Spirit.[10]

But the example of Samuel Sewall's repentance was not followed by John Hathorne, who, according to his great-great-grandson, died unrepentant. In fact, Judge Hathorne left upon the family a blemish of prideful injustice, as well as the curses of those who died under his condemnation. Five generations later, these curses seemed to haunt Nathaniel Hawthorne, leading him to explore their implications in stories set in the New England theocracy of two centuries earlier. These were gothic stories of hidden guilt exposed ("The Minister's Black Veil"), nightmarish escapades in the forbidden forest ("Young Goodman Brown"), alchemy and other occult practices ("Rappacini's Daughter"), or a facial blemish whose root lies in the heart's undisclosed and evil secrets ("The Birthmark").

So obsessed was Hawthorne by his ancestral connection with civil evil, he eventually made it the central theme of his longer fiction, *The Scarlet Letter* and, in 1851, *The House of the Seven Gables*. In both novels, Hawthorne diagnosed a metastasizing spiritual cancer called cynicism. A cynic is marked by that most insidious of human traits: the inability to believe or trust in the motives of others. The result is a reflexive contempt for appearances, a suspicion that everyone else's actions are only a screen behind which to hide darker intentions. Indeed, cynicism's greatest feeding ground is a false religious profession; cynicism's theme, therefore, is an automatic assumption of hypocrisy. So cynicism penetrates and consumes the very soul of a human being, turning apparent goodness into consummate evil, apparent joy into wretched lament, apparent hope into despair. Infecting the spirit of men and women, cynicism is, therefore, the ultimate, all-pervasive destroyer.

For Hawthorne, the moral climate of the New England he recreated was thoroughly polluted by hypocrisy and the cynicism it engendered. Preoccupied by Salem's curses, Hawthorne began *The Scarlet Letter* with a lengthy introductory essay he called "The Custom House." Before introducing his romance about a virtuous adulteress and the vice of the two men who had wronged her, Hawthorne sought to absolve himself of his ancestor's guilt, describing John Hathorne as having had "the persecuting spirit," which contributed to making him so conspicuous in the martyrdom of the witches that their blood may fairly be said to have left a stain upon him. So deep a stain, indeed, that his old dry bones, in the Charter Street burial ground, must still retain it, if they have not crumbled utterly to dust!

Hawthorne professed not to know "whether these ancestors of mine bethought themselves to repent, and ask pardon of Heaven for their cruelties; or whether they are now groaning under the heavy consequences of them in another state of being."[11] Nonetheless, Hawthorne wrote,

At all events, I, the present writer, as their representative, hereby take shame upon myself for their sakes, and pray that any curse incurred by them—as I have heard, and as the dreary and unprosperous condition of the race, for many a long year back, would argue to exist—may be now and henceforth removed.[12]

For Hawthorne, the lingering evil remembered in the Salem of his lineage and recreated by his imagination served as the model for the world gone awry. Salem was a microcosm of moral decay, redeemable only by love and truth, apparently—alas—in too short supply to be effectual. Hawthorne had already demonstrated the fearful influence of this environment in the spiritual collapse of characters such as Goodman Brown; now in *The Scarlet Letter* he would carry forward both his sense of corporate and personal guilt and his need to participate in its expiation. To Hawthorne, the whole village of Salem was to blame for mercilessly punishing Hester Prynne and her daughter Pearl for a sin far less heinous than either a haughty spirit or hypocrisy. But Hawthorne did not fail to condemn individual sin as well; in particular, he charged the Reverend Arthur Dimmesdale with moral cowardice and Roger Chillingworth with heinous moral superiority.

A sketch of plot details scarcely begins to measure the novel's power. By inference, the reader pieces together those elements of the story that precede the narrative as written. A man is forced by circumstances to delay his own emigration to New England, and so the husband sends his wife, Hester Prynne, on ahead and alone. For some three years she has no word from him; meanwhile, she has come under the spell of a young divine, Arthur Dimmesdale, whose oracular preaching barely hints at the emotional fires within. Whether by assignation or happenstance, she meets him in the dark forest where, because paramount evil inhabits such regions, no pious person would dare venture. Spiritual passion becomes erotic desire; a child is conceived, born, and given the name Pearl. Hester is arrested, tried, and convicted of adultery, but she refuses to name the man who has fathered her child. Adamantly rejecting the threats and appeals of her judges, Hester Prynne remains steadfast.

Thwarted by her loyalty, Hester's judges determine that her crime merits punishment in two forms: First, she is exposed to public shame on the gallows platform for three hours; second, she is condemned to wear a self-incriminating letter *A* on her person. In fact, Hester Prynne is more fortunate than some: Hawthorne tells us, in a footnote, that a historical adulteress in New England had the letter burned into her forehead. At the very moment she is placed before the public, she sees in the crowd a face known only to her. It is her mishapened husband; his humped-back spine or any physical deformity serves as a clue to Hawthorne's readers—acquainted with the conventions of gothic literature—that his character is similarly deformed. Newly arrived, her husband passes himself off as one "Roger Chillingworth," a name with Dickensian evocation. Later, he visits Hester, seeking to extract from her the name of the one who has seduced his wife. All he gains from her is a reluctant promise not to reveal his own true identity. Thereupon he sets himself upon the task of discovering and exposing what the judges and he have not been able to learn: the identity of the man who has cuckolded him.

As *The Scarlet Letter* unfolds, Hawthorne heightens the drama by shining the searchlight of conscience upon the weak character of Arthur Dimmesdale, Hester's faithless pastor and paramour, and the corrupted soul of Roger Chillingworth, Hester's vengeful husband. Like Raskolnikov and Porfiry in Fyodor Dostoyevsky's *Crime and Punishment*—a near-contemporary volume published in 1866—a bond develops between the two men: the hunted and the hunter, the offending lover and—unknown to him—the offended husband.

But even as Dimmesdale's secret unravels before Chillingworth's prying and psychologically tormenting presence, a double shift in guilt and blame occurs. First, Chillingworth's vengeance turns him into a monster feeding off the moral frailty and psychosomatic collapse of Dimmesdale. In Chillingworth's obsessive demand for justice, he has canceled any hope of mercy for himself. Second, both men stand accused of faithlessness toward Hester and her daughter, neither man willing to assume his proper role and responsibility as either husband or father. For each of them, the accusation of little Pearl is stingingly accurate: "Thou wast not true!"

For Hawthorne, the violation of the sanctity of the human heart is the unpardonable sin. To be sure, both Dimmesdale and Chillingworth have sinned; but whereas Dimmesdale's sin originated in the heat of passion, the eponymous *Chilling*worth is a cold-hearted killer. Loving no one, he cannot bring himself to forgive, even though Hester pleads with him to do so. Seven years have elapsed since she first promised to keep both men's secrets. Now, believing that she can no longer deceive either, she asks Roger Chillingworth to forgive the man who has fathered Pearl, thereby gaining grace for himself:

> Forgive, and leave his further retribution to the Power that claims it! . . . There might be good for thee, and thee alone, since thou hast been deeply wronged, and hast it at thy will to pardon. Wilt thou give up that only privilege? Wilt thou reject that priceless benefit?[13]

To this appeal Chillingworth offers only a frozen theology and its analogical application. Chillingworth represents the law without any tempering of grace; his Puritan theology is part Calvinistic election and predestination, part pagan fatalism:

> "Peace, Hester, peace!" replied the old man, with gloomy sternness. "It is not granted me to pardon."

He goes on,

> My old faith, long forgotten, comes back to me, and explains all that we do, and all we suffer. By thy first step awry thou didst plant the germ of evil; but since that moment, it has all been a dark necessity. Ye that have wronged me are not sinful, save in a kind of typical illusion; neither am I fiend-like, who have snatched a fiend's office from his hands. It is our fate. Let the black flower blossom as it may![14]

The black flower—the noxious weed—represents the gothic sign of sin's manifestation to the world. In spite of the gardener's best efforts to extirpate it, the telltale plant will reveal its secrets; in fact, one of Dimmesdale's superstitious fears is that, if he dies with unconfessed sin, out of his grave will grow weeds of condemnation. Knowing this, the final judgment of Chillingworth upon his victim and—by virtue of his unforgiving spirit—upon himself is to leave to fate whatever will be. Thus borne down by vengeance, Chillingworth seems to shrink under its weight. Is it not just, therefore, that both Hester Prynne and Arthur Dimmesdale should escape Chillingworth's ultimate revenge, the preacher's public humiliation?

As Herman Melville had perceived and written in his review, Hawthorne's worldview assumed "the power of blackness," the overwhelming capacity of evil to imbue nature and human nature with its presence. Scarcely any other writer has offered so penetrating a view of religion in America. Yet while Hawthorne wrote extensively in his fiction about the visible effects of sin—its moral twistedness, its psychological impairment—almost nothing else exists to tell us about Nathaniel Hawthorne's personal religious faith or lack thereof. We are left to assume that Hawthorne's spiritual choices were shaped by his reaction against the cold and rigid religiosity of his forefathers.

Herman Melville's case is different. The son of Allan and Maria Gansevoort Melville was born in 1819 into a New York City family of Dutch extraction, the third of eight children. Melville's father was eternally optimistic about his fortunes yet financially imprudent and often deeply in debt. The stabilizing force in the family was Maria Gansevoort Melville, who provided her children with spiritual nurture and saw to it that they were baptized and learned the rudiments of Christian faith in the Reformed Church. From an early age, Herman Melville was well acquainted with the English Bible. By 1830, Allan Melville's business failure compelled the family to relocate permanently to Albany, where Maria Gansevoort Melville's family lived. Two years later, the father had died, broken by the burden of his debts. Maria's school-age children were compelled to leave school and find work. Herman took a variety of jobs, eventually teaching school in rural Massachusetts and New York.

In 1838, he took to sea for the first time on a merchant vessel to Liverpool. Later, he saw the world in all its depravity onboard the whaling vessel *Acushnet*, bound for the South Seas, where he jumped ship to enjoy a profligate escapade among the naked islanders. Finally, Melville joined the United States Navy and sailed 'round the Horn. While on these voyages, Melville witnessed the flogging of a seaman, a sight so brutal it turned him forever against any supposition of human perfectability. Furthermore, his views on the effects of Christian evangelism were not enhanced by his encounters with missionaries in the Polynesian or Sandwich Islands. All these impressions subsequently found their way into the adventure novels that followed, *Typee* and *Omoo*.

Upon returning home in 1844, Melville began courting Elizabeth Shaw, daughter of his father's best friend, Lemuel Shaw, chief justice of the Massachusetts Supreme Court; they were married in 1847. Two years later, Melville published *Mardi,* ostensibly another story of the South Sea islands but, in reality, Melville's first attempt at plumbing spiritual and allegorical depths. The book was not well received; in fact, Elizabeth Shaw Melville herself offered a critique well shared by the reading public when, in a letter to her mother, she spoke of "the 'fogs' of Mardi—if the mist ever does clear away."[15]

Melville now had a wife and, soon, children to support; he knew that he must write books that would sell. He had struggled to produce simple tales based on his seagoing adventures; his new books, *Redburn* and *White-Jacket,* were of the same type; but for all their popularity, his heart was not in them. Herman Melville was that anomaly of human nature, a person of comic wit whose seemingly shallow humor barely covers an interior of far more profoundly serious disposition. Except for the failed *Mardi,* his books had been lightweight. Meanwhile his private correspondence—often facetious and amusing—hinted at a soul in struggle with itself and with serious thinking.

For instance, in the winter of 1849, Melville and his wife went to Boston for the birth of their son. Melville spent two months indulging his mind, for the first time reading Shakespeare—as he wrote to Duyckinck, making "close acquaintance with the divine William."[16] His reading also included the works of Sir Thomas Browne, Hobbes, Locke, and Carlyle. On occasion he attended lectures, including one by Ralph Waldo Emerson, of whom he wrote:

I love all men who *dive*. Any fish can swim near the surface, but it takes a great whale to go down stairs five miles or more; and if he don't attain the bottom, why, all the lead in Galena can't fashion the plummet that will.[17]

He too would learn to dive, to take his intellect and emotions "down stairs." Furthermore, he would do so through the vehicle of another adventure story, this time set as a whaling voyage.

By May 1850, three months before meeting Hawthorne, Melville wrote to another new acquaintance, Richard Henry Dana, author of *Two Years Before the Mast,*

> About the "whaling voyage"—I am half way in the work. . . . It will be a strange sort of book, tho', I fear; blubber is blubber you know; tho' you may get oil out of it, the poetry runs hard as sap from a frozen maple tree;—and to cook the thing up, one must needs throw in a little fancy, which from the nature of the thing, must be ungainly as the gambols of the whales themselves. Yet I mean to give the truth of the thing, spite of this.[18]

Clearly, Melville had in mind another book based on his own experience, yet more than mere "blubber." Like "a great whale," Herman Melville was prepared "to go down stairs" into the realm of metaphysics, and take his reading audience with him. But how to extract the oil? How to "give the truth of the thing"?

By late June of 1850, still six weeks before meeting Hawthorne, Melville wrote to inform his English publisher that a new book could be expected by late autumn: "The book is a romance of adventure, founded upon certain wild legends in the Southern Sperm Whale Fisheries, and illustrated by the author's own personal experience, of two years and more, as a harpooner."[19] This description offers no hint of what was to come; perhaps Melville himself hardly knew. For *Moby-Dick* (Melville employed the hyphen to differentiate the book from the whale itself), the book that emerged almost seventeen months later, could scarcely have been advertised as "a romance of adventure."

How did such a transformation, from work in progress to the finished publication, occur? Scholars surmise that Melville's original intention may well have been to construct an adventure tale about a prodigious whale chased by a ship whose crew represented a floating microcosm—an early version of the United Nations. But at some point in the process of writing this book, Melville discovered in his new friendship with Nathaniel Hawthorne the catalytic agent necessary to bring about a fusion of his developing metaphysics with his art. In Hawthorne, he found a compatible spirit, someone whose own soul seemed to validate the significance of Melville's search to probe more deeply the questions of mortality and immortality, the seeming discrepancies between an infinitely loving God and his uncaring natural world, and the inadequacies of a purely conventional religious solution.

The transition from "a romance of adventure" to a metaphysical epic did not come readily. By mid-December 1850, Melville asked Duyckinck to send him "about fifty fast-writing youths" to help him with his work. In the spring of 1851, Melville told Hawthorne that he was headed for New York City, where he hoped to "work and slave on my 'Whale.'" But on June 29, 1851, he wrote to Hawthorne that he had returned to Pittsfield to "end the book."

> Shall I send you a fin of the "Whale" by way of a specimen mouthful? The tail is not yet cooked, though the hell-fire in which the whole book is broiled might not unreasonably have cooked it ere this.

Then Melville revealed "the book's motto (the secret one), Ego non baptiso [sic] te in nomine—but make out the rest yourself."[20]

Such spiritual enigmas and paradoxes filling Melville's mind were not to be resolved easily. Life could not be seen through the easy perspective of either/or; there were always those inscrutable, imponderable problems "from whose visitations," Melville had written of Hawthorne's stories, "in some shape or other, no deeply thinking mind is always and wholly free."[21] Foremost, perhaps, among these was the problem of evil contested, on the one hand, by Calvinists with their doctrine of original sin and innate depravity, on the other, by the romantic liberals with their idealized views of natural man. Melville had learned and witnessed the effects of both: his religious upbringing in the Dutch Reformed Church balanced by his personal experience with the Congregational missionaries and the Polynesian natives. He was certain that truth lay somewhere other than within the purview of these alternatives.

In this quest for truth, Melville recognized the essential predicament of human beings confronted by their need to resolve two conflicting states of being: either the apparent purposelessness of their lives, the aloofness of God, the vindictiveness of nature, or else the possibility of developing a personal reason for being, a personal relationship with the Creator, a full recognition of what it means to be fully human in this universe. But as Melville pondered more and more the problem he had set before himself, he came to believe that truth might be apprehended behind the appearances of nature, hidden from our glance until we penetrate its veneer. If nothing is what it seems, then the serious-minded man or woman looking to unravel life's conundrums would find instead secrets ever more tightly wound, knots no human mind could untie.

To help him find answers, Melville turned back to the Bible he had read as a child. His copy, inscribed in 1850, reveals how closely he read Job and Ecclesiastes in particular. From these deeply searching passages of Scripture, Melville drew in large measure the philosophical basis of his novel. Yet by the time he had finished the book—its dedication reading, "In token of my admiration for his genius, this book is inscribed to Nathaniel Hawthorne"—Melville was convinced that he had "written a wicked book."[22]

As with *The Scarlet Letter,* it would be absurd to attempt an analysis of *Moby-Dick* in the compass of a mere chapter. But one can learn a great deal about the book from the character of Ishmael, the narrator. "Call me Ishmael." With these enigmatic words the novel opens, introducing us to the archetypal wanderer, the permanent outcast. More than any other participant in the narrative, Ishmael is responsible for the metaphysical speculations that weave throughout descriptions of the whaling industry's technique, turning his analogies into a coherent tapestry so that the voyage of life is no longer a cliché but the definitive metaphor of human experience.

To this overriding synecdoche of the voyage must also be added the biblical temper in which the book is forged. From the names of his characters—Ishmael, Ahab, Elijah, Peleg, Bildad—to his parodies of the sacraments of baptism, holy communion, and consecration, Melville holds his book together by the fibres of biblical allusion. But the key, perhaps, to the whole work—its narrative and its meaning—may be found in the remarkable sermon, in chapter 9, preached by Father Mapple on the appropriate topic of Jonah and the whale.

Ishmael is a member of the congregation on the Sunday just before embarking; he devotes two chapters to describing the Seaman's Bethel, a chapel on Johnny Cake Hill in New Bedford, and its unusual pulpit. Then he introduces Father Mapple, whose dire warnings Ishmael can never forget; for when he reaches his peroration, Father Mapple foreshadows the woe or delight awaiting those about to board Captain Ahab's *Pequod*. The preacher begins with a catalogue of woe:

> Woe to him whom this world charms from Gospel duty! Woe to him who seeks to pour oil upon the waters when God has brewed them into a gale! Woe to him who seeks to please rather than to appal! Woe to him whose good name is more to him than goodness! Woe to him who, in this world, courts not dishonor! Woe to him who would not be true, even though to be false were salvation! . . .[23]

As the novel develops, Ishmael will be able to reflect on his own character and that of others upon whom such woes have fallen. But then Father Mapple shifts to prospects of delight:

> But oh! ship-mates! on the starboard side of every woe, there is a sure delight . . . Delight is to him—a far, far upward, and inward delight—who against the proud gods and commodores of this earth, ever stands forth his own inexorable self. Delight is to him whose strong arms yet support him when the ship of this base treacherous world has gone down beneath him. Delight is to him, who gives no quarter in the truth, and kills, burns, and destroys all sin though he pluck it out from under the robes of Senators and Judges.

Delight—top-gallant delight is to him, who acknowledges no law or lord but the Lord his God, and is only a patriot to heaven.[24]

The preacher reaches a crescendo of emotion as he utters,

And eternal delight and deliciousness will be his, who coming to lay him down, can say with his final breath—O Father!—chiefly known to me by Thy rod—mortal or immortal, here I die. I have striven to be Thine, more than to this world's, or mine own. Yet this is nothing; I leave eternity to Thee; for what is man that he should live out the lifetime of his God?[25]

But in spite of such religious ecstasy experienced by the godly Father Mapple, there are always other human beings so full of hubris, they feel compelled to attack every mystery. Melville delivers to us such a man, the heroic and tragic figure named Ahab, a Quaker sea captain "with a globular brain and a ponderous heart,"[26] who by virtue of the loneliness of his life at sea and a deep communion with nature had learned what Melville calls "a bold and nervous lofty language"[27]—in short, a man destined like Jacob to wrestle with God until either blessed or broken.

In Ahab's case, he is broken—branded by lightning, cursed by insomnia, obsessed by a monomania that burns like the fires of hell. For Ahab has also been shorn of his leg in mortal combat with the White Whale, Moby Dick. Out of that catastrophe Ahab emerges "with a crucifixion in his face; in all the nameless regal overbearing dignity of some mighty woe."[28] Ahab bears the weight of nature's apparent cruelty and, in time, comes to such a point of madness that, in the words of Ishmael,

all evil, to crazy Ahab, were visibly personified and made practically assailable in *Moby Dick*. He piled upon the whale's white hump the sum of all the general rage and hate felt by his whole race from Adam down.[29]

And so, Ahab conceives a plan. He engages a whaling ship and hires a crew "with the one only and all-engrossing object of hunting the White Whale" because Ahab "was intent on an audacious, immitigable, and supernatural revenge."[30] From this psychotic obsession, Melville shows a profound and frightening new aspect to Ahab's "fiery hunt." Ahab's goal is not merely to kill Moby Dick but to solve the riddle of the universe—to answer, once and for all, the question Why? It is a question whose very difficulty in answering baffles and eventually blinds to all reason the monomaniacal Ahab.

In a chapter called "The Whiteness of the Whale," Ishmael attempts to explain how, to Ahab, the natural phenomenon of an albino whale typifies nature's ambivalence toward him personally. If in the whiteness of the Milky Way, in the blank colorlessness of light itself, an introspective man finds starkest evidence of nature's unmeasured and unmeasurable expanse, what, then, is man in such an illimitable universe? The very thought corrodes the mind with intimations of annihilation. At the same time, man becomes aware that the universe in which he feels threatened is not itself unintelligible; it is full of meaning deliberately withheld from him. The universe chooses to remain dumb, while disclosing by one clue or another the rich stores of meaning it could open to him, if only it would. So, Ahab's madness tells him, the cosmic answer to his question Why? lies behind "the dead, blind wall" of Moby Dick's colossal body. The only access to truth is to penetrate the physical flesh of the Whale. Thus Ahab's frenzy as he captures the *Pequod*'s crew to his will:

> All visible objects . . . are but as pasteboard masks. But in each event—in the living act, the undoubted deed—there, some unknown but still reasoning thing puts forth the mouldings of its features from behind the unreasoning mask. If man will strike, strike through the mask![31]

Ahab has personalized all evil and named it Moby Dick: "He tasks me; he heaps me; I see in him outrageous strength, with an inscrutable malice sinewing it." Finally, his madness revealed, Ahab declares, "That inscrutable thing is chiefly what I hate; and be the white whale agent, or be the white whale principal, I will wreak that hate upon him."[32]

Ahab sets out upon his epic voyage with a crew consisting of three mates—Starbuck, Stubb, and Flask—a demented cabin boy, and a variety of half-breeds and renegades so diverse as to call to mind "the collective sinful posterity of Adam." Among the pagan harpooners is Queequeg, a cannibal chieftain yet a noble figure whose moral stability and courage stand out among a crew of no-accounts. As the "fiery hunt" is about to commence, Ahab bathes a special barb in the blood of his harpooners, howling deliriously, "Ego non baptizo te in nomine patris, sed in nomine diaboli,"[33] meaning "I do not baptize you in the name of the Father, but in the name of the devil." Later, Ahab gazes at the sea and says to Starbuck, "Who's to doom, when the judge himself is dragged to the bar?"[34] At last, the unspeakable has been spoken: Ahab has rejected his Quaker faith and made a Faustian pact with Satan to set himself as sole arbiter of what is and what is not just; aligning himself with those in rebellion against God, Ahab has determined to sue the judge of all the earth to stand accused himself at the bar of judgment.

By the novel's end, Ishmael has reached no final theological opinion about the universe and his place in it. He knows only that he is the sole survivor of a voyage brought to its doom by an obsession with evil more evil of itself. How far has Ishmael progressed toward spiritual awareness and maturity? Early in the book, Ishmael had made his claim: "I was a good Christian; born and bred in the bosom of the infallible Presbyterian church."[35] Yet soon thereafter, he had forsworn Christian orthodoxy and for a time adopted the heathenism of Queequeg. At midpoint in the novel, in a chapter called "The Funeral," Ishmael describes how the distant sight of a butchered whale's floating remains may be misconstrued and lead a gullible seaman to record in his log, "Shoals, rocks, and breakers hereabouts: beware." Ishmael notes, "And for years afterwards, ships shun the place; leaping over it as silly sheep leap over a vacuum. . . . There's orthodoxy."[36]

Ishmael's derision is consistent. Excepting only Father Mapple, the reader never meets a reputable representative of Christian orthodoxy. They are all either wild-eyed prophets, Shaker fanatics, or moral weaklings, like Starbuck, who—as Father Mapple warned—prefers the woe of seeking "to please rather than to appal." Yet Ishmael is no Ahab, in cahoots with the devil. In "The Fountain," Ishmael is discoursing on the whale's spouting but transposes the animal's natural act into "the act of thinking deep thoughts." Then follows his usual metaphysical clincher:

> And so, through all the thick mists of the dim doubts in my mind, divine intuitions now and then shoot, enkindling my fog with a heavenly ray. And for this I thank God; for all have doubts; many deny; but doubts or denials, few along with them have intuitions. Doubts of all things earthly, and intuitions of some things heavenly; this combination makes neither believer nor infidel, but makes a man who regards them both with equal eye.[37]

Clearly, Ishmael has chosen the role of skeptic; not the disbelieving antagonist but someone caught midway between belief and unbelief; yet he remains susceptible to "intuitions," the intrusion upon his rational consciousness of spiritual truths from beyond himself. Even his skepticism, however, must be qualified by the meditative cast of his private thoughts, for in those moments of contemplation, who could predict what illumination might strike?

So a contemplative Herman Melville appeared to Nathaniel Hawthorne some five years later, when the two men met in Liverpool, England, where Hawthorne was serving as American consul. How well Hawthorne understood his friend and the perplexities of his soul can be found in the entry Hawthorne wrote in his journal for November 20, 1856:

> [Melville] stayed with us from Tuesday till Thursday; and, on the intervening day, we took a pretty long walk together, and sat down in a hollow among the sand hills . . . and smoked a cigar. Melville, as he always does, began to reason of Providence and futurity, and of everything that lies beyond human ken, and informed me that he had "pretty much made up his mind to be annihilated"; but still he does not seem to rest in that anticipation; and, I think, will never rest until he gets hold of a definite belief.[38]

Hawthorne's compassion for a man in spiritual ambivalence shows itself in the concluding passage:

It is strange how he persists—and has persisted ever since I knew him, and probably long before—in wandering to-and-fro over these deserts, as dismal and monotonous as the sand hills amid which we were sitting. He can neither believe, nor be comfortable in his unbelief; and he is too honest and courageous not to try to do one or the other.[39]

But, in fact, Melville was no theological fence-straddler, balancing between belief and unbelief. He was more the wanderer whom Hawthorne describes—a literal Ishmael—and his own figure of speech, found in chapter 114, "The Gilder," traces a pattern of circular repetition through six stages of spiritual anxiety:

There is no steady unretracing progress in this life; we do not advance through fixed gradations, and at the last one pause:— through infancy's unconscious spell, boyhood's thoughtless faith, adolescence' doubt (the common doom), then skepticism, then disbelief, resting at last in manhood's pondering repose of If. But once gone through, we trace the round again; and are infants, boys, and men, and Ifs eternally. Where lies the final harbor, whence we unmoor no more?[40]

Melville's cycle, begun in innocent oblivion, passes into a shallow religiosity—perhaps compelled by parents—too readily taken for granted; thereafter, teenage doubt ensues before giving way to skepticism, then disbelief, and on to ultimate incredulity. *If* is the signal for the diametric opposite of faith, the maximal mistrust. It is the word beginning all attempts at discrediting God: "If God is good, then why . . . ? If God is omnipotent, then why . . . ? If God is loving, then why . . . ?" *If* is rooted in hubris, the overweening pride that deludes a human being into contesting with God, strength for strength. Many modern men and women still follow Melville's description, spinning endless spiritual cycles: reverting to infantile mindlessness, turning over one's faculties to charlatans offering panaceas for a price; or to puerile religious emotionalism, all too soon wilted for lack of depth; then back to doubt, skepticism, and disbelief—forever bound to the wheel of inconstancy. Here is the terror of repeating past errors, like the Bourbon kings of whom Leo Tolstoy wrote, "They have learned nothing and forgotten nothing."[41]

"Where lies the final harbor, whence we unmoor no more?" asked Melville, who never gave up the quest. For another forty years after meeting Hawthorne, after writing *Moby-Dick*, the old sailor who had earned his reputation as the man who had lived among the cannibals and had speculated about heaven and hell sought his own safe haven. Eventually in old age, it appears, Herman Melville may have found calm from his tempestuous doubts and disbelief in a harbor of faith. As W. H. Auden puts it in his poem,

> . . . he cried in exultation and surrender
> "The Godhead is broken like bread. We are the pieces."
> And sat down at his desk and wrote a story.[42]

That story is "Billy Budd, Foretopman," a solemn parable of good and evil. In *Moby-Dick*, the namesake of Hagar's bastard son had asked, "Where is the foundling's father hidden?" In "Billy Budd," Herman Melville provided an answer full of the promise in which he had come to hope for release from the nauseating merry-go-round of denial, the maelstrom of sinking doubt, bringing to the trusting "a far, far upward and inward delight."[43]

"Nature's Abominable Injustice and Indifference"————

Stephen Crane

The violence and insanity of war are a common theme in literature. From the *Iliad* to accounts of modern combat, war's horrific events become a paradigm for life at its best, as well as its worst.

War also helps to shape the profile of Stephen Crane. Born in 1871, six years after Robert E. Lee surrendered to Ulysses S. Grant at Appomattox Court House, Crane came from a long line of warriors, including one who presided at pre-Revolutionary War colonial assemblies; another who was the senior major general in George Washington's army; another, the highest ranking naval officer. As Crane wrote to a friend, he came from a family that did its duty to its country.

Crane's America was a nation struggling to regain the Union so precious to Abraham Lincoln, the Union for which blue had fought against gray. In the North, where Crane was brought up, contempt for the defeated South during the Reconstruction Era fueled a prevaling spirit hostile to the South's cause. Yet, at the age of only twenty-four, Crane created in his mind the most indelible and balanced account of the Civil War, his novel *The Red Badge of Courage*.

This work for which Stephen Crane is known worldwide stands apart from the work of lesser novelists, several of whom had the advantage of having served in the Union or Confederate armies and survived the horrors of Gettysburg and Missionary Ridge. Yet none of them could reproduce from memory the faithful realization of vivid scenes that Crane could only imagine. His short novel, barely one hundred pages long, astonished its early critics, who could not believe its author was not a Civil War veteran. In fact, as Crane told a friend in 1897, at the time of writing he had "never smelled even the powder of a sham battle." Instead, Crane suggested, he had obtained his "sense of the rage of conflict on the football field, or else fighting is a hereditary instinct," in which case, Crane concluded, "I wrote intuitively."[1]

Perhaps it was the very fact of his distance—emotional as well as physical—from the substance of war that gave Crane his characteristically dispassionate tone, his ability to eschew parochialism and partisanship—favoring neither Yankee nor Johnny Reb—in balancing his account of cowardice and courage. Perhaps it was his knowledge of depraved human nature and the possibility of salvation, gained by listening to his Methodist father's sermons, that equipped him to accept the possibility of a coward's redemption.

But while Crane's novel and journalism represented real wars in which real men were shot and bayoneted and killed by real weapons, another kind of war raged within Stephen Crane from adolescence on. This was a war between himself and his father's God, whom he described in one of his short poems as

> Blustering god,
> Stamping across the sky.[2]

What forces impel a child born into a godly home to rebel against his father and his father's God? Stephen Crane was born in Newark, New Jersey, the fourteenth child of a Methodist minister, the Reverend Doctor Jonathan Townley Crane, a graduate of Princeton, and his wife, Mary Helen Peck Crane; his parents were educated, devout, and rigid about their convictions. Not only was Crane's father a pastor and theologian, his uncle and grandfather were also Methodist clergymen; his mother's uncle was a Methodist bishop and one of the founders of Syracuse University. But young Stephen Crane seems never to have been anything other than Peck's bad boy—a preacher's kid at war in the sanctuary, in the parsonage, and in the secret recesses of his own heart. His strictly pious father preached against such profane amusement as the reading of novels. Although Stephen Crane wrote respectfully of his father's "great, fine, simple mind," the elder Crane often punished his youngest son with severe beatings; but even these thrashings seemed bearable when weighed against the sentence of listening to his father's interminable sermons about hell and damnation at the New Jersey Methodist camp meeting at Ocean Grove.

Nor was Stephen the only member of his father's household to disdain his father's teaching. Like many younger siblings, he came under the influence of an older brother. Stephen Crane had not been precocious in his rebellion; rather, it came on gradually, as he told a friend,

> I used to like church and prayer meetings when I was a kid, but that cooled off and when I was thirteen or about that, my brother Will told me not to believe in Hell after my uncle had been boring me about the lake of fire and the rest of the sideshows.[3]

The facetious irreverence of that phrase, "the rest of the sideshows," may offer a clue to the temperament of Stephen Crane. To say that he was persistently irreverent is an understatement; rather, Crane sought always to appear outrageous, more often than not blasphemous, in an era when blasphemy could only appear in print under the disguise of minced oaths and irony. For example, he recalls the seemingly unjust threat from the Decalogue's second commandment and uses a corrupted form of it to headnote a few lines of verse, before turning the venom of his sarcasm against the Divine Bully:

> "And the sins of the fathers shall be visited upon the heads of the children, even unto the third and fourth generations of them that hate me."

93

> Well, then, I hate Thee, unrighteous picture;
> Wicked image, I hate Thee;
> So, strike with Thy vengeance
> The heads of these little men
> Who come blindly.
> It will be a brave thing.[4]

Stephen Crane's résumé reads like that of many a modern rebellious student. He was sent to several schools, including Lafayette College and another brief enrollment at Syracuse, where he was more interested in baseball than in a baccalaureate education. Clearly, his heart was set on writing and women. His interest in writing came honestly enough. His father's sermons had been published; his mother's temperance lectures printed; two of his brothers were correspondents for the *New York Tribune*, for which his mother also wrote a column. But Crane was not content to write in the manner of ease and elegance popular in his parents' style; from his earliest efforts, something about his style shows the jagged edge of realism that was to mark the work of his entire but short-lived life.

The women came almost as soon as the writing. Crane seemed drawn to the very sort of woman his father and other Methodist clergy inveighed against from their pulpits: scarlet women, women of ill repute, temptresses, fallen women. Like the prodigal son, Crane also wallowed in corruption. His love affairs and liaisons included a notorious divorcee, an actress of some renown, and the madame of a brothel, Cora Howorth-Taylor, with whom, in the final years of his life, Crane lived outside the bounds of social and moral convention as common-law husband and wife. But while Crane frequented the harlots of New York City, there was more to him than mere lust: He also had a genuine humanitarian concern for the low-life existence of the urban poor.

During his brief stint at Syracuse University, Crane had written a fictional account of an impoverished young woman whose economic circumstances forced her into prostitution. The original draft was a young man's attempt at imagining a world he as yet did not know. But upon leaving Syracuse and heading for New York City, Crane became personally acquainted with the type he had imagined. Not only did he see their despicable living conditions for himself, but he also knew and supported the efforts of reformers such as Jacob Riis, author of a shocking exposé of tenement poverty, *How the Other Half Lives.* In the summer of 1892, Crane attended a lecture by Riis. The effect of that lecture can be seen in *Maggie: A Girl of the Streets,* published the next year under the pseudonym Johnston Smith.

After his novel *Maggie,* Crane showed himself to be more than merely a libertine bent on violating the religious scruples of his parents. He became an arch opponent of the moralizing hypocrisy of his day. He saw the blight of urban squalor and the poverty that, seemingly, left some women without a reasonable alternative to prostitution; he also witnessed the brutality of police and saw the cynicism it bred in common citizens; he perceived how corrupt politicians and police could demoralize a city and, in his *New York Tribune* pieces and articles for other newspapers, railed against them.

One of Crane's biographers, Robert Wooster Stallman, quotes this statement by Stephen Crane: "The sense of a city is war."[5] In a notorious case, a woman had been arrested for practising prostitution beyond the limits of the Tenderloin district of New York City, just south of today's Times Square. Crane, then writing for William Randolph Hearst's newspaper syndicate, covered her story and took the woman's side, claiming that she was a victim of selective arrest. In the process, Crane earned the ire not only of the cop on the beat but also of such underworld figures as Arnold Rothstein, who, a generation later, would be involved in the infamous "Black Sox" scandal that rigged the 1919 World Series. When even Theodore Roosevelt, then president of New York City's Board of Police Commissioners, failed to defend the prostitute thus falsely accused and harrassed by his own vice squad, Crane took up her cause and appeared in court on her behalf. The fact that the woman was not personally known to Crane made his defense of her all the more notable.

Furthermore, Crane's empathy reached beyond lines of social class and race. In the very era when the Supreme Court of the United States was interpreting the law of the land to permit "separate but equal" facilities, services, and accommodations for so-called negroes, Crane was writing his own minority opinion of *Plessy v. Ferguson*, decrying a social system that would turn every black man into a grotesque. His story, "The Monster," tells about Henry Johnson, a black stableman disfigured in a fire when he attempted to rescue a child—the son of his white employer—from a burning house. Thereafter, the black man—initially hailed as a hero—is turned into "a thing, a dreadful thing." Similarly, for showing compassion to the man who saved their son, Dr. Trescott and his wife are shunned by the community. Before one finishes the story, it becomes clear that Crane intends to identify another and more dreadful monster than Henry Johnson.

But even a far greater monster than the evils of human baseness and cruelty was yet to be tested. A "blustering God" had been cut down to size by Crane's refusal to believe; war had been reduced to so much blood and thunder by foolhardy risk; political thuggery had been undermined by personal courage; racial ostracism had been overcome by love. But what about nature? What of the abominable injustice and indifference of the elements in assaulting a lone human being?

The most significant context in which to find Stephen Crane's description of the struggle between humanity and nature is his story "The Open Boat," published in England in 1898. This fiction derives from an actual shipwreck Crane experienced. Commissioned to report on gunrunning from Florida to Cuba, Crane shipped from Jacksonville on board the tug *Commodore* on New Year's Eve of 1896. Off Daytona Beach, the ship foundered. Crane reported on the event in a dispatch to the *New York Press* datelined "Jacksonville, Fla., Jan. 6, 1897," and headlined as "Stephen Crane's Own Story."

The story places four men in a lifeboat: the cook, the oiler, the injured captain, and the correspondent. From its opening sentence, "None of them knew the color of the sky," Crane's story moves—like the ocean's deadly undertow—toward its inexorably deadly conclusion. The reader seems to be in the boat with the men; their every movement, every word, intensifies the drama as they fight for their lives against the superior strength of the stormy sea.

"The Open Boat" proceeds by episodes during which hope and despair alternate as the men's chances for rescue—shifting ever so slightly—seem to rise or fall. Crane evokes "the subtle brotherhood of men" being established as a result of their common predicament and reliance upon each other. They know the anxiety of their position, tired and hungry. "Shipwrecks are *apropos* of nothing," the correspondent realizes. As the tempest persists, the four men take turns rowing, rowing, and more rowing. They experience exhilaration when a man on the beach waves his coat at them; then desperation as the boat thrashes about in futility. Thereafter the correspondent begins to philosophize about his fate:

> If I am going to be drowned—if I am going to be drowned—if I am going to be drowned, why, in the name of the seven mad gods who rule the sea, was I allowed to come thus far and contemplate sand and trees? Was I brought here merely to have my nose dragged away as I was about to nibble the sacred cheese of life?

He knows—they all know—that they are fighting for their lives against the implacable forces of nature. These forces are both animate and inanimate. A shark whose enormous fin cuts "like a shadow through the water" and a vulture-like seagull, so sinister and ominous to the men, are both fearsome figures whose presence haunts the shipwreck survivors. But both the shark and the bird are out of the boat and are therefore secondary causes for concern. Cowardly as they are, neither the shark nor the bird will attack to feast upon their prey until the boat capsizes and the men lost. More immediate dangers are represented to the struggling men in the form of waves, tides, currents, wind, temperature, and darkness—all elements of nature whose presence in and around the tiny boat threatens the existence of the mariners with unceasing attacks. Against these representations of the natural universe the correspondent and his three fellow survivors are engaged in mortal combat.

Here an argument can be made that the struggle against nature is, in fact, a struggle against Nature, which, in turn, is a surrogate for the ongoing struggle against God. For in spite of all attempts to dismiss the faith of his fathers, Stephen Crane was unable to do so. Amy Lowell, who knew Crane well, wrote of Crane's religious heritage, "He disbelieved it and he hated it, but he could not free himself from it."[6] Crane had long ago separated himself from believing in theophanies, inspired Scripture, or an incarnate Messiah; however, he had not espoused atheism. Rather, he militantly opposed that which mere unbelief could not eradicate from his consciousness. Like Melville's Ahab, Crane carried on his personal hostility against God through the medium of a personified nature.

Thus God, sometimes disguised as nature, remains a character or caricature in Crane's art. This is not to say, fatuously, that because the idealistic pantheist saw nature as the garment of God, Crane saw those garments in tatters. The deeper reality lies in how one perceives God's revelation to humanity. The romantic poet William Cullen Bryant, for instance, could see in the flight of a water fowl the benevolent, guiding hand of God. To him, death was only the passing from this life to a mysterious realm beyond, the transition made as simply as one "lies down to pleasant dreams."[7] But for Crane, there would be a different conception of God. The God Crane recognized was the enemy.

Whether representing the sordid environment of the Bowery or the wretched living conditions of the American pioneers on the Plains, the only God whom Stephen Crane presents to his readers is a God whose implacable wrath and immutable decisions are wreaked upon human beings through the forces of nature and the privations that result from these destructive forces. Hence, God is in nature—no, God *is* Nature—disclosing himself now in mild and calm weather, now in hurricanes and tornadoes; now in a bountiful harvest, now in blight and devastation. As Daniel G. Hoffman notes, Crane's "'Blustering God' wears as his mask the visible forms of Nature. His wrath and rod are our hostile environment."[8]

God is also a bumbling incompetent of whom Crane writes mockingly:

> God fashioned the ship of the world carefully.
> With the infinite skill of an All-Master
> Made He the hull and the sails,

> Held He the rudder
> Ready for adjustment.

Yet, quite unlike Thomas Paine's "great mechanic," God became distracted when "at a fateful time—a wrong called." While God was attending to that emergency,

> Lo, the ship, at this opportunity, slipped slyly,
> Making cunning noiseless travel down the ways.
> So that, for ever rudderless, it went upon the seas
> Going ridiculous voyages,
> Making quaint progress,
> Turning as with serious purpose
> Before stupid winds.

Crane concludes,

> And there were many in the sky
> Who laughed at this thing.[9]

And, one might surmise, at least one Methodist preacher's son who also joined in that laughter.

In "The Open Boat," therefore, Crane presents nature as he does as a means of continuing his personal vendetta against the God whom he both despises yet fears as a bully. Of course, it is a risky critical practice to place too much emphasis upon autobiographical aspects of any art; nontheless, it is true that Crane's own experience in a shipwreck had a prolonged effect on him. Hoffman states that the catastrophe "did not alter his convictions about man's relations to nature; it simply confirmed them."[10] In her letter of June 3, 1900, to Moreton Frewen, Cora Crane tells of her dying husband's heartrending delirium: "My husband's brain is never at rest. He lives over everything in dreams and talks constantly. It is too awful to hear him try to change place in the Open Boat."[11] In the story itself, Crane had explained with what difficulty the balance of the boat might be maintained while places were being shifted so that one man might relieve another in rowing. Such care as the men took to keep the boat afloat is further proof of the fundamental human yearning for self-preservation. Crane's wife seems to be saying that, in the closing days of his life, Crane's subconscious mind appears to have reminded him of the desire to live, so that he concentrated in his feverish ravings upon keeping the boat of life afloat.

Throughout the first five sections of "The Open Boat," the author's language suggests the injustice of God, or Nature, toward humanity. But at the outset of the sixth section, Crane reaches the climax in his courtroom summation of his case against God. For the third time he repeats his incantation—"If I am going to be drowned"—offering logical reasons against a watery grave. So the narrator muses,

> During this dismal night, it may be remarked that a man would conclude that it was really the intention of the seven mad gods to drown him, despite the abominable injustice of it. For it was certainly an abominable injustice to drown a man who had worked so hard, so hard.[12]

Nature's injustice is Crane's first theme. It shows itself in one of Crane's poems, again depicting a powerful deity abusing a puny man:

> A god in wrath
> Was beating a man;
> He cuffed him loudly
> With thunderous blows
> That rang and rolled over the earth.
> All people came running.
> The man screamed and struggled,
> And bit madly at the feet of the god.
> The people cried,
> "Ah, what a wicked man!"
> And—
> "Ah, what a redoubtable god!"[13]

But after recounting the many unjust offenses of God, or Nature, Crane adopts a different posture. For the first time, the language of the story indicates not mere injustice but indifference to man's condition as Nature's only discernible trait. To the men in the boat, from this time on, as Danforth Ross writes, "the ocean is not animated by hostile gods, as with ancient Greeks, but is simply a manifestation of a nature indifferent to their fate."[14] Crane's earlier antagonism against God, centering upon his perception of the injustice of God toward humanity, carries into this new phase.

> When it occurs to a man that nature does not regard him as important, and that she feels she would not maim the universe by disposing of him, he at first wishes to throw bricks at the temple, and he hates deeply the fact that there are no bricks and no temples. Any visible expression of nature would surely be pelleted with his jeers.
>
> Then, if there is no tangible thing to hoot he feels, perhaps, the desire to confront a personification and indulge in pleas, bowed to one knee, and with hands supplicant, saying: "Yes, but I love myself."
>
> A high cold star on a winter's night is the word he feels that she says to him. Thereafter he knows the pathos of his situation.[15]

Note the understated tone of this passage. It merely "occurs to a man," writes Crane; his fictionalized correspondent might rather have argued that such an awareness resulted from the pounding reality of his potential death by drowning. "She would not maim the universe" is almost sarcastically amusing. The correspondent, who perhaps has not heretofore concerned himself much about the place of religion in his life, now "wishes to throw bricks at the temple." Of course, his disbelief has eliminated that option. So he would willingly resort to name-calling as a last resort.

Next, he contemplates pleading with Nature, based on the highest human motivation after altruistic sacrifice: self-preservation. Merely altering one's recognition of Nature's injustice to Nature's indifference has not eased the situation. In actuality, such realization multiplies the pathetic circumstances; for to be unjustly treated and abused may be lamentable, but to be ignored is a hundredfold worse. The latter exceeds the former, but in reverse, as pathos exceeds tragedy only in its folly. Such injustice at least implies recognition by the perpetrator of that injustice; indifference is nothing more than contempt.

No man can endure the sense of being held in contempt without resorting to some demonstration of his own self-importance. And so Crane's correspondent rightly imagines himself—cast adrift on the sea of life as survivors from the derelict ship that God let go rudderless—wishing "to throw bricks at the temple," if only to gain attention from the deity inhabiting that temple. But upon realizing the futility of his act, the correspondent casts himself upon the mercy of "a personification." The picture is awkward with incongruity: a disbeliever "bowed to one knee, and with hands supplicant." It is a vignette of a frustrated man who, after trying all other avenues of escape, now turns as if resigned to acknowledge a Supreme Being. But even in this remarkable image, so unlike the Crane we have come to expect, there is an irreverent note to assure the reader that Crane has not yet repented. The plea in which the bowed supplicant indulges says nothing about acknowledging a divine authority; instead, the correspondent is insistent upon his own worth: "Yes, but I love myself!"

Such is the admission of the egocentric man. His will to live receives its impetus from his desire to please himself. The Westminster Catechism defines "the chief end of man" as the obligation "to glorify God and to enjoy him forever." Crane rejects this religious tenet as so much double-talk and insists on the primacy of the individual as the single motivating current for existence. Yet he himself knows that such a view of life is ironically contradicted by Nature's having negated the value of any single human being. Nowhere is this perception more clearly delineated than in one of Crane's most memorable short poems. Daniel Hoffman has observed that "if man is alone in a hostile universe in Crane's fiction, the conditions of isolation and menace are intensified still further in his verse."[16] This poem stands as a clear example of Hoffman's point.

> A man said to the universe:
> "Sir, I exist!"
> "However," replied the universe,

"The fact has not created in me
A sense of obligation."[17]

Here we have in the finely drawn compression of a poem what Crane had expounded at greater length in "The Open Boat." If a man's mere existence is of no import, then surely no great measures will be undergone by Nature to rescue him from his predicament. God or Nature or Fate—called by whatever name one wishes—is under no obligation to strengthen a human being's precarious hold on life. Crane reworks this same theme in his least successful novel, *George's Mother,* when his hero realizes that "the earth was not grateful to him for his presence upon it." To retaliate, he drinks himself into oblivion, convinced that "the universe would regret its position when it saw him drunk." But what is the reply of the universe to man's cowering under her in petition for his own life? Nothing. Only the remote and indifferent shining forth of "a high cold star on a winter's night."[18]

For Hoffman, "the implication of such a world view is the terrible aloneness with which Crane's puny protagonists must face their fates."[19] Crane himself adequately summarizes the perilous position resulting from such isolation: "Thereafter he knows the pathos of his situation." There is no nobility in pathos, such as characterizes tragedy; no empathy from an audience stunned by pity and fear in a catharsis of identification. There is only the anticlimax of utter futility.

In the final dramatic episode of the story, Crane reiterates Nature's disinterest. He tells of a tower—presumably a windmill—on the distant beach:

> This tower was a giant, standing with its back to the plight of ants. It represented in a degree, to the correspondent, the serenity of nature amid the struggles of the individual—nature in the wind and nature in the vision of men.[20]

In the correspondent's view, the gigantic tower has turned deliberately away from the men, who are represented as mere insects. As he scans the horizon, the correspondent notes two contrasting aspects of the natural scene: "nature in the wind and nature in the vision of men." The blades of the windmill lazily turning suggest "the serenity of nature." This is "nature in the wind," the romantic view of those who perceive—mistakenly, Crane would insist—a kindly, sympathetic Nature; a benevolent and placid Nature under the calming influence of the knowledge that if "God's in his heaven, all's right with the world."

But all is not right, as the correspondent knows. The primitive, savage force of Nature "in the vision of men" is also apparent to them in the unimpeded tossing of their boat. They know all too well that Nature has no regard for equity or justice; in fact, Nature simply does not care. So the correspondent rejects two fallacious worldviews: the sunny optimism of a romantic, and the victimization of someone unfairly suffering. Instead, for him life on the sea, lived in the absolute imminence of disaster, has been an enlarging experience; in fact, he calls it "the best experience of his life." The correspondent has learned a new side of Nature and has reconciled himself to living with this new knowledge. He is not happy with what he has learned; however, he no longer looks to throw bricks at temples.

He realizes with matter-of-factness that Nature "did not seem cruel, . . . nor beneficent, nor treacherous, nor wise." Rather, "she was indifferent, flatly indifferent." Once again, there is a momentary hint at supplication and repentance:

> It is, perhaps, plausible that a man in this situation, impressed with the unconcern of the universe, should see the innumerable flaws of his life, and have them taste wickedly in his mind and wish for another chance.

But Crane, who had listened to many a preacher's altar call and had heard about radical conversion experiences all his life, is not prepared to take seriously his correspondent's wavering toward religion. Even though "a distinction between right and wrong seems absurdly clear to him . . . in this new ignorance of the grave-edge," the correspondent's penitence is limited and, in the end, merely facetious. All that Crane will allow is that "he understands that if he were given another opportunity he would mend his

conduct and his words, and be better and brighter during an introduction or at a tea." In the end, all the correspondent will concede is reform, not repentance; he will behave himself more with
genteel and socially acceptable habits. Gradually the impression
of Nature's indifference begins to work upon the correspondent
in a psychosomatic way. He finds his mind "dominated at this time
by the muscles, and the muscles said they did not care."[21] Like
Nature itself, the body of a man weary with toiling against impossible opposition no longer cares. Total indifference has become
the enlarging theme.

No further proof of Nature's dispassionate unconcern is needed,
but Crane has more to add: The water into which the men are
tumbled, when the boat finally swamps, is not only cold; "the
coldness of the water was sad; it was tragic." In his distraught condition the journalist sees just one more evidence of Nature's apathy toward him and his companions in the chilling temperature
of the sea. "The water was cold." One cannot read this simple
statement without remembering another of Stephen Crane's
equally simple declarations, "God is cold."

> A man adrift on a slim spar
> A horizon smaller than the rim of a bottle
> Tented waves rearing lashy dark points
> The near whine of froth in circles.
> > God is cold.

> The incessant raise and swing of the sea
> The growl after growl of crest
> The sinkings, green, seething, endless
> The upheaval half-completed.
> > God is cold.

> The seas are in the hollow of Thy hand;
> Oceans may be turned into a spray
> Raining down through the stars
> Because of a gesture of pity toward a babe.
> Oceans may become gray ashes,
> Die with a long moan and a roar
> Amid the tumult of the fishes

And the cries of the ships,
Because The Hand beckons the mice.

A horizon smaller than a doomed assassin's cap,
Inky, surging tumults
A reeling, drunken sky and no sky
A pale hand sliding from a polished spar.
God is cold.

The puff of a coat imprisoning air:
A face kissing the water-death
A weary slow sway of a lost hand
And the sea, the moving sea, the sea.
God is cold.[22]

The chilling refrain accompanies the vain struggles of a shipwreck survivor to overcome the traditional three-times-down-and-under of drowning. As Hoffman notes,

> Nature endures—the triple iteration of that last line ["God is cold."] makes it endure—and the God who, Christian doctrine assures us, is concerned with every sparrow's fall, takes not the slightest heed of "A face kissing the water-death," not even to judge his soul. The man is drowned; the sea goes on forever.[23]

Furthermore, the men in the boat need not be told of God's cold indifference. They have known it and realized it ever since first they saw "a high cold star," the perfect symbol of a deity disinterested in their plight.

One more ironic incident, perhaps Crane's most masterly invention in this story. Through the memory of the correspondent flashes the recall of a poem, an undistinguished bit of verse by a forgotten poet. Drawn from the far recesses of his mind, the correspondent "had even forgotten that he had forgotten this verse, but it suddenly was in his mind." The poem itself is typical of memory work once assigned to whole classes in schools. There is nothing especially noteworthy about its structure; only its theme interests us here. A man about to die in a foreign land whimpers over his fate and receives his only comfort from a comrade.

> A soldier of the Legion lay dying in Algiers.
> There was a lack of woman's nursing, there was a dearth of
>   woman's tears;
> But a comrade stood beside him, and he took that comrade's
>   hand,
> And he said: "I shall never see my own, my native land."[24]

As unaccountably yet vividly the poem seeps into his consciousness, the correspondent admits that, although "he had been made acquainted with the fact that a soldier of the Legion lay dying in Algiers, . . . he had never regarded the fact as important." This last statement underscores the situational irony. The correspondent had never considered seriously the plight of an anonymous soldier, a mere character in a narrative poem. One imagines the correspondent-as-schoolboy reciting his own singsong version of the poem; then, the reason for his unconcern becomes clear:

> Myriads of his school-fellows had informed him of the soldier's plight, but the dinning had naturally ended by making him perfectly indifferent. He had never considered it his affair that a soldier of the Legion lay dying in Algiers, nor had it appeared to him as a matter for sorrow. It was less to him than the breaking of a pencil's point.[25]

Like the soldier of the poem, the correspondent is also a dying man, comforted only by the presence of his comrades. But also like the young declamer of the poem, Nature—or God—has grown callous and indifferent to the peril of the doomed man. Incessant repetition of the same tragedy has dulled all compassion. To the schoolboy, the soldier's predicament seems less significant "than the breaking of a pencil's point." Now the correspondent is ready to make the unhappy analogy to his present predicament. While a pencil in the hand of either the schoolboy or the mature correspondent is an important instrument, the breaking of its tip may be frustrating but hardly life threatening. Only minor inconvenience results. In the classroom, a student may resharpen the point; on the battlefield, a correspondent simply reaches for another pencil or whittles a new tip. So, when Nature, or God, senses no anguish nor any feeling at all toward the endangered war correspondent—the human pencil—the loss of his life creates no sense of cosmic or divine obligation. It means nothing more than "the breaking of a pencil's point."

This realization—how many years after the fact?—makes the correspondent belatedly sympathetic toward the soldier of the poem. But is not his sympathy mere self-interested sentimentality because the correspondent hopes that, by displaying some human compassion now, Nature, or God, will take pity on him? When it becomes clear that no evidence of pity may be expected, the correspondent resigns himself. Faced by such absurd unfairness and unconcern, he reasons, a man might actually come to regard his own death as "a comfortable arrangement, a cessation of hostilities accompanied by a large degree of relief." Yet if no one else cares—not God, not Nature, not Fate—human beings care! And because human beings care, we fight against the logical possibility of our own deaths as "the final phenomenon of nature."[26]

In fact, the correspondent does survive; but the oiler who had fought so valiantly does not. With all the forces of Nature opposing the will of men to live, it is only to be expected that Nature will claim some victory. Foiled in the attempt to destroy all four in the open boat, Nature claims the one who had done the most to prevail. Thus the picture Stephen Crane draws of life's combat is stark with injustice and indifference. An earlier communique from his visit to Pennsylvania's coal mines sums up the conditions of human existence:

> It is war. It is the most savage part of all in the endless battle between man and nature. . . . Man is in the implacable grasp of nature. It has only to tighten slightly, and he is crushed like a bug. His loudest shriek of agony would be as impotent as his final moan to bring help.[27]

These, then, were the terms in which Stephen Crane experienced life—an unending struggle for survival in a hostile environment made more so by the ingenuity of men in devising ever more efficient means of inflicting physical and psychological pain upon each other and themselves. Such a view provides a working definition of *naturalism,* for it is life lived in subjection to the hostile forces of Nature yet always combating those forces. And when one substitutes God for Nature, that hostility rises to higher levels. It becomes war—implacable, all-out war—against God.

Halley's Comet and the Mysterious Stranger

Samuel Langhorne Clemens and Mark Twain

The puzzle that is Samuel Langhorne Clemens and his pseudonymous alter ego Mark Twain makes any serious reading of his work—in its turn—baffling, amusing, satisfying, uproarious, searching, and never less than piercing in its analysis of the human predicament. On the surface, at least, is the regional humorist creating or reshaping tall tales from the Western frontier; or the romancer delving into his imagination and love of pomp to reproduce the court of King Arthur or the palace of Henry VIII; or the admirer of nature whose eye can see power and beauty in a muddy, meandering river and evoke from the experience of an urchin boy and his slave companion transcendent illumination worthy of a religious profession. But here too is the acerbic social critic, demolishing with every sentence the mendacious, hypocritical code of life by which his despised society lives and judges others. In time, the reader also meets the embittered misanthrope, thoroughly contemptuous of "the damned human race."[1]

These are only a few aspects of the character known as Mark Twain. One must also recognize the stage performer, the public entertainer; the white-haired, white-suited, stand-up jester whose jokes stabbed both his audience and himself. In spite of this, Mark Twain was loved by the masses as few others in America have ever been; perhaps Will Rogers, W. C. Fields, Jack Benny, Milton Berle, and George Burns together might equal the popularity of Mark Twain alone on stage.

Behind this persona, of course, remained the man himself: Samuel Langhorne Clemens as frontier youth, journeyman printer, riverboat pilot, husband of a respectable wife, Olivia, father, friend, and failing businessman. Deeply beneath these several levels of being lodged the private man, nursing in increasing bitterness the soul of a belligerent—another man at war with God.

Clemens was born in 1835—a year that Halley's comet made its fabled return—in the region then known as the American Southwest, the far side of the Mississippi River. His father, John Marshall Clemens, a Virginian with pretensions to a noble lineage, had taken his family west to improve their fortunes. Settled in the riverside village of Hannibal, north of St. Louis, he managed to become a justice of the peace but failed both in land speculation and in the design of a perpetual motion machine—a failure ironically similar to his son Sam's sixty years later. So poorly did the elder Clemens's paltry fees for his services provide for his family that his wife found it necessary to take in boarders to help meet expenses. In 1846, Judge Clemens announced his candidacy for elected office; yet he could hardly afford the fee to have his name placed on the ballot. Just before the election, he died of pneumonia, leaving his wife, daughter, two older sons, and the almost eleven-year-old Sam.

The younger son needed a stronger father. Already he had begun to drift from the conventional religious orthodoxy he later parodied in Tom Sawyer's Sunday school quiz and scorched throughout many episodes in *Adventures of Huckleberry Finn*. With his father dead and his mother impoverished, Sam Clemens's formal schooling ended, and his life as an opportunistic and enterprising wanderer began. He started as a printer's apprentice at a local newspaper office, then joined his brother Orion at a rival paper, where he had opportunity to have his writing published. Encouraged by his success with brief humorous sketches, Clemens sought grander worlds to conquer. He left his brother for work in St. Louis, New York, Philadelphia, and back in St. Louis; then on to Keokuk, Iowa, and Cincinnati.

In our era of diminishing numbers and influence of newspapers, it may be hard for us to imagine the significance of the nineteenth-century newspaper as a civilizing force in American life, especially in the West. In some frontier settings, the newspaper editor and publisher was also one of the few literate and culturally sophisticated persons in the community, the others being the preacher and schoolmistress. In the case of Samuel Langhorne Clemens, whose formal education had been abbreviated, his apprenticeship and subsequent employment in newspaper offices and printshops could serve—like Melville's experience on whaling ships—to further his education.

But in 1857, Clemens left the newspaper shop for the river, the mighty Mississippi, where he learned the art and science of a riverboat pilot. As with Melville's whaling adventures, the riverboats were for Clemens a microcosm, acquainting him with "all the different types of human nature that are to be found in fiction, biography, or history," he later wrote in *Life on the Mississippi*. Some of these types—thieves, swindlers, con-men of all sorts, met on the vessels Clemens piloted—he portrayed with a filmmaker's sense of *cinema verité*, content to let the camera do the talking.

Perhaps the reason for Clemens's seeming nonchalance toward "the squalid venery" of steamboat life was his growing cynicism and virulent contempt for the hypocrisy of those whom the thieves robbed and the con-men duped. These were the reputedly upright citizens of Southwestern towns whose behavior onboard the paddlewheeler was often at odds with their onshore middle-class morality that governed life back home. Not unlike the climate of today's cruise ship or casino resort, the riverboats proved that shallow religiosity is often little more than a holiday away from exposing its own sham.

Clemens spent only about four years on the river, but as a result of that experience, "Mark Twain" was born. The pseudonym has ambiguous origins. It may stem from the steamboat crew's calling out the river's soundings in fathoms, "Mark twain" meaning that a depth of two fathoms is safe for navigation. But another version suggests a different origin: "Mark Twain" was a nickname applied to Clemens by Western saloon keepers because of his habit of charging two drinks at a time to his account. Still another account of Clemens's self-invention as "Mark Twain" holds that Clemens took the name—some would say he literally pirated it—from another would-be writer, Isaiah Sellers, whom Clemens had ridiculed in print so that Sellers gave up writing.

Whatever the origin of his pseudonym, when Fort Sumter was attacked in 1861, commercial travel on the Mississippi ended, and Clemens left the river forever. His next venue was a brief foray as a second lieutenant in Marion's Rangers, a ragtag company of undisciplined recruits. When word came that Ulysses S. Grant was about to attack, the heart of Marion's Rangers failed. They became a troop of cowards who "knew more about retreating than the man that invented retreating,"[2] Clemens later confessed in his sketch "Private History of a Campaign That Failed." By the summer of 1861, Clemens had rejoined his brother Orion, this time in Virginia City, Nevada, where Orion had been appointed secretary of the Territory of Nevada. Clemens knocked about as a silver miner before returning to write for the *Territorial Enterprise*. On February 1, 1863, he published his first piece under the pseudonym Mark Twain and so uncovered a treasure all his own, a rich lode called the "tall tale."

Moving on to San Francisco in 1864, Clemens became associated with the local colorist Bret Harte, author of stories such as "The Outcasts of Poker Flat." As a contributor to the San Francisco *Call*, and later as correspondent for the Virginia City *Enterprise*, Clemens worked to attain an identifiable voice, a style all his own. In November 1865, he published his sketch "The Celebrated Jumping Frog of Calaveras County," which circulated across the nation and brought Mark Twain his first notoriety. Sent to Hawaii by the Sacramento *Union*, Clemens returned to California with enough humorous material to go on stage as an entertainer. In October 1866, Mark Twain made his debut as a stand-up comic. By 1867, he had collected enough stories and sketches to publish his first book under the title of his now-famous *Jumping Frog*.

This early fame enabled him to make an excursion to Europe. From that trip Clemens obtained sufficient material to publish a satirical account of American tourists and American philistinism in general, *The Innocents Abroad*. This book, published in 1869, was an international success, and for the first time Samuel L. Clemens believed himself to be Mark Twain, the world-famous author. Onboard the *Quaker City,* he had met a fellow passenger who later invited Clemens to his home in Elmira, New York. There Clemens met Olivia Langdon, whom he married in 1870. Establishing their home, first, in Buffalo, New York, then in the sophisticated city of Hartford, Connecticut, Livy Clemens undertook to refine her rough-hewn husband as best she could, curbing his penchant for colorful profanity, his habit of eating, writing, and smoking in bed, his heavy drinking, and his spendthrift ways. Like the women in Huck Finn's life, Livy Langdon Clemens had set out to "sivilize" him against his will. To keep domestic peace, Clemens endured his wife's insistence that he adapt to the niceties of middle-class morality; but he resented in himself the resulting hypocrisy he found blatant in the culture around him.

Conventional religious observance and orthodoxy had always been obligatory in American society; consequently, hypocrisy had also flourished. But a new and riotous flowering of hypocrisy in post–Civil War America was rooted in an essential change in attitudes toward God and man and human destiny. The decades immediately following the surrender of the Confederate States in 1865 brought the rise of industrialization to New England. New machines, new manufacturing facilities and methods now overrode human effort and human significance. Mass production in factories replaced individual cottage craftsmen, making easier both the increase of productivity and profits, but also marking the beginnings of a concomitant loss of human dignity. Mill towns thrived, and the robber barons who owned the mills flourished and grew powerful. But with affluence and power came not only the demeaning of human values but also political corruption, a waning of true religion, and the rise of mere "churchianity" and unmitigated hypocrisy.

Revivalists such as Dwight Lyman Moody of Northfield, Massachusetts, inveighed against the shallow preaching of New England's clerics and pulpiteers, more noted for their oratory than for their spiritual fervor and passion for winning souls to Jesus Christ. Some listeners heard Moody and repented, among them, Henry Fowle Durant, founder of Wellesley College. But for the most part, Americans were ready to worship a new god called technology and pay homage to a new spirit of mechanistic optimism. The human race would save itself from further calamity like the war just concluded by inventing ever newer machines by which to improve the standard of living, an a-theology Justin Kaplan calls "a covert secular religion which, as an unexamined article of faith, believed in perpetual motion instead of eternal life."[3] In the terms that Henry Adams would use in 1907, America—like Europe—had replaced religion ("The Virgin") with technology ("The Dynamo").

To this heterodoxy Sam Clemens himself subscribed, largely because it provided an antidote to the cultural religiosity he despised. Never much for attending church himself, Clemens held in contempt those who posed as cultural Christians yet lived a lie. They were representative of the fraudulence that Clemens and Charles Dudley Warner described in their 1873 novel, *The Gilded Age*. But while this book attacked greed and chicanery and religious hypocrisy, its tone was so facetious that, as a result, its criticism was blunted. So too, his boyhood romance *The Adventures of Tom Sawyer* (1876), an exercise in adolescent foolery, with its parodies of piety in the riverfront town Clemens knew as Hannibal but renamed Petersburg.

But something deeper and more antagonistic than could be combated by mere witticism had lodged in Clemens's soul. As he aged, Clemens was becoming increasingly hostile toward both his fellow human beings and the God whose only attribute he considered to be cruelty. To a society not yet acquainted with the psychological analysis of jesters, clowns, and comedians, the bitterly misanthropic and disbelieving statements of the world-renowned humorist Mark Twain came as a shock. Onstage in his white suit and billowing white hair, he seemed to be free to utter the outrageous and only thinly veiled blasphemies he could not yet publish. Not only had Mark Twain taken to referring to "the damned human race," but he also spoke ironically, sarcastically, of God's "fatherly infatuation,"[4] which demonstrates itself by God's giving life, only to ravage human beings by disease and death.

What brought about this bitterness? Beginning in 1881, it seems, repeated commercial and personal disappointments and losses took their toll. For instance, on the business front, Clemens's heavy investment in a modern production machine had somehow been connected in his mind with that same optimism regarding the human race's potential for technological salvation under the influence of the machine. But the Paige typesetting machine fell short of its promise, and Clemens lost hundreds of thousands of dollars. Next, a publishing company headed by a relative but backed by Clemens collapsed in bankruptcy—a disgrace Clemens sought to overcome with honor by lecturing nonstop to pay his debts.

During a lecture tour of England, his beloved daughter Susy died of meningitis; another daughter Jean, who suffered from epilepsy, died; Livy became an invalid because of depression. These adverse circumstances—personal and financial—afflicted Clemens, who became more and more embittered. As Clemens's faith in the machine as a symbol of human perfectability wavered with failure after failure, the fantasy of human goodness and the reality of unavoidable suffering compelled in him a new sense of the tragicomedy called life. In *Pudd'nhead Wilson*, published in 1894, Twain summed up his estimate of life's value: "Whoever has lived long enough to find out what life is, knows how deep a debt of gratitude we owe to Adam, the first great benefactor of our race. He brought death into the world."[5]

No wonder that by the time he got around to completing the sequel to Tom Sawyer, his masterpiece *Adventures of Huckleberry Finn,* he had wearied of his role as America's funnyman; he was ready to probe the inner recesses of the human spirit and reveal both its full wretchedness and limited glory. He was also determined to expose the emptiness of institutional religion.

In many respects, *Adventures of Huckleberry Finn* is the great American novel. As Ernest Hemingway noted, "All modern American literature comes from one book by Mark Twain called

Huckleberry Finn. . . . It's the best book we've had."[6] But the story of Huck Finn and the runaway slave Jim is also one of the most misunderstood books in American literature, criticized alike by educational purists, misguided social moralists, and persons who lack the powers to perceive irony; thus its history of being trivialized by opponents of its misspellings and reviled by those who are insulted by its common use of racial epithets. Perhaps at the root of these opponents' various problems with the book is their failure to note that the narrator of the novel is neither the real-life Samuel L. Clemens nor his literary persona Mark Twain. The narrator is a creature of fiction, Huckleberry Finn, an early adolescent, semi-literate naif whose candor and common sense about what he sees to be the inconsistencies of human behavior compel him to question what lies behind the veneer of supposed civility and conventional religiosity.

Huckleberry Finn may not be possessed of a formally educated mind, and his heart may be no more pure than any other victim of human depravity; but he has a keen conscience. He knows the difference between truth and falsehood, and he prefers to be one of those who tells the truth. "You don't know about me," the narrator begins,

> without you have read a book by the name of "The Adventures of Tom Sawyer," but that ain't no matter. That book was made by Mr. Mark Twain, and he told the truth, mainly. There was things which he stretched, but mainly he told the truth. That is nothing. I never seen anybody but lied, one time or another, without it was Aunt Polly or the widow, or maybe Mary. Aunt Polly—Tom's Aunt Polly, she is—and Mary, and the Widow Douglas, is all told about in that book—which is mostly a true book; with some stretchers, as I said before.[7]

"That is nothing," says Huck Finn—the equivalent of today's casual utterance "No problem." But it is a problem, especially if the speaker suspects that he is being deceived. The only reason that Huck Finn can reduce the level of his concern as to whether or not Mr. Mark Twain "told the truth, mainly" or indulged himself in "some stretchers, as I said before," is the sorry fact that, in his experience, he "never seen anybody but lied, one time or another." Mendacity—as Tennessee Williams was to emphasize in *Cat on a Hot Tin Roof*—is not the exception but the rule in human discourse and behavior.

Adventures of Huckleberry Finn, therefore, is a novel whose theme is truth telling and the necessary compromises one must make with truth in order to survive. Huck Finn equates the making of such compromises to telling "stretchers" or telling the truth, "mainly." In an ideal world, Huck Finn would agree, truth would not be such a rare commodity; but in the real world he inhabits, even the best people lie "one time or another." The problem he faces lies in weighing the purpose and intent of those "stretchers" and their compromises: Is that purpose to advance self-interest and self-aggrandizement, or is telling a lie vindicated as a means of avoiding the consequences of an injustice worse than falsehood itself?

Huck Finn has come under the influence of the Widow Douglas, who intends to "sivilize" him by reading the Bible to him; even worse, her sister, Miss Watson, attempts to teach Huck the niceties of spelling and social decorum. His discomfort is increased by his own sense of hypocrisy. He hates pretense and sham; yet there he sits in his starched collar and woolen trousers, listening to the story of "Moses and the Bulrushers," when he would prefer to be enjoying a smoke in the woods. The Widow disapproves of smoking, although she is herself a user of snuff—acceptable, of course, because she does it. In even so trivial a matter, Clemens introduces polite society's double standard for judging the uprightness of someone else.

Clemens uses such characters as the Widow and her sister and their peccadillos to advance his case against conventional morality and orthodox religion. For instance, in an early chapter, Miss Watson lectures the boy about prayer, assuring him that "whatever I asked for I would get it." Huck Finn has his doubts.

> But it warn't so. I tried it. Once I got a fish-line, but no hooks. It warn't any good to me without hooks. I tried for the hooks three or four times, but somehow I couldn't make it work. By-and-by,

one day, I asked Miss Watson to try for me, but she said I was a fool. She never told me why, and I couldn't make it out no way.[8]

Huck Finn wants to believe. Even his disappointment over not being able to "make it work" does not entirely quash his willingness to test the power of God to answer prayer. He mulls the matter over:

> I says to myself, if a body can get anything they pray for, why don't Deacon Winn get back the money he lost on pork? Why can't the widow get back her silver snuff-box that was stole? Why can't Miss Watson fat up? No, says I to myself, there ain't nothing in it. I went and told the widow about it, and she said the thing a body could get by praying for it was "spiritual gifts." This was too many for me, but she told me what she meant—I must help other people, and do everything I could for other people, and look out for them all the time, and never think about myself. This was including Miss Watson, as I took it. I went out in the woods and turned it over in my mind a long time, but I couldn't see no advantage about it— except for the other people—so at last I reckoned I wouldn't worry about it any more, but just let it go.[9]

Gradually the boy's cynicism toward religious profession intensifies as he encounters the gullibility of the devout adults who are easily duped by his father's fraudulent conversion. But a change is coming for Huckleberry Finn when he meets an authentically decent human being in the kindly person of the runaway slave Jim. Huck Finn escapes to an island in the middle of the Mississippi, where he finds Jim, one of Miss Watson's slaves, who has risked his life by running away. Together they construct a raft and set out to float down the river.

In the Southwest of that period, provisions of the Missouri Compromise of 1820 obtained. In that year, Congress had agreed to admit into the Union both the state of Maine as a free state and Missouri as a slave state. Then in 1850, Congress passed the Fugitive Slave Law, which exacerbated the tension between defenders of "the peculiar institution" of slavery and advocates of emancipation. Regarded by the federal government as legitimate property, slaves who escaped from their masters were liable to be hanged; those who fled to free territory were not to be welcomed as if delivered from bondage but were to be returned across state lines to their owners. For a citizen of a free state not to comply was tantamount to stealing someone else's belongings.

This, then, is the ethical and moral climate in which Huck Finn finds himself when he learns that Jim intends to flee further down the river to freedom in Illinois at Cairo, where the Ohio river meets the Mississippi. As their raft approaches Cairo, Huck recalls,

> Jim said it made him all over trembly and feverish to be so close to freedom. Well, I can tell you it made me all over trembly and feverish, too, to hear him, because I begun to get it through my head that he was most free—and who was to blame for it? Why, me. I couldn't get that out of my conscience, no how nor no way. It got to troubling me so I couldn't rest; I couldn't stay still in one place. It hadn't ever come home to me before, what this thing was that I was doing.[10]

What troubles Huck Finn's conscience is the fact that he knew Jim's intention to run away and had done nothing to prevent it or report Jim to the authorities. In his culturally twisted mind, even Miss Watson becomes a victim:

> Conscience says to me, "What had poor Miss Watson done to you, that you could see her nigger go off right under your eyes and never say one single word? What did that poor old woman do to you, that you could treat her so mean? Why, she tried to learn you your book, she tried to learn you your manners, she tried to be good to you every way she knowed how. That's what she done."[11]

By Huck's reasoning, matters worsen when Jim tells him that, when he gets to free territory, he intends to work hard, save enough money to buy his wife—a slave on another farm near Petersburg—and two children owned by yet another slaveholder. "And if their master wouldn't sell them, they'd get an Ab'lition-ist to go and steal them," Huck recalls in horror.

> It most froze me to hear such talk. He wouldn't ever dared to talk such talk in his life before. Just see what a difference it made in

him the minute he judged he was about free. . . . Here was this nigger which I had as good as helped to run away, coming right out flat-footed and saying he would steal his children—children that belonged to a man I didn't even know; a man that hadn't ever done me no harm.[12]

Irony always loses power if it is subjected to analysis. Like explaining a joke, the effect of verbal play—whereby a phrase or an incident must be understood to mean its very opposite—becomes ineffectual. Yet here, Clemens is deliberately compounding irony upon irony: A teenage boy, conditioned by the ethos of his culture to accept slavery as legal, is appalled that another human being would violate those laws, not only by seeking his own freedom and that of his wife but also considering further illegality in abducting his own children from their slavemaster. The ironies begin with the boy's distortedly equating mere *ethics*—the standards of his society—into *morality*—the higher standards of religious sensibility. The ironies continue when one realizes that Jim also accepts the ethos and assumes that, in seeking his and his family's freedom, he is—as Huck says—lowering himself. Then there is the irony that slavery exists at all in a nation brought into being by a declaration that states as its premise,

We hold these truths to be self-evident: That all men are created equal; that they are endowed by their Creator with certain unalienable rights; that among these are life, liberty, and the pursuit of happiness . . .

Finally—and most ironic of all—is the fact that, twenty years after the Emancipation Proclamation and the war that divided the Union, some of Sam Clemens's readers did not perceive these ironies at all. So also it is today.

Huckleberry Finn attempts to do what his ethics would call the right thing. Clearly, on the narrative graph that Clemens/Mark Twain is sketching, two lines are being drawn to describe Huck Finn's ethical values and moral virtues. His ethical line is falling off sharply; his moral line is rising steeply. Those who miss the author's ironies also misread the graph. Thus they are unprepared

121

to recognize the novel's genius and lasting power, which stem from its conflict over what Clemens considered genuine good and genuine evil: human fortitude at war with decadent religious superstition. For Clemens, the symbols of this religious superstition were belief in heaven and hell. In his latter years, Clemens almost never ceased to occupy himself by combating such beliefs, more often with acid humor. For instance, when the pious Miss Watson begins threatening Huck with the dire prospects of hell and insists on her own likely heavenly destination, Huck tells us, "Well, I couldn't see no advantage in going where she was going, so I made up my mind I wouldn't try for it. But I never said so, because it would only make trouble, and wouldn't do no good."[13]

This theme of choosing hell over heaven presents itself at the most critical moment—indeed, the narrative climax—of the novel. In chapter 31, Huck Finn discovers that Jim has been apprehended and is being held in grave danger at the Phelps farm. Once again Huck begins to reason: Should he or should he not write a letter to Miss Watson, telling her the truth about her slave's whereabouts? Would Jim be better or worse off? And what about his own reputation?

> It would get all around, that Huck Finn helped a nigger to get his freedom; and if I was to ever see anybody from that town again, I'd be ready to get down and lick his boots for shame. . . . The more I studied about this, the more my conscience went to grinding me, and the more wicked and low-down and ornery I got to feeling. And at last, when it hit me all of a sudden that here was the plain hand of Providence slapping me in the face and letting me know my wickedness was being watched all the time from up there in heaven, whilst I was stealing a poor old woman's nigger that hadn't ever done me no harm, and now was showing me there's One that's always on the lookout, and ain't agoing to allow no such miserable doings to go only just so fur and no further, I most dropped in my tracks I was so scared.[14]

So scared, in fact, because he realizes that "people that acts as I'd been acting about that nigger goes to everlasting fire."

Huckleberry Finn has reached the point at which his ethical acuity and moral awareness are at their most distant opposites.

And what does Sam Clemens/Mark Twain have him do? Huck Finn prays; more accurately, he tries to pray.

> So I kneeled down. But the words wouldn't come. Why wouldn't they? It warn't no use to try and hide it from Him. Nor from me, neither. I knowed very well why they wouldn't come. It was because my heart warn't right; it was because I warn't square; it was because I was playing double. I was letting on to give up sin, but away inside of me I was holding on to the biggest one of all. I was trying to make my mouth say I would do the right thing and the clean thing, and go and write to that nigger's owner and tell where he was; but deep down in me I knowed it was a lie—and He knowed it. You can't pray a lie—I found that out.[15]

So too did Hamlet's uncle Claudius, who in his remorse attempts to pray the prayer of the penitent. Yet even in the act of kneeling, Claudius asks, "But, O, what form of prayer / Can serve my turn?" Not willing to give up that which he gained by his misdeeds, he knows full well that his prayer is nothing short of hypocritical. Still, he is enough of a practical politician to go through the motions of prayer, to "try what repentance can. What can it not? / Yet what can it, when one cannot repent?" So, like Huckleberry Finn, he kneels until, at last, he too admits the truth:

> My words fly up, my thoughts remain below;
> Words without thoughts never to heaven go.[16]

Unlike the murderer Claudius, however, Huck Finn finds a solution. He decides to write the letter to Miss Watson, "then see if I can pray." The change is astonishing: "I felt good and washed clean of sin for the first time I had ever felt so in my life, and I knowed I could pray now." He writes the letter; but just before prayer, Huck is distracted by

> thinking how good it was all this happened so, and how near I come to being lost and going to hell. And went on thinking. And got to thinking over our trip down the river; and I see Jim before me, all the time . . . ; and then I happened to look around, and see that paper.[17]

Here is the moment of crisis. With everything sacred on the line—eternal destiny in the balance—Huckleberry Finn makes a choice between his prevailing culture's ethics and a natural morality.

> It was a close place. I took it up, and held it in my hand. I was a trembling, because I'd got to decide, forever, betwixt two things, and I knowed it. I studied a minute, sort of holding my breath, and then says to myself: "All right, then, I'll go to hell"—and tore it up.[18]

By so exposing the bankruptcy of mid-nineteenth century Christian ethics in favor of innate human decency, Clemens was declaring war not only on racism and its demeaning of human life; he was also and principally attacking those institutions that had promoted the ethics of slavery and continued to advance the cause of "separate but equal." Foremost among these institutions was the church.

In much of Clemens's later work—*A Connecticut Yankee in King Arthur's Court* (1889), "The Man That Corrupted Hadleyburg" (1899), "The Mysterious Stranger" (posthumous, 1916)—he rails against the American social class system, the *status quo,* and in particular a smug religiosity, by which he meant hypocrisy. Yet Clemens was guilty himself of seeking to have it both ways: Making his assaults on conventional Christianity but doing so under the disguise of humor and satire; or worse, in the estimate of his critics, deliberately delaying publishing his work until after his death so as to maintain his popularity and earning capacity as a humorist. One of these critics, Van Wyck Brooks, in *The Ordeal of Mark Twain,* deplores the timid and devious manner of Clemens in carrying out his anti-religious sentiments. Brooks blames both the cowardice of Clemens himself and the repressive influences of his wife, Livy, and friend William Dean Howells—himself the author of *A Modern Instance,* the first American novel about divorce—for Clemens's failure to publish whatever representation of blasphemy or, at least, minced oaths might have been possible for publishers of his era. For instance, "Captain Stormfield's Visit to Heaven" was withheld for forty years, Brooks claims. When

Clemens consulted Howells about releasing the story, Howells conservatively advised Clemens to publish it first in England, where its endorsements "will draw some of the teeth of the religious press, and then reprint it in America."[19]

In his wife, Olivia—his beloved Livy—Clemens found both his single greatest inspiration and impediment to his art. She provided the seemingly rootless vagabond with the refinements of a home and a stable environment in which to work; but these very refinements also carried with them her disapproval of anything she considered coarse and crude. Thus, Brooks contends, it was Olivia Langdon Clemens's Calvinistic conscience that imposed upon Mark Twain a censorship that prevented him from giving vent to the full scope of his social criticism. Other critics, however, blame Samuel Langhorne Clemens for having sold himself short. Instead of writing the acidic and blasphemous critique that might have challenged the conventional morality of his time, Clemens seemed to content himself with merely poking fun at evident absurdities.

Yet there is much antagonism and hostility intended against the God of his wife's polite society; or, if not against that God, certainly against the professing worshipers of that God. One needs only to examine "The Man That Corrupted Hadleyburg" to see the direction in which Mark Twain's readers were being led, even if unknowingly and against their will. Beginning with a rhapsodic description of Hadleyburg as "the most honest and upright town" and its citizens' inordinate pride in their self-righteousness, Mark Twain moves quickly to expose the dangers of a community content to be "sufficient unto itself" and which "cared not a rap for strangers."[20] All that is needed is to appeal to the curiosity and greed of persons over-confident in their own probity and goodness. To test the residents' capacity for hypocrisy, a stranger concocts a scheme by which someone will be able to claim a reward for recalling the exact words spoken during an act of kindness. But there never was such an act, nor any memorable statement; it is all a ruse to show how readily the incorruptible people of Hadleyburg will yield with an embarrassing lack of shame. In time, one of Hadleyburg's citizens realizes that the town's reputation for honesty is "*artificial* honesty, and weak as water when temptation comes." She acknowledges that "this town's honesty is as rotten as mine is."[21]

At the story's end, Hadleyburg's official seal is changed from "Lead Us Not into Temptation" to "Lead Us into Temptation," which—in Mark Twain's estimate—makes it "an honest town once more." How so? It is the opinion of Samuel L. Clemens, who, like one of his characters, is "a frank despiser of the human species,"[22] that corruptibility is truer to human nature—and therefore a more honest appraisal—than is the pretense of self-righteousness.

The evaporation of idealism, especially to the sentimental and romantic mind, is always accompanied by bitterness and cynicism. Religious disaffection and social disgust pervaded most of Clemens's last years—although he retained as one of his closest friends a Hartford clergyman, the Reverend Joseph Twichell. But even so negative a portrait of human frailty as "The Man That Corrupted Hadleyburg" did not prepare Mark Twain's admirers for the final vision he offered, pointing in the direction toward personal annihilation, articulated in his unfinished allegory, "The Mysterious Stranger." All the darkest terms apply to Mark Twain's depiction of human existence: pessimistic, bleak, inexorably despairing. Here Satan states to "the damned human race" the nihilist's creed:

> There is no God, no universe, no human race, no earthly life, no heaven, no hell. It is all a dream—a grotesque and foolish dream. Nothing exists but you. And you are but a thought—a vagrant thought, a useless thought, a homeless thought, wandering forlorn among the empty eternities.[23]

Furthermore, Mark Twain inveighs against

> a God who could make good children as easily as bad, yet preferred to make bad ones; who could have made every one of them happy, yet never made a single happy one; who made them prize their bitter life, yet stingily cut it short; who mouths justice and invented hell—mouths mercy and invented hell—mouths Golden Rules, and forgiveness multiplied by seventy times seven, and invented hell; who created man without invitation, then tries to shuffle the responsibility for man's acts upon man, instead of honorably plac-

ing it where it belongs, upon himself; and finally, with altogether divine obtuseness, invites this poor, abused slave to worship him![24]

Shortly before he died, Samuel Langhorne Clemens said, "I came in with Halley's comet in 1835. It is coming again next year, and I expect to go out with it. It will be the greatest disappointment of my life if I don't go out with Halley's comet. The Almighty has said, no doubt: 'Now here are these two unaccountable freaks, they came in together, they must go out together.' Oh, I am looking forward to that."[25]

Clemens had his wish fulfilled in death. Within a few days of the comet's 1910 return, he died at Redding, Connecticut. His friend William Dean Howells eulogized him as "the Lincoln of our literature," and Henry L. Mencken called him "the true father of our national literature." But, for all such plaudits, Samuel L. Clemens is also the forerunner of twentieth-century disbelief. Upon completion of *A Connecticut Yankee,* Clemens had written to Howells,

> Well, my book is written—let it go. But if it were only to write over again there wouldn't be so many things left out. They burn in me; and they keep multiplying; but now they can't ever be said. And besides, they would require a library—and a pen warmed up in hell.[26]

One cannot read such words without recalling a similar passage in a letter from Herman Melville to Nathaniel Hawthorne: "I have written a wicked book, and feel spotless as the lamb." Not so, Samuel L. Clemens. For all his subtle declarations of war against God, he never satisfactorily exorcised himself of the demons that possessed him.

7

Eluding the Hound of Heaven

The English Neo-Pagans

By the middle of the nineteenth century, the England of Thomas More and Thomas Cranmer, of Oliver Cromwell and Oliver Goldsmith's "Vicar of Wakefield," of John Bunyan and John Wesley had changed dramatically. The structure and mood of society, particularly toward the practice of established Christianity, had been disrupted by economic forces that shattered the British ethical system. The commercial triumph that was the Industrial Revolution had transformed England from a bucolic and agrarian landscape, dominated by neatly cultivated fields surrounding tiny villages and their parish churches, into a cauldron of foundries and belching smokestacks and rows of tenements. In only a half century, the population had doubled, and the industrialized centers of manufacturing had swelled with people, many of whom had no voluntary religious inclination whatever.

Accustomed to centuries of conformity to the rituals of class consciousness, the British aristocracy and its serving class were both shaken when the Industrial Revolution created a new breed: the middle class, with its rising expectations of wealth derived not merely from consanguinity and birthright, not merely from hard work, but from ingenuity and invention. Men without breeding, without education, without manners, but possessed of extraordinary imagination and the ability to turn the new machines to human advantage, were suddenly rich almost beyond reckoning.

Such a cataclysm in the social order meant that all the categories were overturned. The aristocrats still claimed their titles and their land, but they no longer possessed all the money. Those whose lot in life had once seemed fixed as members of the serving class saw new openings in manufacturing and business. In such topsy-turvy economic conditions—as every social scientist knows—conventional morality, distinct from religious conviction, often depends on one's level of financial security and confidence. When a segment of society discovers that its financial base is shrinking, one natural reaction is to retreat from any semblance of faith to cynicism. Similarly, when another segment of society finds itself unaccountably increasing in wealth, a frequent reaction is not a more intense piety but an unrestrained greed for even greater gain.

Formal religion, especially as represented by the established church, was in major disarray. For with the growth of middle-class affluence came a lessening of dependence upon the God who had been relied on to "supply all your needs according to his riches in glory by Christ Jesus" (Phil. 4:19 KJV). The census of 1851 had already determined that, on a given Sunday—it happened to be March 30—only 7.2 million out of almost 18 million in England had attended any form of religious service; of those who had attended some church or chapel, only 52 percent had entered a sanctuary belonging to the Church of England.

Part of the reason for this endemic apathy toward formalized religion may have been the nature of the Church of England's elitism, especially at the parish level. In an era in which illiteracy was still not uncommon among village folk, bishops often required that their clergy be educated both at university and at theological college and be fluent in the Hebrew and Greek texts of Scripture. The parish priest saw himself—not without some cause—as a member of both the learned class and the gentry. Meanwhile, at least some of his people languished in conditions of periodic economic distress, rampant disease, infant and child-bearing mor-

129

tality, debtors' prisons, and Dickensian poverty. By the 1890s, the last Victorian decade, the established church had fallen even more deeply into its long decline, accelerated thereafter by the general disillusionment created by the Great War of 1914–1918. Aristocrats and working class alike, professionals and tradesmen, industrialists and artisans, turned away from institutionalized religion to something else.

Among some writers and other artists, that something else was neo-paganism. Like the late-twentieth-century renewal of neo-paganism called "the New Age," the nineteenth-century movement also derived from a revival of romanticism extended into aestheticism: the glorification of nature, vegetarianism and anti-vivisectionism, sexual license and exhibitionism, all in the name of personal and political liberty. Accompanying these manifestations of neo-paganism came a new sense of freedom from religious constraints and an open hostility to Christianity and its God. Some writers discovered that they could now expend their literary energies expressing their contempt for institutionalized religion, especially that of Great Britain. For them, their enmity against God and the vacuum created by the extirpation of conventional faith was filled by a new paganism called aestheticism. The essence of aestheticism is emotion elevated above reason, the supremacy of feelings engendered by the perception of beauty or pain or love or the quest for personal and social liberty, and its appeal to the senses over logical argument.

The anti-intellectual and heterodox roots of aestheticism reach back into the eighteenth century and the mysticism of William Blake. Influenced by his father's Swedenborgianism, Blake believed that he was in constant communication with the spirit world of demons and angels. Blake thought of himself and all other poets, including John Milton, as being "of the Devil's party without knowing it"[1] because they advocated liberty and love as the highest human aspirations. He saw Hell as a place in which to celebrate "the enjoyments of Genius, which to Angels look like torment and insanity." In *The Marriage of Heaven and Hell*, Blake explained that he and his "particular friend"—an angel transformed into a devil—"often read the Bible together in its infernal or diabolical sense."[2]

Rather than conform to any orthodoxy, Blake followed a religion of imagination, one of whose principle doctrines was freedom, which Blake treasured; thus, both the revolt of the American colonies in 1776 and the French Revolution of 1789 were divinely inspired events, prototypes of what should be appropriated by all individuals and extended through all societies. In an essay addressed "To the Christians," he wrote,

> I know of no other Christianity and of no other Gospel than the liberty both of body and mind to exercise the Divine Arts of Imagination—Imagination, the real and Eternal World of which this Vegetable Universe is but a faint shadow.[3]

In this pursuit of personal liberty, Blake advocated a necessary anarchy and purifying antinomianism. "To cleanse the face of my spirit by self-examination," he wrote,

> I come in self-annihilation and the grandeur of inspiration,
> To cast off rational demonstration by faith in the Savior.[4]

Rather, he looked to the glowing example of Jesus himself. In "The Everlasting Gospel," Blake described the effect of the incident recorded in John 8:

> Was Jesus chaste? or did he
> Give any lessons of chastity?
> The Morning blushed fiery red:
> Mary was found in adulterous bed;
> Earth groaned beneath, and Heaven above
> Trembled at discovery of Love.
> Jesus was sitting in Moses' chair,
> They brought the trembling woman there.
> Moses commands she be stoned to death,
> What was the sound of Jesus' breath?
> He laid His hand on Moses' law;
> The ancient heavens, in silent awe,
> Writ with curses from pole to pole,
> All away began to roll.[5]

Under the rubric of philosophical anarchy, therefore, aestheticism becomes heightened to a cult, the worship of beauty.

But neo-pagan aestheticism also transcends the romantic poet's fancy upon seeing "a host of golden daffodils"[6] or even the sentimental thrill of lost love. Aestheticism is essentially a religious and political movement led by the artist himself, who becomes both priest and promulgator of laws.

In 1821, Percy Bysshe Shelley—who had been dismissed from Oxford for espousing atheism—completed an essay, "A Defense of Poetry," in which, like Blake, he contrasted "reason and imagination," proposing that

> the former may be considered as mind contemplating the relations borne by one thought to another, however produced, and the latter as mind acting upon those thoughts so as to color them with its own light, and composing from them, as from elements, other thoughts, each containing within itself the principle of its own integrity.[7]

"Reason," Shelley stated, "is to imagination as the instrument to the agent, as the body to the spirit, as the shadow to the substance." He then went on to claim that "poets are the unacknowledged legislators of the world" because the poet

> not only beholds intensely the present as it is, and discovers those laws according to which present things ought to be ordered, but he beholds the future in the present, and his thoughts are the germs of the flower and the fruit of latest time.[8]

What Shelley and other poets perceive that the rationalist does not is that "the great secret of morals is love." So, "Poetry thus makes immortal all that is best and most beautiful in the world. . . . Poetry redeems from decay the visitations of the divinity in man."[9]

According to Shelley, "Poetry is indeed something divine. It is at once the center and circumference of all knowledge." If so, is not the poet also "at once the center and circumference"[10] of all that matters? Therefore, aestheticism recreates an old order—East of Eden—in which the self is pre-eminent and one's own perception of reality becomes paramount. For if, as John Keats wrote, "'Beauty is truth, truth beauty,'—that is all / Ye know on earth, and all ye need to know,"[11] then the message of the Grecian Urn—and, by extrapolation, the meaning of all art—becomes essentially a solipsistic reduction of truth to whatever beauty may be found in the eye of each beholder. And what higher beauty—therefore, what higher truth?—can the self discover than that residing within?

This was the pagan creed of aestheticism. Under the aegis of nineteenth-century critics such as John Ruskin and the poet and designer William Morris, an image of the artist emerged as polymath and, therefore, sole arbiter of ethical and moral right and wrong, based on individual taste. For instance, Morris added to poetry both interior decorating—the Morris chair, tapestries and carpet, along with elegantly bound books—and utopian politics as a means of altering Victorian ugliness. In the early 1880s, Morris left the Liberal party to help found the Social Democrat Federation; yet within six years, he had abandoned this party in disillusionment.

In *Modern Painters,* Ruskin wrote, "Great art is produced by men who feel acutely and nobly; and it is in some sort an expression of this personal feeling."[12] The artist was presumed, therefore, to possess heightened powers by which to determine taste and style, a code of living different from other mortals doomed to a middle-class mentality and conventional living. Under the guise of defending personal liberty or human rights, a glamorized self-indulgence—no matter how scandalous or outrageous, no matter how socially reprehensible—began to be countenanced with impunity. This, then, is the essential character of neo-pagan aestheticism, raised to a high level of self-absorption by the successors to Blake, Shelley, and Keats.

First among them is Edward FitzGerald, whose "transmutation," as he termed his work, of the twelfth-century Persian poet Omar Khayyam's "Rubaiyat" created a sensation in Victorian England. Born in 1809, FitzGerald graduated from Trinity College, Cambridge, and returned to Suffolk, where he lived as a country gentleman with more than a passing interest in ancient languages. For example, in his midfifties, FitzGerald took up the study of Persian with a Cambridge professor. In only six years, he had sufficient mastery of that language to attempt an English version of Omar's epic, published in 1859, the same year that saw Charles Darwin's *Origin of Species*.

Omar Khayyam had been a mathematician and astronomer in the royal palace at Babylon, where he earned fame for his work on a new calendar; he also produced a treatise on algebra. But his lasting acclaim was for the five hundred quatrains he wrote on many themes, including the poet's fatalistic vision of life; his daring hostility against Allah, the prophet Mohammed, and conventional Islam; his celebration of an infidel's folly. Yet scholars who know the original poem object that FitzGerald's "transmutation" accentuates more than did Omar the themes of skepticism, agnosticism, and outright unbelief in rebellion against God; in fact, FitzGerald largely overlooks those parts of Omar's poem calling for religious devotion. So in the guise of representing a distant and foreign worldview, FitzGerald was actually representing his own contrary values. Like many of the seventeenth-century metaphysical poems—Andrew Marvell's "To His Coy Mistress," for example—the principal theme of FitzGerald's "Rubaiyat" is *carpe diem*, seize the day. In an orgy of self-indulgence, FitzGerald's speaker cries out,

> Come, fill the Cup, and in the fire of Spring
> Your Winter-garment of Repentance fling;
> The Bird of Time has but a little way
> To flutter—and the Bird is on the Wing.

> Whether at Naishapur or Babylon,
> Whether the Cup with sweet or bitter run,
> The Wine of Life keeps oozing drop by drop,
> The Leaves of Life keep falling one by one.

> . . . .

> A Book of Verses underneath the Bough,
> A Jug of Wine, a Loaf of Bread—and Thou

Beside me singing in the Wilderness—
Oh, Wilderness were Paradise enow!

Some for the Glories of this World; and some
Sigh for the Prophet's Paradise to come;
Ah, take the Cash, and let the Credit go,
Nor heed the rumble of a distant Drum!

. . . .

Ah, make the most of what we yet may spend,
Before we too into the Dust descend;
Dust into Dust, and under Dust, to lie,
Sans Wine, sans Song, sans Singer, and—sans End!

. . . .

Oh threats of Hell and Hopes of Paradise!
One thing at least is certain—*This* Life flies;
One thing is certain and the rest is Lies—
The Flower that once has blown forever dies.

Strange, is it not? that of the myriads who
Before us passed the door of Darkness through
Not one returns to tell us of the Road,
Which to discover we must travel too.

. . . .

The Moving Finger writes, and, having writ,
Moves on; nor all your Piety nor Wit
Shall lure it back to cancel half a Line,
Nor all your Tears wash out a Word of it.

. . . .

Ah, Love! could you and I with Him conspire
To grasp this sorry Scheme of Things entire,
Would not we shatter it to bits—and then
Remold it nearer to the Heart's Desire![13]

FitzGerald invested his "transmutation" of a Persian poem with his own fatalism and idealization of love. But at the core of his "Rubaiyat" lies also an idolization of self; for it is the speaker of the "Rubaiyat" himself who is the focal point. His version of an

Islamic nobleman is contrary to the very principle of submission that the word *Islam* represents. Instead, FitzGerald paints a portrait of a rebel, an unrepentant libertine, a drunken profligate who risks all for wine, women, and still more wine.

This was a portrait increasingly popular among aesthetes of the later nineteenth century, for whom affectation of strange attire and outrageous personal conduct became an obligation. Algernon Charles Swinburne, Oscar Wilde, Aubrey Beardsley, among others, typify this phenomenon. Swinburne, a brilliant student of the classics who left Oxford before receiving a degree, had an early connection there with the Pre-Raphaelite Brotherhood; but he moved quickly beyond their mild protests to establish his own reputation for "feverish carnality," as one critic described his first published poems. Before the age of thirty, Swinburne had written "Atalanta in Calydon," a drama in verse replicating a Greek tragedy. One phrase in the opening chorus speaks of "the hoofed heel of a satyr." This hint at sexual debauchery defined the paganism which Swinburne espoused: Not only a fascination with classical and Germanic mythology but also an ardent opposition against conventional morality and its religious underpinnings in Christian theology. Elsewhere in "Atalanta in Calydon," Swinburne wrote of "the supreme evil, God"—a line which so offended Christina Rossetti, she erased it in her copy.

In his "Hymn to Proserpine," the goddess of the Underworld, Swinburne borrowed the legendary dying exclamation of the Roman emperor Julian, half brother of Constantine. Reared a Christian, Julian had defected in his young manhood, thereafter earning the nickname "the Apostate." When he became emperor, late in 361, he set about to institute policies of religious tolerance, welcoming the return of pagan worship alongside his half brother's imperial church. The following year, Julian the Apostate helped to organize the pagan priesthood in ways similar to the church's hierarchy. He attempted to rebuild the temple at Jerusalem, but his work was thwarted by an earthquake, which Christians interpreted to be the intervention of God. After this, Julian turned hostile to the church, imposing taxes on the clergy, preventing Christians from teaching in schools, and promoting pagans to political office. In 363, he was killed in battle. Allegedly, his final words were *"Vicisti, Galilaee!"* "Thou hast conquered, O Galilean!" In Swinburne's version, the text is more than a resigned capitulation; it is a continuing declaration of hostilities based on the speaker's assessment of the damage done by the Galilean's triumph: "Thou hast conquered, O pale Galilean; the world has grown grey from thy breath."[14]

What does Swinburne the Apostate mean by his acquiescence and accusation? In what sense has the "pale Galilean" conquered? Whom has he conquered? Evidently, not Swinburne. Does the speaker mean that, since the civilized world of his day is known as Christendom, Jesus Christ has conquered? Or does he mean, perhaps, that because the Christian ethic has prevailed—compelling its cold, passionless, moral rectitude; proscribing sexual relations except in marriage, never for the joy and pleasure of sensuality, only for the sole purpose of procreation: Is this how Christ has conquered? Whatever he means, the consequences of that victory are seen in only the most baleful and gloomy light: ". . . the world has grown grey from thy breath." Rather than inspiring each human being with resurrection life, the figure of Christus Victor infects those upon whom he breathes with the curse of death. A disease called conventional morality, an illness named conformity, a plague called religion, ravages the would-be pagan aesthete. So, for Swinburne, the fitting response to the conquering Christ was bold rebellion:

> Though all men abase them before you in spirit, and all knees
> bend,
> I kneel not, neither adore you, but standing, look to the end.[15]

As evidence of his rebellion, after the "Hymn to Proserpine," Swinburne turned to themes almost too depraved for publication in the Victorian age.

This is the same stance struck by one of Swinburne's contemporaries, William Ernest Henley. In 1874, Henley, an aspiring poet and tubercular patient in Edinburgh Infirmary—having lost one foot to infection—was in danger of losing the other also. His physician, the renowned Joseph Lister, hoping to save him, encouraged him to write about his experiences during his hospitalization. Henley wrote a series of sonnets—"Enter Patient," "Waiting," "Staff-Nurse: Old Style," "Staff-Nurse: New Style," and others—which were published, first, in *The Cornhill Magazine,* later collected as a volume entitled *In Hospital.*

While Henley recuperated, the *Cornhill* editor, Leslie Stephen, introduced him to a fellow patient and fellow contributor to the magazine, Robert Louis Stevenson, also confined in Edinburgh Infirmary with tuberculosis. One of Henley's vignettes of hospital life is "Apparition," in which he describes Stevenson as

> Buffoon and poet, lover and sensualist;
> A deal of Ariel, just a streak of Puck,
> Much Antony, of Hamlet most of all,
> And something of the Shorter-Catechist.[16]

Henley himself had none of "the Shorter-Catechist" in his disposition; in fact, he despised institutional religion and opposed any hint of a loving God. The presence of disease and suffering was evidence enough against such a notion; when his young daughter died, Henley became resolute in his disbelief. In his poem "Space and Dread and the Dark," he speaks of being possessed by "some enormous, rudimentary grief." Henley's worldview is wholly pessimistic: Life offers little more than "haunting loneliness" and "a desperate sense, / A strong foreboding."[17]

A man who lives from his youth with the spectre of death may be understood for his fatalistic views but hardly excused when his malignancy corrupts a former friend's reputation. An explanation, however, may be found in Henley's worldview, which dispenses with weakness in others and finds strength only in the adamantine fatalism of one's own determinism. If remembered for nothing else, William Ernest Henley is known for his poem "Invictus."

> Out of the night that covers me,
> Black as the Pit from pole to pole,
> I thank whatever gods may be
> For my unconquerable soul.

In the fell clutch of circumstance
I have not winced nor cried aloud.
Under the bludgeonings of chance
My head is bloody, but unbowed.

Beyond this place of wrath and tears
Looms but the Horror of the shade,
And yet the menace of the years
Finds, and shall find, me unafraid.

It matters not how strait the gate,
How charged with punishments the scroll,
I am the master of my fate;
I am the captain of my soul.[18]

Headnotes in student anthologies sometimes introduce this poem as an example of "rugged individualism" and "Emersonian self-reliance." No doubt about it: The persona who speaks—seemingly for Henley—in this poem is certainly secure in his self-reliance. Nothing undermines his resolve to remain unassailable, impenetrable, invincible. But this poem is more than a declaration of personal independence; it is an invocation to spiritual rebellion, even though the speaker is compelled to acknowledge some power beyond his own. Ironically, the speaker is not able to swear only by himself and his own veracity. He must invoke some higher order; so he chooses to thank "whatever gods may be" for himself and his all-sufficiency. This speaker is nothing if not resilient. He has taken the worst the malignant universe has to offer. Bad luck, misfortune, happenstance, circumstance, or chance: None of these has been able to summon from him the slightest whimper. Nor will he succumb to any sentimental fear of the unknown after death. Neither "the Horror of the shade" nor "the menace of the years" can shake him.

The speaker knows that he is flying directly in the face of the Bible's warnings: "Strait is the gate, and narrow is the way," said Jesus of Nazareth; the scroll of Scripture is indeed "charged with punishments" against offenders; but the speaker is resolute in his rebelliousness: "I am the master of my fate; / I am the captain of my soul." On one level, these final lines may be read as an admirable assertion of personal responsibility. In spite of religion's hectoring—in spite of Christianity's dire warnings—the speaker has willingly accepted whatever consequences may result from his decision to reject divine authority and submission to it. Rather, he will rely solely on himself and blame no one else; he is master and captain of the ship he sails. But on another level, the poem reveals a puerile mind, ranting at an unacknowledged transcendence, cursing the very darkness he prefers, congratulating himself on those choices that limit and constrain, and calling himself free.

He is free, of course, because the God he scorns will not compel worship—not yet. He is free to blaspheme and idolize himself. C. S. Lewis wrote in *The Great Divorce*, "There are only two kinds of people in the end: those who say to God, 'Thy will be done,' and those to whom God says, in the end, '*Thy* will be done.' All that are in Hell choose it."[19] So, the self-centered disbeliever gains the very eternity of his fondest choice, the hell of his own making.

Etymology often uncovers curious derivations of words, with sometimes even more curious applications. Two words that, to the conventionally religious, possess almost exclusively pejorative connotations are *pagan* and *heathen*. For most English-speaking persons, these words classify animists, idolaters, and sensualists, setting them apart from orthodox believers. Upon hearing either word, our imaginations provide impressions, perhaps, of fanatical devotees before some gigantic statue of a patron goddess, engaged in the horror of human sacrifice, or, as in Romantic poetry, a sensualist's adoration of nature and its phenomena.

But both words, *pagan* and *heathen*, have far more innocent origins. A pagan is merely someone from the *pagus*, the Latin word meaning "countryside." By the nature of human social development, city dwellers in Rome or Carthage refined the religious practices brought with them from their rural homes. Their former bucolic practices tended to be more primitive than sophisticated cities would tolerate. For example, while Ephesians may have enjoyed their orgies at the Temple of Diana, they were well beyond believing that the divine huntress nightly rode the moon as her chariot. They would have regarded with scorn the simple traditions and practices still carried on, in the name of the same goddess, in the *pagus*. To call someone a pagan, therefore, was something like our referring to an Appalachian resident as a "holy roller" or "snake handler"—an epithet of disrespect carrying all the status superiorities of geography, education, culture, and religious refinement implicit in the speaker's use of the term.

In the New Testament account of the early church's growth, the Acts of the Apostles makes it clear that Christian evangelists first preached in cities. It seems probable, therefore, that Christian usage also described a pagan as someone who remained subject to the old mythological religions or, worse, to the ancient Canaanite rituals: someone who had not yet moved from the provinces of Satan to become a citizen in the city of God.

In much the same manner, the word *heathen* comes from the Old English and its Christian influence under kings and scholars such as Alfred, Canute, and the Venerable Bede. A word similar to ours designated those *heath-men* who literally lived "on the heath." Therefore, while Christianity flourished in the Briton of Augustine and Anselm, at Canterbury and Old Sarum and York, the isolation of those heath-men from these centers of Christian worship kept them from being converted. In their ignorance they continued to obey Druid and other superstitions to which their ancestors had appealed. Chief among all such superstitions were those addressed to the mediating powers of good and evil revealed in nature, thereby binding human beings to worship the elements of air, water, earth, and fire.

Leaping across the centuries, as we have already seen, the nineteenth century brought to English letters a new period of paganism. Charles Darwin's *Origin of Species*, the hectoring of Thomas Huxley, and liberal theology's doctrine of melioration may have led some proponents to an all-encompassing theory of material and scientific progress; however, a contrary attitude toward life and art also re-emerged at that time. Appearing to grow out of the earlier romantic imagination of William Blake, William Wordsworth, Samuel Coleridge, and other poets, its earnestness in advocating human capacity to learn enduring lessons from nature, its glorification of the past, and its emphasis upon personal liberty were expressed in optimism and passion for reform.

But to more serious neo-pagans, such romanticism seemed merely puerile. Their authentic pagan roots were to be found in the aesthetics of the Renaissance, in the mysteries of medievalism, in classic Greek and Roman art with its sense for beauty even in the struggles of daily life. Like his predecessor, the new pagan found life to be oppressed by morbidity and decadence, governed by fate and doom, subject to dark and brooding memories. The brevity of life was deeply troubling; its only recourse, the immediacy of experience. In nature, the pagan artist found little consolation but only further evidence of mankind's isolation—a freak in a sterile environment inhabited by elemental spirits hostile to human life. For comfort, the artist chose aesthetic pleasure, a heightened sensuality more important than the intellect.

Thus, neo-paganism sanctioned the cult of the beautiful, whose rites depend upon experience leading to self-indulgence; in short, to hedonism and, in particular, sexual perversion. The pagan element in art correlates with the degree of the artist's absorbing fascination with himself, his body, his passions. It is sensuality transferred from the nerves to the canvas, the marble block, the page. In language, paganism accentuates its rhetoric until the writer's voice becomes tremulous with feeling, his emotions elevated to the pitch of Percy Bysshe Shelley's cry, "I shrieked, and clasped my hands in ecstasy."

If Edward FitzGerald's "Rubaiyat of Omar Khayyam" is the keystone poem of neo-paganism—hedonism's love-song—then its argument is spelled out in Walter Pater's *Studies in the History of the Renaissance*. Walter Horatio Pater, born in 1839, received his education at King's School, Canterbury, and Queen's College, Oxford. Upon receiving his degree, Pater began a career in the environs of Oxford as private tutor and man of letters. His essays on Leonardo da Vinci, Michelangelo, and other Renaissance artists were collected and published in 1873 as his *Studies in the History of the Renaissance*. Other works followed: *Marius the Epicurean* (1885) and *Plato and Platonism* (1893) indicate Pater's commitment to a blend of classicism and preciousness. He wrote with intensity and passion, attracting a small circle of devotees—including, among others, Oscar Wilde, William Butler Yeats, and James Joyce—to his aesthetics, which he summed up in the memorable phrase, "the love of art for art's sake."[20]

This phrase comes at the conclusion of his *Studies,* where Pater writes,

> We are all *condemned,* as Victor Hugo says: we are all under sentence of death but with a sort of indefinite reprieve, . . . we have an interval, and then our place knows us no more. Some spend this interval in listlessness, some in high passions, the wisest—at least among "the children of this world"—in art and song.[21]

Now Pater reaches his peroration:

> For our one chance lies in expanding that interval, in getting as many pulsations as possible into the given time. Great passions may give us this quickened sense of life, ecstasy and sorrow of love, the various forms of enthusiastic activity, disinterested or otherwise, which come naturally to many of us. Only be sure it is passion—that it does yield you this fruit of a quickened, multiplied consciousness. Of this wisdom, the poetic passion, the desire of beauty, the love of art for art's sake, has most; for art comes to you professing frankly to give nothing but the highest quality to your moments as they pass, and simply for those moments' sake.[22]

In terms of strict comparative religion, paganism is often defined by its worship of gods made in the image of man; thus, the model for worship becomes the human craftsman himself, the maker of the god or goddess. For aesthetic paganism, the icons constructed may perhaps be more sophisticated than those of which Bishop Reginald Heber of Calcutta wrote: "The heathen in his blindness bows down to wood and stone"[23]; but the model for aesthetic paganism is nonetheless drawn from its theological counterpart. Aesthetic paganism also venerates the artist mirrored in his own artifact, setting up no higher standard than "art for art's sake"— the sensual self-indulgence by which the artist appeals to his own domineering ego. Nowhere is this preening more evident than in homosexuality's fascination with its own image.

In the final three decades of the twentieth century, homosexuals in force have largely shed their secrecy and become a political party in Western Europe and America. Their hold upon the arts—dance and theatre especially—and those related industries of publishing, advertising, and broadcast media has become dominant. In spite of the outbreak of the HIV virus and the still-incurable disease known as AIDS, their insistence upon a manner of living deemed perverse by both natural and moral law has become a deadly rebellion, decimating an entire generation of young men in particular.

Such a climate of fist-shaking in the face of death clouds common discourse, making it almost impossible to recall a time when social convention alone suppressed and discouraged open homosexuality. Yet, in Victorian England—where syphilis and other sexually transmitted diseases attacked heterosexual prodigals—social convention shunned homosexuals, and civil law mandated their imprisonment for homosexual predilections and acts. So, at a time when any hint of public accusation or acknowledgment of sexual deviance led to opprobrium—if not incarceration—Pater's personal life appears to have been a struggle to keep his homosexual tendencies as private as possible. Still, he risked being closely associated with notorious sodomites, and his rhetoric was full of *double entendre* descriptions of Greek and Roman male statuary, as well as direct references to "romantic, fervid friendships with young men."[24]

However timid Pater may have been about his sexual preference, the homosexuality toward which he leaned points toward an undisguised aesthetic paganism, anticipating its revival at the end of the twentieth century in militant homosexual and lesbian politics, reducing the cult of the beautiful to its basest terms so that an idealized search for moral beauty declines into a decadent and ego-centric perversion called solipsism. For it must be clear that when a human being constructs his or her spiritual ideals upon the sands of aesthetic subjectivity—whatever pleases me alone is art and thus is worthy of worship—human beings invariably rise no higher than their own criteria for passionate self-satisfaction and self-absorption. Behind this neo-pagan slogan lies hidden the destroying power of the seven deadly sins: "food for food's sake," which is gluttony; "possessions for possession's sake," which is avarice; "sexual pleasure for sex's sake," devoid of loving responsibility, which is lust; and so on. Chief among these sins is pride: "Everything for my sake."

At its most elemental, aesthetic paganism—of whatever century—has no higher plane than self-gratification. The cult of the beautiful becomes, at last, the cult of egoism, whose ultimate expression is same-gender sexual politics and moral revolt against biblical precepts. If pride is at the heart of neo-paganism, we ought not to be surprised to find—from Omar Khayyam's hedonism to the militant anti-religious stance of homosexuals, lesbians, and bi-sexuals in such current organizations as ACT-UP, Queer Nation, and various mainline denominational factions such as the Episcopal group called Integrity—a steady pattern of social and spiritual estrangement coiling inward.

8

"A Dyed and Figured Mystery"

Thomas Hardy and William Butler Yeats

Homosexuality is not the only expression of a neo-pagan resistance to God. There is also a spiritual rebellion expressed by the refusal to honor what one has once professed to be true. As evidence, turn to the life and work of Thomas Hardy, English novelist and poet.

Born in 1840, Hardy lived through the most tumultuous period of industrial and economic change in English history, dying in 1928. Victoria was the young queen when he was born; her grandson George V was on the throne when Hardy died. At Hardy's birth, England had barely entered the age of mechanical invention; by his death, aviation had already surpassed the oxcarts and drovers he had known as a boy. But this was also a period of social and moral change throughout Great Britain. From the Crimean War to the Boer War to World War I, England's confidence in a caring and protective God had been shaken; with this, the established church's hold upon the souls of Englishmen had been weakened, in part by the church's timidity in the face of Darwin's inquiry and Huxley's scientism and in part by the church's rapturous adoption of German theologians' accommodations to the science of so-called "higher criticism."

As a young man in Puddletown, his Dorset village, Thomas Hardy contemplated a vocation in the Church of England. The fact that he was not encouraged by the Bishop of Salisbury, William Kerr Hamilton, because of Hardy's inferior social standing was promoted by allusion in one of his stories, "A Tragedy of Two Ambitions,"

> To succeed in the Church, people must believe in you, first of all, as a gentleman, secondly as a man of means, thirdly as a scholar, fourthly as a preacher, fifthly, perhaps, as a Christian—but always first as a gentleman.[1]

This sarcastic attitude toward the clergy may have developed in Hardy's midlife, but recent biographers contend that Hardy was not anticlerical. Among his best friends was Horace Moule, the youngest son of a local vicar, Henry Moule, much admired for his strong Christian convictions and social conscience. The Moule family, renowned for scholarship at Cambridge and for leadership in the church, had a strong influence upon Hardy. One aspect of the Moule family's influence upon Hardy was its insistence that the Dorset youth begin to lose his provincial outlook by reading London periodicals such as the *Saturday Review*. There Hardy— accustomed to the bucolic news of local newspapers—became aware for the first time of the wretchedness and scandal of both urban and rural life, as well as the heterodoxy of relative morality that the *Saturday Review* espoused. For instance, its writers proclaimed that social conditions created by greedy landholders contributed to moral depravity; so the two-room cottage led to incest. A pervading cynicism emanated from the *Review*'s pages, to which Hardy would eventually respond in developing his own ironic worldview.

Another influence upon the young Hardy was his reading of Darwin's *Origin of Species* and the 1860 publication *Essays and Reviews,* in which the reliability and authority of the Bible were severely questioned. Still, Hardy remained a believer. On Easter 1861, he purchased a Bible and a copy of *The Book of Common Prayer,* in which he made notes. He also owned a copy of John Keble's volume, *The Christian Year: Thoughts in Verse for the Sundays and Holidays throughout the Year,* a devotional companion tracing the Christian calendar. A brilliant scholar at Oxford, Keble had a major role in "the Oxford Movement" during the 1830s. According to John Henry Newman, Keble's simple piety, evident in *The Christian Year,* "woke up in the hearts of thousands a new music."[2] This was the sort of literature with which Thomas Hardy was intimately acquainted. In his *Young Thomas Hardy,* Robert Gittings reports that Hardy's annotations in his prayer book and in his copy of Keble's poems "form a kind of diary of the church services he attended, the actual church and the dates of attendance."[3] Gittings also notes that Hardy repeatedly marked two passages in his own Bible: 1 Kings 19, the account of Elijah's hearing the still, small voice of God, and St. Paul's argument for the authenticity of the resurrection in 1 Corinthians 15.

For some time in his early twenties, Hardy deliberated his need for an adult baptism to reaffirm his infant christening. Clearly, he was a committed and thinking Anglican churchman. Yet, upon the advice of Horace Moule, Hardy chose to pursue a career in architecture rather than holy orders. He joined a firm in London and worked there until age twenty-five, when, growing tired of his work, he decided to pursue theology and inquired about enrolling at Cambridge. His annotations in his copy of *The Christian Year* indicate that he was still attending services, at least occasionally. But within a few months, Hardy seems to have set aside permanently any clerical aspirations and begun to abandon his faith.

Some biographers of the Victorian era note that their subjects discovered—somewhat to their surprise—not that they had lost their faith in God but that they had never truly possessed such a faith, only a cultural adornment. Not so Thomas Hardy. The evidence of a sincere devotion and spiritual discipline throughout his young manhood is too well documented in his books and Bible. But also evident in his fiction and poetry is the dismay—if not contempt—that eventually swept over him as he became older and increasingly hostile toward the church and the faith that had once been his.

For instance, his 1895 novel, *Jude the Obscure,* presents as its protagonist Jude Fawley, a man of unpretentious country manners with a consuming passion to serve God in the Church of England. In many respects, Jude is the mirror image of Thomas Hardy himself. Like Hardy, Jude faces all manner of impediments to fulfilling his sense of call, not the least of whom is his cousin Sue Bridehead, who is almost equally possessed by her antagonism toward the church and Christianity as therein represented. In his notes for the novel, Hardy had written, "Sue and her heathen gods set against Jude's reading the Greek testament; . . . Jude the saint, . . . Sue the Pagan."[4]

In fact, she calls herself "a Corinthian," thereby identifying herself with the most licentious of the Greeks. For this reason alone, the Bishop of Wakefield found sufficient cause to burn a copy of *Jude the Obscure* in protest against Hardy's alleged obscenity. The hopeful scholar and would-be theologian Jude is set in contrast with an early prototype of the modern liberated woman, who becomes convinced by the misfortunes of their relationship that Jude's God of providence is powerless to effect good. Rather, it is nature's law of "mutual butchery" that succeeds. In this realization Sue steels herself against the weakness of Jude's faith; so she survives, while he dies in wretchedness.

Another of Hardy's novels, *Tess of the d'Urbervilles,* published in 1891, presents the most striking contrast between his versions of innocent paganism and defiled Christianity. Not surprisingly, one of the early advocates of the novel was the editor William Ernest Henley, who sympathized with Hardy's struggle against religion. In relating the troubles of a naive girl sexually compromised by a scoundrel who is obsessed by her beauty, Hardy argued that he was daring to do what few other writers would: Express candidly "the position of man and woman in nature, and the position of belief in the minds of man and woman."[5]

Hardy begins his case with the subtitle of the novel, describing its heroine as "A Pure Woman." Throughout the plot her purity—as judged by conventional moral standards—is challenged and Tess victimized, first by her irreligious lover, Alec—who, unaccountably succumbs to an intense but short-lived religious conversion, only to relapse into passion for Tess—but also by other

149

hypocrites, among them two ironically named Angel and Mercy. Through betrayal and religious sham, Tess falls prey before the God of her fathers, whom Hardy depicts as no better than the pagan deities of King Lear's era: "As flies to wanton boys are we to the gods; / They kill us for their sport."[6] There is no caring God to protect Tess. As Tess moves inexorably toward her disastrous relationship with Alec, Hardy writes, "In the ill-judged execution of the well-judged plan of things the call seldom produces the comer, the man to love rarely coincides with the hour for loving."[7] And later, following Alec's seduction of Tess, the narrator asks,

> But, might some say, where was Tess's guardian angel? where was the providence of her simple faith? Perhaps, like that other god of whom the ironical Tishbite spoke, he was talking, or he was pursuing, or he was in a journey, or he was sleeping and not to be awaked.[8]

By comparing—not contrasting—the Christian God with the baal of Elijah's day, Hardy condemns the God who answers by fire as no god at all. He echoes St. Augustine of Hippo, "Thou hast counselled a better course than Thou hast permitted."[9] Tess comes to know that she inhabits a blighted star and, in time, rejects her Christian faith, recognizing herself to be a heathen. She is most at home, therefore, at Stonehenge, where she serves as a fitting sacrifice to the whims of Fate. Hardy has his most bitter jab at Christianity in the famous sentence in the novel's final paragraph, as he writes sarcastically, "'Justice' was done, and the President of the Immortals, in the Aeschylean phrase, had ended his sport with Tess."[10]

But Hardy was not done with attacking the God he had once worshiped. Although he ceased writing novels in 1897, the poetry he wrote thereafter and published almost until his death in 1928 is full of caustic antagonism and disbelief. Hardy's view does not presume a malevolent deity bent upon destroying his creation; rather, Hardy projects a variety of uncaring forces—God, nature, whatever—passively pursuing their ordained tasks. In the absence of provident God, accident must be the rule; so, a poem reminiscent of the verse of Stephen Crane, "Hap"—meaning "chance"—reads,

> If but some vengeful god would call to me
> From up the sky, and laugh: "Thou suffering thing,
> Know that thy sorrow is my ecstasy,
> That thy love's loss is my hate's profiting!"
>
> Then I would bear it, clench myself, and die,
> Steeled by the sense of ire unmerited;
> Half-eased in that a Powerfuller than I
> Had willed and meted me the tears I shed.
>
> But not so. How arrives it joy lies slain,
> And why unblooms the best hope ever sown?
> —Crass Casualty obstructs the sun and rain,
> And dicing Time for gladness casts a moan. . . .
> These purblind Doomsters had as readily strown
> Blisses about my pilgrimage as pain.[11]

The notion of an indifferent deity prevails throughout this poem. In Crane's poem, "A man said to the universe, / 'Sir, I exist,'" the universe has the courtesy, at least, to reply, "The fact has not created in me / A sense of obligation." In Hardy's "Hap," there is no communication between the speaker and "some vengeful god." There are only "Crass Casualty," "dicing Time," and "These purblind Doomsters."

Another poem of similar bent, "The Subalterns"—meaning those in subordinate positions—offers the excuses of the powers that most affect the human race for merely doing their job:

> "Poor wanderer," said the leaden sky,
> "I fain would lighten thee,
> But there are laws in force on high
> Which say it must not be."
>
> —"I would not freeze thee, shorn one," cried
> The North, "knew I but how

To warm my breath, to slack my stride;
But I am ruled as thou."

—"Tomorrow I attack thee, wight,"
Said Sickness. "Yet I swear
I bear thy little ark no spite,
But am bid enter there."

—"Come hither, Son," I heard Death say;
"I did not will a grave
Should end thy pilgrimage today,
But I, too, am a slave!"

We smiled upon each other then,
And life to me had less
Of that fell look it wore ere when
They owned their passiveness.[12]

So, too, in one of his most famous poems, "The Convergence of the Twain," which commemorates the sinking of the *Titanic* on April 14, 1912. Here Hardy brings together the great ship, whose origins are "the Pride of Life that planned her," and "A Shape of Ice," formed by "The Immanent Will that stirs and urges everything." The two objects are not hostile toward each other, merely *there* and, in the nature of things, bound for collision by the whims of Fate, "the Spinner of the Years," in Hardy's terms. To Hardy, it is one of his "Satires of Circumstance" that these two objects should meet.

Alien they seemed to be;
No mortal eye could see
The intimate welding of their later history,

Or sign that they were bent
By paths coincident
On being anon twin halves of one august event,

Till the Spinner of the Years
Said "Now!" And each one hears,
And consummation comes, and jars two hemispheres.[13]

Once Hardy had knelt and prayed, in the language of *The Book of Common Prayer,* to the "Almighty and most merciful Father." Now the names by which he acknowledged any Power beyond had changed to Fate, Chance, Hap, Crass Casualty, the Spinner of the Years, and two names more. In a poem called "Nature's Questioning," Hardy supposes that, like himself and other human beings, "Field, flock, and lonely tree" ask the reason for their existence: "We wonder, ever wonder, why we find us here!" In answering their own question, the personifications of Nature inquire,

> "Has some Vast Imbecility,
> Mighty to build and blend,
> But impotent to tend,
> Framed us in jest, and left us now to hazardry?
>
> "Or come we of an Automaton
> Unconscious of our pains? . . ."[14]

"Vast Imbecility" or "an Automaton." One remembers the words of Herman Melville's Ishmael in *Moby-Dick* and of Stephen Crane in "The Open Boat." First, Melville's narrator Ishmael muses,

> There are certain queer times and occasions in this strange mixed affair we call life when a man takes this whole universe for a vast practical joke, though the wit thereof he but dimly discerns, and more than suspects that the joke is at nobody's expense but his own.[15]

Thereafter Ishmael refers to God as "the unseen and unaccountable old joker." But in Crane's story, the correspondent, trapped in the desperately threatened lifeboat, knows only that the joke has been carried too far. He sees no whimsical humor by a divine Practical Joker; not even the "abominable injustice" of an unfair and imbecilic God; he sees the coldly mechanical indifference of Hardy's "Automaton."

By the end of his life, Thomas Hardy had turned so against the church, he despised the sham and pretense of its ministers. The poem "In Church" typifies his attitude:

"And now to God the Father," he ends,
And his voice thrills up to the topmost tiles:
Each listener chokes as he bows and bends,
And emotion pervades the crowded aisles.
Then the preacher glides to the vestry-door,
And shuts it, and thinks he is seen no more.

The door swings softly ajar meanwhile,
And a pupil of his in the Bible class,
Who adores him as one without gloss or guile,
Sees her idol stand with a satisfied smile
And re-enact at the vestry-glass
Each pulpit gesture in deft dumb-show
That had moved the congregation so.[16]

The undoubtedly adverse effect upon the Bible class pupil is left for the reader to assume.

But nonetheless, Hardy could not quite forsake the faith of his youth. His poem "The Oxen" is set on Christmas Eve. Seated in comfort before the fireplace, the speaker and an older person discuss the legend, that at midnight the cattle all kneel in their stalls. The speaker carries the poem forward:

So fair a fancy few would weave
In these years! Yet, I feel,
If someone said on Christmas Eve,
"Come; see the oxen kneel,

"In the lonely barton by yonder coomb
Our childhood used to know,"
I should go with him in the gloom,
Hoping it might be so.[17]

Such poignancy over the admitted loss of faith suggests that the "gloom" in which Hardy's speaker lingers is more than a convenient rhyme; rather, it is the dimness of doubt turning to the darkness of disbelief. Yet, like Emily Dickinson, Hardy would almost admit—"Hoping it might be so"—that even an *ignis fatuus* is better "than no illume at all."

At the same time that the young Thomas Hardy was puzzling over his call to become an Anglican priest, an architect, or a writer, a child was born, in 1865, near Dublin, Ireland. William Butler Yeats was to become the most versatile and renowned poet to bridge the nineteenth and twentieth centuries, belonging simultaneously to the ages of modernity and myth.

In his lifetime occurred the great events marking the modern era, and Yeats was very much a man of his times, spanning the period from mid-Victorian expansion of the British Empire to the outbreak of World War II. Active in the Irish Renaissance, he was a principal behind the founding of the national Abbey Theatre and eventually became a senator of the Irish Free State; like Matthew Arnold before him, Yeats served as school inspector and described himself, in "Among School Children," as "a sixty-year old smiling public man."[18]

But privately Yeats also possessed—or was possessed by—an imagination largely shaped by Celtic mythology. As a young boy, living both in London and in County Sligo, where his mother had been raised, he had made it his practice to seek out and listen to simple peasants and their tales of faeryland, leprechauns, trolls, and other denizens of fantasy or spirit realms. Throughout his youth and young manhood, as his household shifted between London and the Irish countryside, Yeats came under the influence of his painter-father's Pre-Raphaelite acquaintances and their agnosticism or his mother's rural family and their neighbors. Yeats fed on rumors of the supernatural. His mother's family claimed to be in communication with spirits, and no occasion passed when the young Yeats was not subject to their stories of psychic phenomena. He grew up accepting as routine what most other modern men might have assumed were abnormal experiences. So his fascination with the occult received its early implanting.

Counteracting these influences, but ineffectually, were his paternal grandparents, evangelical Anglicans. As a boy, Yeats accompanied them to church, where, we are told, he enjoyed the hymns and sermons and took a special interest in two books of the Bible, Ecclesiastes and Revelation. But the relationship between the established church and state—Anglican in England, Roman Catholic in Ireland—left Yeats hungry for a religious passion he could not satisfy in either church's vapid complacency. As Austin Warren has said of Yeats, he showed "the devotion of a young man in search of symbolism and audacity."[19] Instead, in Anglicanism he found literalism and respectability; in Catholicism, priestcraft mired in dogma.

So, while Yeats retained intellectual respect for Christian narratives and for the literary masterpiece that is the English Bible, he could not commit himself to accept the primary tenets of orthodox Christianity by acknowledging faith in Jesus Christ as Savior and Lord. Instead, Yeats adapted what appealed to him from Christian doctrine. He never doubted the mythic efficacy of incarnation, sacrificial atonement, or resurrection as found in the Gospels because the Christ-event corresponded to many hints and shadows in his mind gained from his wonderment over myth; but Yeats never allowed the supernatural to take on personification in the figure of Jesus of Nazareth. Unable to believe in either Christian doctrine or the new science that attacked Christian faith, Yeats became, by his own admission, an unwilling disbeliever. At age seventy, he wrote, "I am very religious, and deprived by [Thomas] Huxley . . . whom I detested, of the simple-minded religion of my childhood, I had made a new religion."[20]

This "new religion" was Yeats's own neo-paganism, the strangest amalgam conceivable, consisting of selected Christian teachings, Celtic legends and fables, demonology, astrology, Hindu religion, magic, Rosicrucianism, cabalism, and other odd bits of the occult invented by himself. He took from his knowledge of William Blake and delved into Swedenborgianism; he became acquainted with Madame Helena Blavatsky, founder of the Theosophical Society, and borrowed ideas from her. His wife participated, contributing her own incantations written while in a trance, claiming them to have come directly from the spirit world. At the same time, Yeats was on friendly terms with notable antagonists of Christianity, such as William Ernest Henley, Oscar Wilde, and Aubrey Beardsley. Perhaps, once again, the influence of Henley upon a fellow writer's disbelief can be discerned. But while Henley might have counseled Yeats toward atheism, Yeats was consumed by his own form of syncretism. Accepting what Henley's

"Invictus" denied—the reality of supernaturalism—and making it his lifelong obsession, the world of *other*-ness, other dimensions, remained wholly real to him.

Yeats saw his mission as a poet: It was apostolic and evangelistic. If the proclamation of his pagan syncretism was enigmatic, he nonetheless knew its intent, as the following quatrain shows:

> God loves dim ways of glint and gleam
> To please him well my rhyme must be
> A dyed and figured mystery
> Thought hid in thought, dream hid in dream.[21]

Yeats's poetry is his scripture, and—like an oriental carpet—its arabesques taken as a whole appear as "a dyed and figured mystery." Upon closer analysis, however, those intricacies may be unraveled, although any thorough riddling out of Yeats's arcane theology must remain a lifetime endeavor for scholars. Here it may be sufficient to look at one of his best-known poems and see in it the pattern of his paganism.

The Second Coming

Turning and turning in the widening gyre
The falcon cannot hear the falconer;
Things fall apart; the centre cannot hold;
Mere anarchy is loosed upon the world,
The blood-dimmed tide is loosed, and everywhere
The ceremony of innocence is drowned;
The best lack all conviction, while the worst
Are full of passionate intensity.

Surely some revelation is at hand;
Surely the Second Coming is at hand.
The Second Coming! Hardly are those words out
When a vast image out of Spiritus Mundi
Troubles my sight: somewhere in the sands of the desert
A shape with lion body and the head of a man,
A gaze as blank and pitiless as the sun,
Is moving its slow thighs, while all about it
Reel shadows of the indignant desert birds.

The darkness drops again; but now I know
That twenty centuries of stony sleep
Were vexed to nightmare by a rocking cradle,
And what rough beast, its hour come round at last,
Slouches towards Bethlehem to be born?[22]

"The Second Coming" may be the most familiar of Yeats's poems, rivaled only by "Sailing to Byzantium" and "Among School Children." Indeed, some might argue that "The Second Coming"—along with T. S. Eliot's "Love-Song of J. Alfred Prufrock"—may be the definitive poems of the twentieth century. Lines and phrases from the poem appear as book titles, as allusions in political speeches, sermons, and editorials. Yet, for all its quotability, the poem remains far from transparent.

To begin, the problem for any reader modestly acquainted with Christian doctrine lies in the title and the sole connotation it evokes almost exclusively. The second coming has particular meaning and reference, difficult for even the nominal Christian to share with any other meaning; it can hardly be spoken merely to suggest that someone who was here just last week plans to return. As such, the phrase is restrictive; in fact, a Christian might very well try to avoid using the phrase in any context other than eschatological. But in Yeats's potpourri of imagery and symbols, ritual and magic, no religious reference can be expected to stand in isolation from the total complexity of his theological warp and woof.

The poem must also be read in light of its contemporary setting. The year of its composing is 1919. The bloodbath of World War I had just ended on the Continent, but in Ireland the carnage of another struggle continued as Republicans battled Unionists. In Russia, the Bolshevik Revolution's reign of terror was underway. Thus, some of the allusions to violence in the poem need to be related to chilling events through which Yeats and his readers were living: the Easter Rising of 1916, the overthrow of the Czar in 1917; the final butchery on the Western Front in 1918; the continuing banditry of the Irish Republican Army; and throughout Europe, apprehension and dismay, revulsion over fresh evidence of man's inhumanity to man.

158

But to grasp a fuller meaning of this poem, we must also know something of Yeats's idiosyncratic view of history. Professor J. I. M. Stewart describes Yeats's scheme as "telescoping a traditional astrological determinism with some irregular derivative of the Hegelian dialectic."[23] We may begin to comprehend what Stewart means if we think of history, not in Christian terms as a line proceeding from its beginning to its eventual end, but as a cosmic wheel containing lesser wheels. From the hub of each wheel project two cones called gyres. The whole mechanism is constantly in motion, the wheels turning, the gyres spiraling. A full cycle measures epochs of approximately two thousand years, called by Yeats, "the Great Year."

This cyclical view of history is familiar, of course, in pagan worldviews; but to its unending repetition Yeats added the interpenetrating eccentric spirals or gyres to describe paradoxes of personal experience within the larger scope of history. These turnings are the passage from primary condition to its antithesis and subsequent resolution or synthesis in a return to the primary state. To add complexity to his model, the two gyres in Yeats's scheme are dynamically inverse to each other, the primary expanding toward its eventual merger in the antithetical, its negative opposite. The primary gyre impels itself to disintegrate in catastrophe, whereupon the whole process repeats itself in the antithetical. Meanwhile, the wheel of historical inevitability grinds on.

Yeats attempted to explain all this in *The Vision*, written in the mid-1920s but unpublished until 1937, two years before his death. The poet's prose explication of his model for history is muddled by clumsy attempts at bending facts and dates to suit his mysticism. But the system remains, nonetheless, a major constituent to our understanding his poem, "The Second Coming."

The poem begins with "the widening gyre," a visual image, not yet a metaphysical model for history. Yeats evokes the sport of falconry, an ancient pastime with strict rules of tradition and order. The later word "ceremony" supplies something of the same tone, for falconry—like other oriental and later chivalric sports—was always conducted according to prescribed forms. Yet here, the unthinkable is occurring: The falcon, spinning in its climb, has passed beyond the control of its handler. The bird's gyrations have turned ceremony into chaos.

The famous third line, "Things fall apart; the centre cannot hold," expands upon the initial sporting figure of speech to register a fact of physics. Every orbit, every object in motion, has its center, its point of balance and control. If the rotating shaft of a great ship's propeller should somehow become damaged and lose its absolute centricity, the shaft will eventually break in pieces. An Olympic cyclist in the velodrome or a sprinting runner on Madison Square Garden's tiny oval soon learns how to accommodate to the laws of centrifugal and centripetal force—or else he or she ends up sprawled over the edge of the banked track. In each case, loss of control at the center results in damage, if not destruction.

In this poem, we find result preceding cause: "Things fall apart" because "the centre cannot hold." The speaker does not immediately specify which "things" related to which "center." To know their context, one must continue reading. Soon we come upon the cause: Anarchy. The word *anarchy* may, of course, mean different things to different speakers. To some, the quiet refusal of Henry David Thoreau to pay his poll tax, in protest against the collaboration of the Commonwealth of Massachusetts in supporting the Fugitive Slave Act, is pure anarchism. The more popular impression of anarchy is probably related to xenophobia, to pictures of sunken-eyed, black-bearded foreigners pointing pistols and tossing bombs. What, then, does "mere anarchy" suggest in this poem? Is it used in the same degree that C. S. Lewis means, when he speaks of "mere Christianity" as the simple, unvarnished, unadulterated, unadorned reality? Similarly, does Yeats mean anarchy with no holds barred? If so, the phrase eliminates any sense of melioration to what is happening. The word *mere* serves as a synonym for *elemental* or *absolute,* words meant to indicate anarchy so far advanced that it carries with it no admixture of noble purpose or of ends to justify means. In blunt terms, it is anarchy for the hell of it!

The speaker's tone condemns the conditions he describes, but it is clear from his rhetoric that neither he nor anyone else is in control. The passive verb "is loosed" recurs ominously: "Mere anarchy is loosed . . . / The blood-dimmed tide is loosed." What comes to my mind is a ferocious animal of some kind, like the Weimarauner dog that once attacked me on a road run. But there is no need to leave the poem itself to find an explanation. The primary attacker Yeats would have us see is the peregrine falcon, diving like a kamikaze—at almost two hundred miles per hour—to strike its victim. Out of the falconer's control, however, and attacking at will rather than by command, the bird satisfies its blood-lust; it also fulfills the frightening effect conveyed by the phrase, "Mere anarchy is loosed . . ." So, too, in its secondary meaning, the predatory falcon represents the loss of order in human society and the chaos and bloodshed that result from human will run amok.

Such anarchy also appears to be universal, for "everywhere / The ceremony of innocence is drowned." The whole world is engulfed by "the blood-dimmed tide," a phrase certain to call up in the mind of any Bible reader prophecies of the sea's turning to blood. But the tide described by Yeats is more than oceanic; it is also religious in that it affects the character of those it overwhelms. The disorder inundating the world has swept away "the ceremony of innocence," by which Yeats may be referring to all those primary joys to which anarchy stands opposed: civil order against riot and confusion; quiet reflection as against mob rule; domestic tranquility as against public mayhem; and the rites of passage from infancy to responsible adulthood—including, perhaps, the ceremonies of infant baptism and confirmation with which Yeats was familiar—as against a baptism in blood and revolution. Whatever meanings the phrase possesses, "the ceremony of innocence" clearly and boldly contrasts with "mere anarchy" and its fateful consequences.

Those consequences reveal themselves in the behavior of human beings, "the best" and "the worst." Perhaps no more telling statement describes the character of this century than these two lines:

> The best lack all conviction, while the worst
> Are full of passionate intensity.

161

In the context of Yeats's own experience during the struggle for Ireland's independence, he grieved over this fact of human nature. But may not the same be said in every age? Apathy, unconcern, lack of conviction plague every worthwhile endeavor, from a local school board referendum to presidential elections. Those who might contribute most to the general welfare take the least interest; meanwhile, their opposites appear to possess undiminished energy and enthusiasm to bring about the further collapse of order.

Thus the first stanza of "The Second Coming" declares the present state of conditions, as the gyre of orderly and stately ceremony winds its way into oblivion. The poet has recorded his observations, from which any reader might very well draw frightening and depressing intimations of impending doom. A world no longer governed but subject to the passionate whims of its worst inhabitants is hardly a world worth fighting for. But "The Second Coming" is not a doomsday poem like Eliot's *The Waste Land* or "The Hollow Men." Yeats's understanding of history has no terminal point, no consummation, whether with a bang or a whimper. The wheel of fate continues endlessly—"Turning and turning in the widening gyre"—and as one element explodes in fragments, its very disintegration launches a new dialectic.

This, then, is Yeats's apocalyptic, his revelation not of the returning and conquering Christ, the Lord of the cosmos, but of a new age and its new gyre, perhaps more horrifying even than that of the present. In *The Vision*, Yeats offers his own summary of this fusion into confusion, one gyre's melding into another: "The loss of control over thought comes towards the end; first, a sinking in upon the moral being, then the last surrender, the irrational cry, revelation—"As one era becomes its opposite, the poet anticipates revelation, the disclosure of dark truths, unintelligible and irrational. The single word *revelation*, in the first line of stanza two, is the ironic obverse of the Apostle John's vision; not the Christian doctrine of "the blessed hope—the glorious appearing of our great God and Savior, Jesus Christ" (Titus 2:13). For while the title phrase appears twice, its very exclamatory repetition yields to an ironic complexity of images drawn from occultic sources.

Yeats's familiarity with a concatenation of astrologers, sorcerers, and other practitioners of the black arts had led him, in 1887, to join a Rosicrucian sect. Through this fellowship of so-called "Christian Cabalism," Yeats had been introduced to some of the deep works of European mysticism. Among these was *De occulta philosophia* by Heinrich Cornelius Agrippa, a physician-turned-magician in the early sixteenth century. In this treatise Yeats found a blending of the occult with Christian orthodoxy and a scheme dividing the universe into three worlds: physical, celestial, and spiritual. Here too Yeats discovered the *Spiritus Mundi,* the World-Soul or "collective unconscious" developed later by C. G. Jung. For Yeats, as for Jung, the idea of a deeply rooted mythic memory, consisting of archetypes or primordial images, helped to explain the sudden flash of illumination that so often serves to universalize private conceptions. From this depth of intuitive memory comes now a specific image.

But, as we have already noted, it is not the transcendent Lord descending from heaven with a shout and with the voice of the archangel. Yeats overturns such Christian expectations with a vision which, in the speaker's own words, "troubles my sight." It is the monstrously appalling figure of the Sphinx, half-human, half-lion, and it is this beast whose second coming the poem heralds. Known throughout antiquity and popularized both in the Oedipus myth and in the colossal monument at Giza, the Sphinx is a classic symbol of voracity and terror. The picture Yeats describes is necessarily out of focus, shadowy, ambiguous, yet unmistakable. An archetype of cruelty, of implacable fury, the very animation of pagan power to destroy, rises and commences its progress toward supremacy.

The second coming of the Sphinx? Yes, for Yeats had postulated his cycles of history on revolutions approximately two thousand years apart. The present "Great Year" had begun with the birth of Jesus, and so its end must soon be anticipated. But the preceding cycle must then have had its start at about the same time that the great Wonder of the World was being constructed on Egypt's sands. So, as "the darkness drops again," shutting out the poet's mythic illumination, he knows the portent of a cataclysm to come. Again his question, "And what rough beast . . . ?" finds its answer in the poem itself.

The stone statue, or at least its spiritual reality, has been dormant for twenty centuries. Now it moves in awful omnipotence, its sleep disturbed "by a rocking cradle." How astonishing that such a gentle, loving image should arouse a sleeping monster! But this is no ordinary cradle. The reference to Bethlehem, in the poem's final line, leads us to assume that Yeats points unequivocally to the birth of Jesus, the incarnation of the Word. That event had ended the pagan era, inaugurating the present primary gyre. But as, in Yeats's determinism, primary must yield to antithetical, so order and innocence brought through Christ must give way to some vast, nameless power; its rebirth—as the cycle of history sees "its hour come round at last"—or its second coming means nothing less than a cosmic nightmare.

The final imagery seems puzzling, outrageous, blasphemous, ironic, and comic all at once. The monster, inert for two thousand years, has finally been awakened, "vexed" into motion. At first glance, the verb "vexed" seems a doubtful choice, too weak to bear the tonnage, too superficial for the emotional burden. But perhaps closer reading shows more: The apparent cause of vexation, "a rocking cradle," raises only irritation in the beast, but even that minor annoyance shows that the Sphinx has power to wreak bad dreams upon civilization. So, it is a distempered although not yet angry monster we see, stirring, shambling, slouching its way toward Bethlehem "to be born"—or, in this case, re-born. The sight would be laughable, were it not so dire. For once arrived at its point of origin, the rebirth that takes place there will shake the world.

Yeats himself suggested what that birth will mean. Speaking of the rise of social economics and the applications of physical science to technology, Yeats projected the dissolution of the present age and emergence of the next: "These movements and this science will have for their object or result the elimination of intellect."[24] This is exactly as it must be, according to Yeats's system of belief. At the onset of this present era, the incarnation of the Word brought God's intelligible message of redemption to humankind. The Logos became flesh in the person of Jesus of Nazareth. But in its succeeding gyre, antithesis must occur. Unintelligibility must replace communication; the Word must yield to the Act: stones turned into bread, daring leaps from the pinnacle, obeisance before the presence of paramount evil.

Is it not possible that the mysterious vision in Yeats's poem is, after all, drawn from a source beyond all his comprehending, beyond all categories of psychology or the occult—drawn, that is, from the very core of divine truth, however distorted and wrenched it may appear? Is it not possible that the poem parallels the rise of Antichrist, whose coming will usher in an era of turmoil and nauseating fear? Certainly, if the Sphinx embodies nothing else, it is at least the personification of pagan barbarism, the apotheosis of brute instinct and of consummate evil.

For Yeats, such a fate spells human disaster, the falling apart of civilization from a center now replaced by the vortex of irrationality. And to this inevitable prospect Yeats had been compelled by his syncretism. Yet in a poem called "All Souls Night," written about the same time as "The Second Coming," Yeats—as he does so often—recognizes another profound truth. In the poem, the speaker relives some of his experiences with friends now dead and, like a medium, attempts to communicate with them. He summons MacGregor Mathers, a theosophist and Rosicrucian, one of the so-called Christian Cabalists. Now, as it were from beyond the veil, Yeats can recognize the consequences of obsession with occult study, that "dyed and figured mystery" leading to madness:

> For meditations upon unknown thought
> Make human intercourse grow less and less.[25]

Again, the words of Emily Dickinson come to mind:

> The abdication of Belief
> Makes the Behavior small—

Yeats's final word comes in the poem "Under Ben Bulben," in which he dictates his epitaph. The mountain looms, the County Sligo graveyard is named, and Yeats recalls three details:

> An ancestor was rector there
> Long years ago, a church stands near,
> By the road an ancient cross.[26]

It is almost as though Yeats cannot pass from this life without reaching out toward his first and long-forsaken teaching—the cross brought by Saint Patrick stands fixed, abolishing forever the turning wheel, the widening gyre, reaching across the centuries from God to man. The fact that William Butler Yeats remembered all this makes even more poignant the words he supplied for his tombstone:

> Cast a cold eye
> On life, on death.
> Horseman, pass by!

"... A Heretic and Immoral Too"

James Joyce and D. H. Lawrence

Epochs rarely coincide or mesh neatly with time measured by centuries. The era that marked the end of serfdom and the beginning of individualism and the right of private judgment began not on January 1 of any particular year but on October 31, 1517, when a monk named Martin posted his ninety-five contentions on the door of the church at Wittenberg. The era we know as the atomic age may be noted as having had its origins, not on New Year's Day, but on August 6, 1945, when the *Enola Gay* dropped its deadly cargo over Hiroshima.

In the art of letters, the modern period was ushered in by the events combining around the death of the last nineteenth-century novelist of manners, Henry James, in 1916, and the publishing that same year of a tract in the form of fiction by a disbelieving former novice for the Roman Catholic priesthood. More than any other writer of his time, Henry James had struggled and succeeded in shaping the novel into the nearest possible reflection of life itself. Almost singlehandedly, James had wrenched narrative fiction from its cloying mid-Victorian sentimentality to portray a stronger, clearer re-creation of life. But even in the hands of Henry James, the novel remained delicately aloof from sexual experience and largely from hostility to religion, except by indirect and discreet allusion.

When James died, an era ended in which the novel of social observation had flourished, in which protagonists and antagonists represented not so much themselves as their respective classes: rich and titled Europeans in conflict with *nouveau riche* Americans. History in the form of the Bolshevik Revolution the following year would confirm the appropriate demise of the novel of aristocratic ideals. To take its place—indeed, to signal the arrival of another age in consort with the new poetry of Ezra Pound and T. S. Eliot—a slim novel was published in 1916. It appeared first in New York, although its author was an Irish expatriate living in Switzerland. That book was *A Portrait of the Artist as a Young Man* by James Joyce.

The book begins with baby talk: "Once upon a time and a very good time it was there was a moocow coming down along the road and this moocow that was coming down along the road met a nicens little boy named baby tuckoo . . ."[1] But it quickly proceeds upon adult issues and complexities which—as Professor J. I. M. Stewart succinctly summarizes—deal with

> the imaginative and unathletic small boy, hardpressed by the narrow orthodoxies and hovering brutalities of a Jesuit boarding school; his growing realization of his family's drift into squalor, and the pride and arrogance which he progressively summons to his aid; the overwhelming sense of sin into which the severity of Catholic doctrine precipitates him upon the occasion of his untimely sexual initiation; the breaking of his nerve and his phase of anxious and elaborate religious observance; his stumbling but implacable advance, through reverie and through conversation with whatever acquaintances will listen, upon an understanding of the realm of art and his elected place in it; the crisis of his break with Church and family, and the exalting moment of revelation and dedication on the strand: all these are vividly realized and rendered experiences.[2]

This "imaginative and unathletic small boy" is named Stephen Dedalus—a name evocative of both the first Christian martyr and the mythic artist; however, he might as well be called James Joyce, for the author and his fictitious hero are one and the same. In short, *The Portrait of an Artist as a Young Man* is a thoroughly genuine account of the childhood and adolescence of a real person.

Born in Dublin in 1882, Joyce was the son of somewhat shabby-genteel parents, John and Mary Jane Joyce; his father was a tax collector for the city of Dublin. At the age of six, Joyce was sent to the Clongowes Wood College, a strict Jesuit school whose main building had formerly been a castle and whose principal form of discipline consisted of threatened and fulfilled brutality. Joyce's contemporaries at school are bullying characters who appear in *The Portrait of an Artist,* including one George Reddington Roche—"Nasty Roche was a stink"—and Charles Wells, who really did push little James Joyce into a cesspool, causing him to contract a fever.

At age eleven, Joyce enrolled at another Jesuit institution, Belvedere College, to prepare for university. There for a time, Joyce—like Stephen Dedalus—followed a pious course toward what might have been a vocation in the priesthood. At Belvedere, he was twice granted the highest honor in his school by being elected prefect of the Sodality of the Blessed Virgin Mary, a student society devoted to her adoration. During his sixteenth year, a spiritual retreat in honor of St. Francis Xavier moved him greatly. But also like Stephen Dedalus, Joyce took an early interest in creativity, winning national competitions for essay writing and acting in school productions. When his parents took him to see a play, he told them, "The subject of the play is genius breaking out in the home and against the home. You needn't have gone to see it. It's going to happen in your own house."[3] This arrogant youth objected to the views of anyone who did not agree with him or expressly use his terms.

The course of his life—including his supposed vocation for the priesthood—was rapidly changing. In 1898, Joyce matriculated at University College, Dublin, where he took his degree in modern languages, mastering Latin, Italian, French, German, and Norwegian in order to read the plays of Henrik Ibsen in his native language. Upon graduating, he left Dublin for Paris to study medicine. By the age of twenty, he had renounced faith in the Roman

Catholic Church and shunned his homeland; he returned to Dublin as his mother was dying, but he refused her last wish, that he reaffirm his faith—just as Stephen Dedalus would also decline all appeals. A year later, in the fall of 1904, he again left Ireland to live abroad with Nora Barnacle, whom he had met a few months earlier. His efforts at writing—submitted, curiously enough, under the pseudonym of Stephen Daedalus—found some success in a periodical called *Irish Homestead*; but Joyce's teaching at the Berlitz schools in Pola and Trieste supported them and their son, Giorgio. He began an extended autobiographical story, on which he worked for seven years; but by 1911, discouraged by publishers' refusals to issue the book, he threw the manuscript into a fire. Only the imagination and energy of his sister Eileen saved it for posterity.

Troubled by persistent eye disease, by poverty, by the refusal of publishers to consider his work, Joyce struggled for another three years until, in 1914, both an early version of his autobiographical narrative and his collection of stories, *Dubliners,* found publishers willing to take a risk with Joyce's work. A magazine, aptly named The Egoist, serialized the proto-version of *A Portrait of the Artist* over an eighteen-month span, not without difficulty because Joyce missed two publishing deadlines. Another publisher brought out *Dubliners,* whose tales confirmed Joyce's narrative method: personal observation of the common experiences of life, set in motion by political or ecclesiastical or domestic oppression, sanctified by both wit and warmth of human love.

By 1916, Joyce had finished his narrative and obtained a publisher in New York for *A Portrait of the Artist as a Young Man.* The modern literary era had begun. Joyce helped carry it forward with the publication, in 1922, of the most controversial book of the century, *Ulysses,* whose court battles over alleged obscenity were finally resolved in 1933, when New York State Judge John M. Woolsey declared that *Ulysses* was not pornographic. Again, in 1939, Joyce published *Finnegans Wake,* perhaps the most representatively chaotic book of the century, with its stream-of-consciousness technique by which the book shapes its own rhetoric. These two novels not only established James Joyce as an innovator of narrative forms but also as a leading revolutionary in the intellectual and artistic war against social convention, religious convictions, and the Christian faith.

An exile from his homeland, Joyce and his family found themselves caught by adverse family circumstances at the outbreak of World War II. His daughter Lucia, suffering from acute mental illness, had been hospitalized in Vichy, France. For a time, Joyce attempted to live near her, but in 1940, he and his wife were compelled to leave hostile territory for the neutrality of Zurich, Switzerland, where he died in January of 1941.

When *A Portrait* begins, Stephen Dedalus is a little boy whose speech is baby talk; he is a university student as the book closes. Over the span of a dozen years, he has developed from child to man, from a reciter of nursery rhymes to a poet himself. More significantly, he has changed from dependence upon his mother and father and submission to his elders to self-assertion and refusal to submit to any authority other than his own aesthetics.

The novel begins with Stephen's recollections of a warm and loving family and their neighbor friends, the Vances. Stephen's father invents stories to tell him; his mother plays the piano while his father dances a sailor's hornpipe; his relatives adore him, the neighbors are close enough that Stephen has already decided to marry Eileen Vance when they both grow up. Suddenly Joyce shifts the scene to the playing field of a Jesuit boys' school where the six-year-old Stephen is enrolled. In this extended introductory episode, Joyce compresses many autobiographical and fictitious events into a single day in October, a technique he would later use in *Ulysses*. After a few weeks at school, Stephen is miserably homesick. He is being bullied by bigger and stronger boys; bullied also, less intentionally but no less painfully, by bigger and stronger men, representative of an oppressive, patriarchal society. Already he perceives himself as nonathletic, preferring aesthetic pleasures to physical prowess because Stephen feels "his body small and weak amid the throng of players."

Stephen already recognizes that he is different from his schoolmates and so is tortured by the conflict between what he must do to get along in the brutish world of his school and what he feels as aesthetic yearnings. He prefers to ponder the sounds and meanings of words; he finds poetry even in his spelling drill book; his senses are attuned to the slightest changes of sound, odor, and touch, cold and warmth; he responds to color, with a special preference for lavender, cream, and pink. At only six years of age, Stephen Dedalus is already being set apart by James Joyce as the potential artist who, by definition, must think beyond the scope of mere men around him. But the artist is also a human being with a heart; in Stephen's case, he is heart-sick, "if you could be sick in that place."[4]

Evening prayers in the chapel conclude the school day, and Stephen not only takes part in the litany but also, later, kneels by his bedside and offers his own prayer for his parents, his brothers and sisters, his aunt and uncle. He blesses himself with the sign of the cross, confident now that "he would not go to hell when he died." The prefect turns out the dormitory light; left in the dark, Stephen is terrified by thoughts of pale, strange faces, until he repeats the words of the common prayer, "Visit, we beseech Thee, O Lord, this habitation and drive away from it all the snares of the enemy. . . ."[5]

Overnight he dreams of going home for the holidays but awakens to the noise of his schoolmates "rising and dressing and washing in the dormitory: a noise of clapping of hands as the prefect went up and down telling the fellows to look sharp."[6] Stephen feels weak and sick; encouraged by an older boy, he remains in bed and hears the others discussing how his illness is related to his having been shoved into the ditch. The villain Wells pleads with Stephen not to report him, and Stephen remembers his father's dictum, "never to peach on a fellow." Stephen realizes that the bully is actually afraid of him and the truth he might tell. The prefect returns and escorts Stephen to the infirmary where Brother Michael is in charge. Stephen thinks about the fact that a brother in religious orders is not the same as a priest or father.

Later in the infirmary, Stephen speculates on the possibility of his own death and fantasizes his funeral, with all his schoolmates dressed in black and refusing to speak to the bully Wells, whose shoving contributed to Stephen's death. "And Wells would be sorry then for what he had done. And the bell would toll slowly." At the thought of the death knell, Stephen indulges in an aesthetic moment of revelation: "A tremor passed over his body. How sad and how beautiful! He wanted to cry quietly but not for himself: for the words, so beautiful and sad, like music. The bell! The bell! Farewell! O farewell!"[7] So his day as a patient goes; and so Joyce introduces his narrative, setting the tone of intimacy and reflection and aesthetic judgment, even in the musings of so young a child.

The next episode occurs on Christmas Day. Along with his parents, his great-uncle Charles, a neighbor lady known as Dante Riordan, and John Casey are present. As the food is served and eaten, Joyce provides the dialogue around the table, a banal discussion of no particular matter until the subject of politics and religion arises. Stephen's father thinks that if priests took no more than "a fool's advice they would confine their attention to religion." Dante disagrees: "It is religion. They are doing their duty in warning the people." Mr. Casey and Mr. Dedalus attack her position, protesting any priest's right to "preach politics from the altar." Mrs. Riordan stands firm: "Am I to sit here and listen to the pastors of my church being flouted? . . . They are the Lord's anointed. They are an honour to their country." But Stephen's father and John Casey disagree: "We are an unfortunate priestridden race," says Simon Dedalus. To this, Casey replies, "No God for Ireland! We have had too much God in Ireland. Away with God!"[8] This dinner-table conversation, heard by the young Stephen, is an essential moment in his development. Mrs. Riordan has expressed the conventional attitude toward the church's authority over the individual and the state—a convention of blind compliance with the dictates of the clergy. But she also rightly predicts that this conventional attitude will eventually be rejected by Stephen as a result of the disrespect his father and others have shown:

O, he'll remember all this when he grows up, said Dante hotly—the language he heard against God and religion and priests in his own home. . . . The blackest protestant in the land would not speak the language I have heard this evening.[9]

Four years later and enrolled at Belvedere College, Stephen engages in a dispute with friends over the merits of several writers. Stephen believes John Cardinal Newman to be the greatest writer of prose; but when others put Tennyson forward as the greatest poet, Stephen nominates Lord Byron. A friend dismisses Byron as "a heretic and immoral too."

> I don't care what he was, cried Stephen hotly.
> You don't care whether he was a heretic or not? said Nash.[10]

No, Stephen Dedalus does not care about the religious orthodoxy of any artist. In fact, he cares less and less about the manners and mores in which he has been reared. Stephen defends Byron and fights off his detractors until they leave him, "half blinded with tears, clenching his fists madly and sobbing." Increasingly thereafter, Stephen sets himself apart as a rebel. He has no reluctance to become—like Byron—"a heretic and immoral too."

He descends suddenly into lust and carnality, satisfying himself with whores, caring little "that he was in mortal sin." In fact, "He wanted to sin with another of his kind, to force another being to sin with him and to exult with her in sin."[11] Like Hamlet's uncle Claudius, he knows that there is no forgiveness possible while he exults in his sin:

> He had sinned mortally not once but many times and he knew that, while he stood in danger of eternal damnation for the first sin alone, by every succeeding sin he multiplied his guilt and his punishment. . . . Devotion had gone by the board. What did it avail to pray when he knew that his soul lusted after its own destruction?[12]

Still, Stephen keeps up the appearances of "a good catholic." With his schoolmates, he goes on a spiritual retreat in honor of St. Francis Xavier, the Jesuit missionary. The homilist preaches a powerful sermon about death and judgment. "Every word of it was for him," Stephen realizes.

Conscience stricken, Stephen seeks out a strange church in which to make his confession. At age sixteen, he shocks an elderly priest by the depths of his debauchery; yet the priest offers hope and absolution to the young man, whom Joyce afterwards describes:

He strode homeward, conscious of an invisible grace pervading and making light his limbs. In spite of all he had done it. He had confessed and God had pardoned him. His soul was made fair and holy once more, holy and happy.[13]

For a time Stephen's redemption holds. He sets apart each day as a holy day: "His daily life was laid out in devotional areas," says Joyce, and "he drove his soul daily through an increasing circle of works of supererogation."[14] In other words, Stephen Dedalus becomes a religious fanatic, demanding of himself more than God demands. As with Joyce himself, however, Stephen's religiosity all too soon collapses under the weight of his own pride. He begins to indulge in what the narrator calls "his own proud musings," especially those in which he pictures himself as "The Reverend Stephen Dedalus, S. J."

But Stephen's vocation is not the priesthood: It is art to which he feels called. In a moment of mystical insight, he recognizes that "this was the call of life to his soul." In the same epiphany, Stephen Dedalus sees the vision of a beautiful woman, which forever settles his choice between the life of a celibate priest and that of a romantic artist:

Her image had passed into his soul for ever and no word had broken the holy silence of his ecstasy. Her eyes had called to him and his soul had leaped at the call. To live, to err, to fall, to triumph, to recreate life out of life! A wild angel had appeared to him, the angel of mortal youth and beauty, an envoy from the fair courts of life, to throw open before him in an instant of ecstasy the gates of all the way of error and glory. On and on and on and on![15]

Now at the university, he engages in dispute with various fellow students and members of the faculty over the nature of art, the authority of the church, and politics. Stephen is committed to the role of nonconformist. He writes, "When the soul of a man is born in this country there are nets flung at it to hold it back from flight. You talk to me of nationality, language, religion. I shall try to fly by those nets." Stephen devotes much of his time to attempting to frame an aesthetic theory by which to live. One morning Stephen awakens in a frenzy of inspiration: He has come to realize a similarity between himself as artist and the Virgin Mary: "O! In the virgin womb of the imagination the word was made flesh."[16] Like the Virgin Mary, idealized and adored by many Roman Catholic men, the artist is giving birth to an incarnation of deity. A poem in the form of a villanelle—a poem structured around the repetition of the first and third lines of its initial stanza—shapes itself "from his mind to his lips," and thence to paper.

> Are you not weary of ardent ways,
> Lure of the fallen seraphim?
> Tell no more of enchanted days.
>
> Your eyes have set man's heart ablaze
> And you have had your will of him.
> Are you not weary of ardent ways?
>
> Above the flame the smoke of praise
> Goes up from ocean rim to rim.
> Tell no more of enchanted days.
>
> Our broken cries and mournful lays
> Rise in one eucharistic hymn.
> Are you not weary of ardent ways?
>
> While sacrificing hands upraise
> The chalice flowing to the brim,
> Tell no more of enchanted days.
>
> And still you hold our longing gaze
> With languorous look and lavish limb!
> Are you not weary of ardent ways?
> Tell no more of enchanted days.[17]

Many readers have noted that this poem is a key to understanding Stephen Dedalus and also, perhaps, James Joyce; but few have connected Joyce's invention of the villanelle with the religious rebellion that both he and his alter ego—the Artist as a Young Man—celebrated sexually. In his book, *Degenerate Moderns,* E. Michael Jones contends that "modernity was rationalized sexual misbehavior."

> All the intellectual and cultural breakthroughs of modernity were in some way or other linked to the sexual desires their progenitors knew to be illicit but which they chose nonetheless. Their theories were ultimately rationalizations of the choices they knew to be wrong.[18]

So it is with Joyce and his protagonist: Rebellion against authority—whether parental, institutional, governmental, or ecclesiastical—manifests itself in violation of conventional sexual mores. Thus, the poem attributed to Stephen Dedalus is more than an artistic experiment; it is his confession of *eros rampant* and the inevitable weariness that accompanies "ardent ways" and "enchanted days" when one is more enraptured by *eros* than by *agape.*

The artist's poem is a conflicted declaration of love and war, albeit disguised as veneration. For the poem is addressed to the archetypal woman, made to be man's partner, yet condemned to be the cause of man's downfall. But if she embodies the power of feminine magnetism present in Eve, in her legendary predecessor Lilith, in every woman, it is because her charms extend beyond human temptation: She is also identified as the "lure of the fallen seraphim," the object of Satanic seduction. Furthermore, her appeal is ongoing: "With languorous look and lavish limb," she continues to "hold our longing gaze."

Some biblical hermeneutics suggest that the temptation in Eden to taste forbidden fruit was more than merely visual and good to the taste. Eve's act of disobedience, her husband Adam's collusion, and their subsequent shame at their nakedness are all sexual. The first Adam is seduced by the woman, who had already been seduced by the serpent. What, then, of the second Adam, the sinless Son of God? How can he be preserved from sexual sin? Only if the principal woman in his life herself is impervious to temptation, however challenging to her virtue. Yet if all women since Eve are defiled by her disobedience, who escapes what another Irish Roman Catholic, Gerard Manley Hopkins, calls "man's smudge," the curse of original sin? This was the very question asked by the astonished young woman of Nazareth, when the angel Gabriel appeared to her with the news, "You will be with child and give birth to a son." "How will this be," she replied, "since I am a virgin?" The messenger assured both the Virgin Mary and, later, her faithful betrothed Joseph that she would not be impregnated by anyone other than the Holy Spirit, so that "the holy one to be born will be called the Son of God" (Luke 1:30–35).

But if this strange news is God's plan to redeem the human race, would not Satan have a counterplan to oppose it? Would not Satan desire to repeat with Mary what he had achieved with Eve: through seduction, the collapse of God's best plan for the human race? So, suppose that Satan had presented himself first in the guise of an angel of light? How would she know the difference? Roman Catholicism overcomes such preposterous doubts and satisfies its quest for the perfect woman by creating the cult of the ever-blessed, ever-chaste Virgin Mary as the object of pure love to the sexually repressed and tormented male worshiper. Thus, the Roman Catholic Church promulgates as dogma the Virgin's immaculate conception, perpetual virginity, sinless life, and even her bodily assumption—all shadow parallels to doctrines about her Son.

But for the apostate Joyce, his irreligion permits him to depict his increasingly confused and skeptical young Artist's infatuation with the Mother of God. With this devout distraction, Stephen Dedalus can deflect his carnal desire for prostitutes by fantasizing his idealized eroticism for the unattainable Virgin. Furthermore, by means of his poem he can accomplish two purposes at once: First, he can shower the object of his passion with praise for her beauty and sexual appeal; at the same time, he can apologize for the unseemliness of that passion—shared by all men—by asking the rhetorical question, "Are you not weary of ardent ways?"

Is the Virgin's answer yes or no? The poem seems to suggest that she continues to revel in her universal attractiveness to men, for she still appeals, holding "our longing gaze / With languorous look and lavish limb!" What does that exclamation point seek to convey? Is it too outrageous to suggest that, perhaps, like the Samaritan woman at Jacob's well in Sychar, the Virgin Mary of the Joyce/Dedalus poem is something of a coquette, flirtatious with the Stranger, as suggested by the tone of her initial questions? At the same time, she is protecting herself against any hint of unorthodox behavior by cover of the "eucharistic hymn," sung "While sacrificing hands upraise/ The chalice flowing to the brim."

The reality of this poem is that Joyce uses its ambiguity and sexual innuendoes to represent Stephen Dedalus as the complete rebel—"a heretic and immoral too"—willing to confess to sexual desire even for the Virgin Mary. From the writing of the poem on, Stephen's spiritual destiny is set. A few pages later in the novel, he echoes the words of Lucifer, declaring, "I will not serve." His mother has asked him to attend an Easter celebration of the Eucharist. He will not do so. While he admits that, as a child at school, he once believed in Christ, today he neither believes nor disbelieves in the efficacy of the Eucharist; he simply sees himself as a changed man. He has become someone else.

> I tried to love God, [Stephen] said at length. It seems now I failed. It is very difficult. I tried to unite my will with the will of God instant by instant. In that I did not always fail. I could perhaps do that still . . .[19]

But he will not; he will not serve because he has lost his faith. The thought has occurred to him that "Jesus was not what he pretended to be."[20] He fears that if he participates in the sacrament of Holy Communion, he will yield to "the chemical action which would be set up in my soul by a false homage to a symbol behind which are massed twenty centuries of authority and veneration."[21]

And thus he gives final utterance to his personal anarchy:

> I will not serve that in which I no longer believe whether it calls itself my home, my fatherland or my church: And I will try to express myself in some mode of my life as freely as I can and as wholly as I can. . . . And I am not afraid to make a mistake, even a great mistake, a lifelong mistake and perhaps as long as eternity too.[22]

Joyce gives to his Artist words that echo those of John Milton's Satan:

> To reign is worth ambition, though in Hell:
> Better to reign in Hell than serve in Heaven.[23]

Michael Jones, in *Degenerate Moderns,* assesses the so-called "postmodern age" as "just thinkers following the ever-constricting ruts of sexual liberation in increasingly compulsive, increasingly self-negating ways."[24] If he is correct, then David Herbert Lawrence—a contemporary of James Joyce—is in the vanguard of such compulsive self-negation. Born near Nottingham, England, in 1885, D. H. Lawrence suffered through a wretched childhood as the son of a brutish miner and his love-starved wife. Lawrence's mother attended church and took her children with her. Irregularly educated—as was true for most sons in the working class—Lawrence did everything in his power to avoid joining his father in the mines. As a teenager, he taught school for three years before winning a scholarship at age twenty-one to Nottingham University. After a brief return to teaching, he set out to become a writer and never turned back.

No effort here will be made to analyze the canon of D. H. Lawrence's stories, novels, poetry, and criticism: *Sons and Lovers, Women in Love, Lady Chatterly's Lover, Studies in Classic American Literature,* and others. What matters in concluding this chapter and its argument is that Lawrence—like so many other artists—also chose deliberately to reject, then militantly attack, the religion of his childhood. For Lawrence, that attack was more intense, more unrestrained, than modern literature had yet known. As Diana Trilling says, in her essay introducing *The Portable D. H. Lawrence,*

> One would be hard put to name another writer . . . who so thoroughly rejects the moral and emotional premises of modern life—not along the traditional literary forms, but also the whole modern Christian ethos.[25]

Whatever their private antagonism against God, Christ, the church, the Scriptures—and however vitriolic their private rant-ings—no other widely read author in the previous century—and few of his twentieth-century contemporaries, including James Joyce—had dared to express himself as did Lawrence in hostility against Christianity and what he considered to be its deadening control over society.

To combat the God of Christianity, Lawrence chose the weapon of primitive sexuality. He saw in myth the relationship between "The Great God Pan, . . . father of fauns and nymphs, satyrs and dryads and naiads," and "the devil of the Christians . . . who is responsible for all our wickednesses, but especially our sensual excesses—this is all that is left of the Great God Pan."[26] So Lawrence praised what he found in the American Southwest, where he and his Frieda resorted to combat his illness: the still-active nature worship of the native peoples and the sexuality of Pan.

Lawrence respected only the sexual nature of the uncivilized, unrefined, and therefore uncorrupted man or woman; he despised the early-twentieth-century's self-congratulatory sexual enlightenment, which he considered yet another form of Victorian prudery; he despised equally all forms of politicized sexuality—the noisy cant of feminists and libertines to make a political point. For these and most other ills of modern society Lawrence blamed the Christian religion's attempt to rid the human race of its darkest passions, to bring light where darkness had once reigned.

In this, Lawrence runs counter to typical liberal progressive thought, which usually assumes that, in the best of all possible worlds, humanity moves from benightedness to illumination; but not in Lawrence's worldview, which J. I. M. Stewart calls "the search for his own Dark God."[27] For Lawrence, the paradox is that to be "dark" is to be enlightened and free; the opposite condition of so-called "enlightenment" is bondage to conventional morality and slavery to the worst effects of religion. In addition to all this talk about "the dark threshold" and "the lower self," Lawrence was obsessed by "blood," the life force that pulsated through a man to make him what his nature intended him to be. Lawrence spells out his conviction:

> My great religion is a belief in the blood, the flesh, as being wiser than the intellect. We can go wrong in our minds. But what our

blood feels and believes and says, is always true. The intellect is only a bit and a bridle. What do I care about knowledge. All I want is to answer to my blood, direct, without fribbling intervention of mind, or moral, or what-not.[28]

Paganism, physical materialism, naturalism, atheism: All are components of D. H. Lawrence's art and personal choices. Add to these his natural inclination toward the outrageous—a juvenile insistence on attention getting for its own sake—and one finds some reasonable explanation for Lawrence's excesses. Beyond the notoriety gained by his pleasure in publishing the "f-word" in *Lady Chatterly's Lover,* perhaps Lawrence's most direct and intentional offense comes in his story "The Man Who Died."

In 1929, Lawrence had written an essay, "The Risen Lord," in which he argued that the church prefers to preach "Christ cruci-fied" more than "Christ Risen." For Lawrence, any semblance of truth to be found in conventional Christianity must contain this:

> Christ rises, when He rises from the dead, in the flesh, not merely as a spirit. He rises with hands and feet, as Thomas knew for cer-tain: and if with hands and feet, then with lips and stomach and genitals of a man. Christ risen, and risen in the whole of His flesh, not with some left out.[29]

Lawrence advances his argument:

> If Jesus rose as a full man, in full flesh and soul, then He rose to take a woman to Himself, to live with her, and know the tender-ness and blossoming of the twoness with her; He who had been hitherto so limited to His oneness, or His universality, which is the same thing. If Jesus rose in the full flesh, He rose to know the ten-derness of a woman, and the great pleasure of her, and to have children by her . . . to know the responsibility and peculiar delight of children . . . to have friends . . . and how much more wonder-ful this than having disciples![30]

So, "The Man Who Died" departs from the account of the four Gospels to tell—according to Lawrence's own description—how Jesus, having somehow survived the crucifixion, "gets up and feels very sick about everything, and can't stand the old crowd any more—so cuts out." He repudiates his former teachings, especially his empty doctrine of love, and wanders throughout the Roman world, takes up with a pagan priestess, fathers a child, and lives the pagan ideal, which he learns is "far more marvellous than any salvation or heaven."[31]

This Jesus has discovered what D. H. Lawrence knew all along, that philosophy and theology are pointless; only "touch" matters; only "the soft warm love which is in touch."[32] For Lawrence, neither romantic love nor fundamental human compassion rank with essential physical passion to measure the meaning of existence. "There is no god," he writes,

> apart from poppies and the flying fish,
> men singing songs, and women brushing their hair in the sun.[33]

Yet, like so many of his fellow antagonists against God, not even Lawrence can quite bring himself to the ultimate negation. He remembers hymns from his childhood and, in a poem written just before his death, in 1930, he affirms that when "strength is gone, and my life / is only the leavings of a life,"

> then I must know that still
> I am in the hands of the unknown God,
> he is breaking me down to his own oblivion
> to send me forth on a new morning, a new man.[34]

The Lost Generation

F. Scott Fitzgerald and Ernest Hemingway

Among American writers, few have been so romanticized and mythologized as have the sometime friends, F. Scott Fitzgerald and Ernest Hemingway. Born fully a century ago, their dominant period in history, popularized by their novels and notorious living as "the Roaring Twenties," has long since faded; yet their books continue to sell by the millions, and the myth of "the lost generation" survives. What is this fascination by which these two fast-living and essentially failed human beings hold succeeding generations of English-speaking readers? If nothing else, it is a fixation upon two recurring themes found in their fiction and in their biographies, themes which stir any deeply thinking person. These themes—set in a context devoid of serious religious faith—are the hope for a new beginning and the terror of lost love.

Francis Scott Key Fitzgerald, born in St. Paul, Minnesota, in 1896, may be viewed by some as an American James Joyce, his near contemporary and model for rebellion against Irish Catholicism. A major difference between them, however, is the fact that Fitzgerald appears to have had little against which to rebel. Unlike the Joyce family, the Fitzgeralds hardly took their religion seriously at all; it is never mentioned as a factor in Scott Fitzgerald's upbringing. For his family, materialism and the appurtenances of a lavish lifestyle were more important than devotion. Yet the Fitzgeralds were far from wealthy; their riches existed only in tradition. While one ancestor had composed "The Star-Spangled Banner," celebrating the valor at Fort McHenry, the branch into which Scott Fitzgerald was born knew only financial insecurity. To please his wife and her expectations of affluence, Fitzgerald's father sought to rent unaffordable houses as near as possible to St. Paul's Summit Avenue and the mansion of James J. Hill, founder of the Great Northern Railroad.

Not surprisingly, Scott Fitzgerald grew up preoccupied with the conflict between wealth and poverty. The difference he perceived and his sense of inferiority dominated Fitzgerald's values throughout his life and produced in him a competitive and even combative attitude toward persons whom he feared considered him inferior. The awkwardness of his family's economic standing became compounded when, through the generosity of a relative, Fitzgerald was sent from St. Paul to the Newman School, a Roman Catholic college-preparatory boarding school in New Jersey, where he found himself an unhappy poor boy in a school for the sons of rich men. From school, Fitzgerald went on to Princeton University, where he seemed to find greater success in the things that mattered to him. He attained membership in one of the university's most exclusive eating societies; he was elected to the board of the most influential literary magazine; he saw one of his theatricals produced by the Triangle Club and was in line to be elected president of that prestigious troupe. But of greatest importance to Fitzgerald was his standing with the most eligible and monied young women whom he met at parties.

Fitzgerald knew himself well. He wrote in his notebook, "I didn't have the two top things: great animal magnetism or money. I had the two second things, though: good looks and intelligence. So I always got the top girl."[1] Fitzgerald's mission in obtaining "the top girl" intended to capitalize on winning a woman whose family wealth could sustain his ambitions and allow him the luxury of time to become a man of letters or of the theatre. To achieve this goal, Fitzgerald was willing to risk his little to gain much. But Fitzgerald's plans miscarried initially because he neglected his academic obligations, requiring him, first, to take a strategic leave of absence, then, in November 1917, to withdraw altogether from Princeton to join the United States Army. He was posted eventually at Camp Sheridan, near Montgomery, Alabama. There he committed his second blunder: He met and became enchanted by a popular debutante named Zelda Sayre. He was a poor army officer from the alien North, a plebian among aristocrats, an Irish Catholic in what Henry Mencken would soon label "the Bible Belt." He had none of the financial resources needed to court and woo such a prize; yet the marvel is that he succeeded, on the strength of persistence, coupled with great personal charm, in once again winning "the top girl"—and this time, for love. It was, of course, a victory for which both of them would later pay dearly.

Discharged from the army in February 1919, he went to New York, working in an advertising agency by day and attempting to write at night. He sold only one story; Zelda Sayre was not impressed and, by early summer, withdrew her promise to marry him. Fitzgerald's solution was to leave New York and return to St. Paul to write full-time. For some time he had been working on the manuscript of a novel. Its original title, *The Romantic Egotist*, became *This Side of Paradise*, published by Scribner's in 1920, an autobiographical account of life in a university. Its principal character, Amory Blaine, is the first of a catalogue of Fitzgerald's college men—Dexter Green in "Winter Dreams," Nick Carraway in *The Great Gatsby*, Anson Hunter in "The Rich Boy"—who know little more than the superficialities of life until faced by an ultimate issue, before which they crumble.

This Side of Paradise achieved instant success, providing a financial cushion for its author and making his name widely known, even in Montgomery, Alabama. With an advance on royalties from its publication, Scott Fitzgerald once again wooed and married Zelda Sayre. This first novel's popularity gave Fitzgerald a taste of two by-products of his art: fame and money. He understood that neither of these was as important as critical recognition as an artist, and in his own way, Fitzgerald never lost sight of that priority. But buoyed by early acceptance and an aura of romance that clouded the reality of their extravagances, the Fitzgeralds set out together on a course doomed to disaster. Their public and private dissipation—which took Scott Fitzgerald farther and farther away from his primary goal as an artist—contributed further to the makings of a tragedy, in spite of their genuine love for each other.

His primary asset was the speed with which he could turn out commercial fiction in the form of magazine stories. With the income from these stories, the Fitzgeralds enjoyed a prodigality that ignored the future, flitting from a New York penthouse to a Riviera beach hotel, from an estate in Delaware or on Long Island Sound to an apartment in Paris—finally, however, to an expensive sanitorium in Switzerland, where Zelda was confined. When their excesses left them deeply in debt, Fitzgerald simply churned out the kind of story that could sell at high premium. Fitzgerald was too gallant ever to blame his wife for what was happening to him as an artist. "We have a good way of living, basically, for us," he wrote to a friend. To another, however, he confided, "I really worked hard as hell last winter, but it was all trash and it nearly broke my heart as well as my iron constitution."[2] In time, Fitzgerald grew more and more dependent upon his self-acknowledged hackwork, enabled by a fifth of gin before noon; from such dependence and the despair with which he produced his work developed a corresponding belligerence toward other writers and critics who disapproved of his waste of talent. Foremost among these was his rival Ernest Hemingway.

Born in Oak Park, Illinois, in 1899—three years after Scott Fitzgerald—Ernest Hemingway was the son of a doctor and his devout wife, who saw to it that her children received a solid grounding in Christian faith and practice. The young Hemingway attended church regularly and—unlike Fitzgerald—gave every evidence of accepting conventional Christianity as a part of his life.

But at the same time, another religion was being taught—the worship of a rugged masculinity in an equally rugged environment. At age three, Ernest Hemingway had announced himself as "'fraid-a-nothin'"[3] and maintained that same bravado throughout his life. Dr. Clarence E. Hemingway introduced his son at an early age to the rituals of camping, hunting, and fishing at the family's summer home on Walloon Lake in Northern Michigan. From his father, Hemingway learned the protocol of setting a tent, aiming a rifle, and casting a line. These almost sacred rules governed the behavior, determined the character of the camper, the hunter, the fisherman, and also shaped the narratives that Hemingway eventually told to exorcise the demons of his memory. For Hemingway had much to forget. First, he had gone to war at an early age and was severely wounded by shrapnel; next, his first great love betrayed him; finally, just as Hemingway was ending his twenties, his father committed suicide by shooting himself in the head. Once more, the father would set the model for the son.

In school, Hemingway had shown some aptitude for writing. Upon graduation, he chose not to enter college but left home, at age eighteen, for Kansas City and a cub reporter's position with the *Star.* When the United States of America became a belligerent in the Great War, Hemingway attempted to enlist in the American Expeditionary Forces. Rejected on medical grounds, he was finally accepted by the American Field Service's ambulance corps as a driver and sent to the Italian front. On July 8, 1918, just two weeks before his nineteenth birthday, Hemingway was severely wounded at Fossalta di Piave. In a Milan hospital for five months, he fell in love with his nurse, Agnes von Kurowsky. Like most such affairs of the heart, this one was doomed by factors beyond the lovers' power to control: She was eight years older, mature enough to recognize the folly of a hospital ward relationship; he was a man under orders, subject to the vagaries of war. Discharged and sent home at the beginning of 1919, Hemingway's recovery was interrupted in March by a letter from von Kurowsky, informing him of her new involvement with an Italian officer. Hemingway claims to have "cauterized" his new pain with "booze and other women"; however, his wounds and the disappointment of this first great romance of his life became a dominant reference point for Hemingway's later fiction.

By summer of 1919, Hemingway was able to retreat from the Chicago suburbs to the wilderness of Northern Michigan. There his recuperation took on metaphysical as well as physical dimensions; there he began the purgation of himself through solitude and the discipline of his writing. Seeking to stabilize his emotions, Hemingway found in nature and art the elements to heal his damaged equilibrium. Thus began the laborious process of articulating the experiences of a youth who, before reaching his maturity, had seen so much of life at its worst. His early sketches, vignettes, and stories drew upon a reservoir of his childhood summer experiences, the camaraderie of adolescence, the horrors of war at first hand, the indescribable psychological tensions of a returning veteran. But Hemingway was not ready to publish his work. He returned to Oak Park, married Hadley Richardson, and with the promise of a correspondent's stipend from the *Toronto Star* sailed for Europe. In Paris, Hemingway joined the literary coterie of Gertrude Stein, contributing to the myth of "the lost generation." At her home on rue de Fleurus, her salon audience included a rare mixture of painters and other artists, poets and novelists, expatriate dabblers and socialites: Henry Matisse, Pablo Picasso, Andre Gide, Ford Madox Ford, John Dos Passos, and Ezra Pound, among others. Most of the artists and would-be artists who met at the flat of Gertrude Stein and Alice B. Toklas had some firsthand experience in the recently concluded conflict, fought as "the war to end all wars." There too Hemingway was introduced to F. Scott Fitzgerald.

As Fitzgerald wrote in *This Side of Paradise*, his was the generation that had "grown up to find all Gods dead, all wars fought, all faiths in man shaken."[4] But the Great War also introduced a new epoch full of new opportunities. It was, first, "the Jazz Age," as Fitzgerald called the era. Whether at home or abroad, Americans were becoming caught up in the frenzy of popular music's new hold on culture through the developing media of piano rolls and other recordings, burlesque and musical theatre, and especially the accompaniment to silent movies, whether in small-town halls or glamorous palaces like the Roxy, and eventually radio. Music meant dancing, and dancing meant parties; parties meant frivolity and license and drunkenness and casual sex; in short, "the Jazz Age" meant hedonism on a grand scale.

It was also "the Roaring Twenties," a period of zany behavior prompted by a wide array of newly discovered social liberties and moral abandonment. The motor car was becoming increasingly available to the working class; women's suffrage and women's presence in the workplace set free "the weaker sex" to exercise political and economic power; money seemed to be in greater abundance, with ways for the underclass to rise more rapidly than ever before through industry or the stock market. It was also the time called Prohibition, the worst period of institutionalized hypocrisy in American history. In 1919, the Eighteenth Amendment to the Constitution was ratified; the Volstead Act followed, banning the manufacture, sale, and transportation of intoxicating beverages. The high-minded intentions of those who saw the consumption of hard liquor, beer, or wine as the root cause of evil and believed that it could be driven from custom and preference and pleasure by edict failed to account for human nature and human ingenuity. Part of such ingenuity included the growth of illegal means of making liquor available, whether by "moonshiners" in Appalachia or bootleggers and their murderous gangster bosses in Chicago and other cities.

So too, it became the epoch of disbelief, starting not in the gutter, where confiscated bathtub gin was dumped, nor even in the Congress, where bad laws were passed. Rather, the most militant hostility against Christian orthodoxy began in seminaries and church-related colleges, where modern theological scholarship debunked the Bible; it carried over eventually into churches, where modernist preachers offered their listeners agnosticism in place of the atonement. On the political and judicial levels, in 1925, the State of Tennessee indicted a high school teacher named John Scopes for teaching the theory of evolution. His trial, in Dayton, at which Clarence Darrow dueled with William Jennings Bryan, became the object of scorn among those who had already dismissed the God of Creation and his authority over the human race.

As America careened toward the Great Depression of 1929 and the Fascist threat that led to World War II, Fitzgerald and Hemingway documented their times and its environment of confusion and radical change. As storytellers for their generation, each relied heavily upon his personal experience and thinly veiled biographical material; so, their novels are like scrapbooks of memorabilia from the period, peopled by characters whose moral bankruptcy anticipated the fiscal crash and its aftermath.

For Fitzgerald, the enduring work is *The Great Gatsby,* published in 1925, and still selling copies in the hundreds of thousands a lifetime later. The love story itself is simple, its framework derived from the Scott-and-Zelda saga a few years earlier; however, his narrative is far more complex in Fitzgerald's telling than any mere formula for "boy meets girl, boy wins girl, boy loses girl." Pieced together, the story is this: A young man named Jimmy Gatz, a roaming spirit from the Upper Midwest, is posted to an army base near Louisville, Kentucky. An idealist, a memorizer of aphorisms from *Poor Richard's Almanac,* self-disciplined and endlessly ambitious, he meets and falls in love with the belle of Louisville, Miss Daisy Fay. From the start their love is fruitless, for she cannot marry a poor young soldier with no prospects beyond his own optimism. Sent to Europe, he first receives an officer's short-term appointment at Oxford, then is decorated for valor by the government of Montenegro. He returns to America at the outset of the Prohibition era, determined to make enough money to win Daisy away from Tom Buchanan, a wealthy Chicago polo player, to whom she has made a marriage of social convenience.

The aspiring lover's means of aquiring money quickly is bootlegging and other forms of racketeering, at which he becomes mysteriously and phenomenally successful. He learns Daisy's whereabouts and purchases an estate across a Long Island bay from her home. Then he sets about to erase the present and retrieve a past that never was. To achieve all this, he renames himself Jay Gatsby and takes on a persona which—Fitzgerald writes—"sprang from his own Platonic conception of himself."[5] Gatsby's method of winning Daisy will be to impress her with his extravagance: He hosts flamboyant parties for the riff-raff rich and infamous of the Prohibition era, one of whom—a girl named Lucille—says, "I like to come. I never care what I do, so I always have a good time."[6] Gatsby hopes that the notoriety of these affairs will attract Daisy and her boorish husband, Tom Buchanan, to attend purely out of curiosity. When this doesn't happen, Gatsby prevails upon his neighbor—by coincidence, Daisy's cousin Nick Carraway—to invite her to his cottage next door for a surprise reunion.

Nick Carraway is the novel's narrator, telling his story two years later. He is a moralist in the midst of depravity, a reactionary disgusted by his brief sojourn into the "riotous excursions" of East Coast moral squalor. Naive at the outset of his narrative, Nick has difficulty suppressing his natural and perhaps culturally derived sense of moral superiority: He regards himself as "one of the few honest people that I have ever known."[7] Conversely, the cast of characters with whom he finds himself consorting during that summer of 1922 are casually dishonest: His adulterous cousin, Daisy, and her philandering husband, Tom, "careless people . . . who let other people clean up the mess they had made"; Daisy's friend Jordan Baker, who cheats at golf; Meyer Wolfsheim, the gambler who fixed the 1919 World Series; Tom's trashy mistress, Myrtle Wilson; and Jay Gatsby himself. By the novel's end, Nick has retreated back to the safe public morality of the Midwest.

On one level, Gatsby's quest presumes all the folly of sheer romanticism; but some readers attuned to the New Testament's language contend that there are clues and hints that point toward the possibility that F. Scott Fitzgerald may have had something more in mind than the mere retelling of a lovelorn tale. The novel is about "the last and greatest of all human dreams"—the hope of starting all over again. Out of the recesses of his Roman Catholic upbringing and as a consequence of his apparent irreligious sentiment, Fitzgerald may have been rewriting portions of the New Testament—in particular, the Gospel according to St. John—describing another kind of new birth, the incarnation of a new messiah. First are the similarities between Nick and Nicodemus, who—like Carraway—encounters the most remarkable man he has ever met only after night has fallen, then later becomes his defender to a hostile public and one of the few mourners at his burial. The message of Jesus of Nazareth to the inquiring Pharisee is clear: "You must be born again" (John 3:7); so too, Gatsby to Nick. The message of Nicodemus to the Sanhedrin is also clear:

Don't condemn anyone on hearsay (John 7:50–51); so too, Nick Carraway to his audience. The presence of Nicodemus and Nick at the respective gravesites speaks for itself.

Twice elsewhere in the novel Fitzgerald borrows directly from Scripture to describe the apotheosis of Jimmy Gatz into Jay Gatsby. "He was a son of God," says Nick Carraway, "a phrase which, if it means anything, means just that—and he must be about His Father's business, the service of a vast, vulgar, and meretricious beauty."[8] Fitzgerald's seemingly slighting reference to the meaning of his descriptive phrase, "a son of God," begs the questions, Son of *which* God? About *which* Father's business? If indeed that business is no more than "the service of a vast, vulgar, and meretricious beauty," then the deity who is his Father may well also be the Father of lies; thus the rumors circulating about Gatsby soon include one that suggests he may be "a nephew or a cousin of Kaiser Wilhelm's"—certainly the most demonized man of his time—and another that makes Gatsby "second cousin to the devil." In any case, his business is to advance every cheap and trifling appeal to the lust of the flesh, the lust of the eye, and the pride of life. To this gospel of self-indulgence Gatsby commits himself, so that the fundamental structure of Fitzgerald's novel becomes a series of parties and alcoholic binges. Early in the novel, he writes, "The party has begun." But by the book's next-to-last page, Nick Carraway observes definitively that "the party was over."

Whoever Gatsby appears to be, he knows both his authentic origins and the source of his eventual transformation. Prior to meeting Daisy, he had been only James Gatz, a St. Olaf's College dropout and the very caricature of what today is known as a "wanna-be." Drawn by his infatuation for the unattainable woman, he experiences an epiphany of sorts on one of those rare evenings when he and Daisy are alone together. Five years later, he recalled the event for Nick Carraway. The challenge of obtaining Daisy's love would not come without sacrifice; it required her suitor to weigh his options between either winning her heart or attaining those heights where he would be free to continue his insatiable quest for wonder. But he must choose one or the other; he cannot have both the woman and the wonder. He settled his choice in the paragraph that follows, painted by Fitzgerald in prose more nearly poetry than any other passage in the novel:

> His heart beat faster and faster as Daisy's white face came up to his own. He knew that when he kissed this girl, and forever wed his unutterable visions to her perishable breath, his mind would never romp again like the mind of God. So he waited, listening for a moment longer to the tuning-fork that had been struck upon a star. Then he kissed her. At his lips' touch she blossomed for him like a flower and the incarnation was complete.[9]

Here is the birth or rebirth of a new messiah, like the enfleshment of Zeus or Apollo or the Frog Prince—or any of the other gods and demigods of carnal love—brought to new life by a kiss.

In Fitzgerald's mythology, however, it is only fitting that Gatsby should be betrayed and killed. His betrayer is none other than his lover, Daisy; his murderer, the cuckolded husband of Tom Buchanan's mistress, Myrtle Wilson. Having just discovered the evidence of Myrtle's infidelity, George Wilson is readily duped into believing that Gatsby is both his wife's seducer and cowardly hit-and-run killer. The grieving husband mourns both his wife's death and its circumstances in the gasoline filling station he operates.

Just outside his station window looms an unusual billboard—a set of spectacles over a pair of eyes—advertising the professional services of an oculist named Dr. T. J. Eckleburg. A friend tries to comfort George Wilson, asking him if there is any pastor who might be contacted. Wilson responds absently, "God sees everything." Immediately the friend replies, "That's an advertisement," hoping to dismiss Wilson's taking consolation from a mere billboard. Nonetheless, the apparent spiritual imagery has been noted, and to the unsuspecting reader Fitzgerald would seem to be suggesting both the omnipresence and judgment of a personal God represented by "the eyes of Dr. T. J. Eckleburg."

Here, however, that reader becomes the victim of a hoax perpetrated as sophomoric "hidden meanings." In fact, "the eyes of Dr. T. J. Eckleburg" are an instance of an author's reaction to one of publishing's most common adages: You can't tell a book by its cover. The cause was the annoying gulf between an author's conception of his book and a commercial artist's rendering of a dust-jacket illustration. In Paris, Fitzgerald received from his editor in New York a copy of the artwork chosen by Scribner's for the dust-jacket of *The Great Gatsby*: A pair of eyes presumably meant to suggest Daisy Fay Buchanan's "flapper" look. Fitzgerald was outraged and demanded withdrawal of the sketch. To his dismay, he learned by cablegram that the dustjacket was already in production; nothing could be done to change the book's cover. But he was still able to make changes in the text. With only a few weeks to go before publication, he added the passages about "the eyes of Dr. T. J. Eckleburg" to accommodate the book's despised jacket.

So, far from a deeply symbolic representation of God's all-seeing attributes, the signboard is only a strategic afterthought whose primary purpose is to deflect the author's disappointment over a marketing decision. In so doing, Fitzgerald makes a bad joke out of God's omnivision. Yet Fitzgerald may also have overreached himself, thereby losing control of his own text—as he had already lost control of his life and art. For the effect of his last-minute editing upon the text presents any reasonable reader with the impression that George Wilson's musings are more than mere delusion. Whatever the author's intentions, by spiritualizing a roadside advertisement, Wilson turns that signboard into a sign that "the eyes of the Lord run to and fro throughout the whole earth" (2 Chron. 16:9 KJV).

At the same time that Scott Fitzgerald was laboring frantically to complete *The Great Gatsby,* his sometime friend and rival Ernest Hemingway was also at work in Paris on his first collection of stories and subsequent longer fiction. *In Our Time* appeared in 1925, the same year as *Gatsby*—and to far greater public acclaim. These brief stories, many of them autobiographical sketches, were bound together by even briefer vignettes, some of which foreshadow later novels and their dominant themes. For instance, in chapter 6, the protagonist Nick has been wounded and dragged by his comrades to rest against a shattered wall. His friend Rinaldi, also wounded, lies facedown nearby. Nick thinks about the meaninglessness of his efforts on behalf of world peace, then declares his own armistice, his own moratorium on killing, "a separate peace," adding his disclaimer: "We're not patriots." This is the perquisite of the individual, the right to set his own terms—to proclaim his own truce—which defines the Hemingway hero as a man deliberately set apart from the rest of society.

One excerpt in particular demonstrates the type: chapter 7 begins with a slice of life that recreates the author's probable trench prayers, recalling childhood petitions learned from his mother and in the Oak Park church he attended and also reveals how readily he was willing to acknowledge the prevailing influence of religious faith, even after it had been rejected. The complete vignette follows:

> While the bombardment was knocking the trench to pieces at Fossalta, he lay very flat and sweated and prayed, "Oh Jesus Christ get me out of here. Dear Jesus, please get me out. Christ, please, please, please, Christ. If you'll only keep me from getting killed I'll do anything you say. I believe in you and I'll tell everybody in the world that you are the only thing that matters. Please, please, dear Jesus." The shelling moved further up the line. We went to work on the trench and in the morning the sun came up and the day was hot and muggy and cheerful and quiet. The next night back at Mestre he did not tell the girl he went upstairs with at the Villa Rossa about Jesus. And he never told anybody.[10]

"Soldier's Home" is the connected story that follows this vignette. It begins, "Krebs went to the war from a Methodist college in Kansas."[11] It might well have read, "Hemingway went to the war from a Presbyterian church in Illinois." The parallels in tone and attitude between the soldier of fiction and the Oak Park ambulance driver are striking: Harold Krebs has returned to his hometown in Oklahoma, somewhat after the welcoming of veterans has passed. To gain any notice at all, he must lie about his war experience, and his lies nauseate him. He wants a life that is as uncomplicated as possible; thus he avoids any relationship with a girl: "He did not want any consequences. He did not want any consequences ever again."[12]

Over breakfast one morning, his mother poses the question, "Have you decided what you're going to do yet, Harold?" When he answers no, she pressures him, as no doubt the well-meaning Grace Hall Hemingway had importuned her son upon his return from his hospitalization in Milan.

> "God has some work for everyone to do," his mother said. "There can be no idle hands in His Kingdom."
> "I'm not in His Kingdom," Krebs said.
> "We are all of us in His Kingdom."[13]

His mother's retort dictates how unthinkable is her son's assertion of independence from God's economy; that Krebs should have forsaken his Methodist upbringing is—to her—simply inconceivable. Her maternal insistence, however, provokes Krebs to insult her, for which he then feels remorse. She seizes that moment to force prayer upon him.

> "Would you kneel and pray with me, Harold?" his mother asked.
> They knelt down beside the dining-room table and Krebs's mother prayed.
> "Now, you pray, Harold," she said.
> "I can't," Krebs said.
> "Try, Harold."
> "I can't."
> "Do you want me to pray for you?"
> "Yes."
> So his mother prayed for him and then they stood up and Krebs kissed his mother and went out of the house. He had tried so to keep his life from being complicated. Still, none of it had touched him. He had felt sorry for his mother and she had made him lie. He would go to Kansas City and get a job and she would feel all right about it. There would be one more scene before he got away.[14]

Hemingway's fame was asssured by the publishing, in 1926, of his first novel, *The Sun Also Rises,* its title and theme derived from the Book of Ecclesiastes. Hemingway depicted a group of war-weary and world-weary young people, whose philosophy of life exemplifies what the Preacher called "vanity and a striving after wind." The Great War has robbed their lives of meaning; their futility can be summed up in an exchange on the novel's final page: "We could have had such a damned good time together," says Lady Brett Ashley, to which one of her erstwhile lovers replies, "Isn't it pretty to think so?" Hemingway's message is clear: The empty life is not worth living.

But the novel that most poignantly depicts the Hemingway hero's alienation and loss of faith is the mostly autobiographical love story, *A Farewell to Arms*. Hemingway tells the story of Frederic Henry—like himself, an American in the Italian ambulance corps, wounded and taken to hospital. There he falls in love with his nurse, Catherine Barkley. Having recuperated and been returned to his company, Frederic Henry is caught in the debacle of the Italian retreat from Caporetto. Now borrowing from his earlier vignette, Hemingway gives his hero the opportunity to settle his fate for himself: He decides to desert and flee to neutral Switzerland because he has determined to make "a separate peace." He is joined by Catherine, pregnant with his child.

In a hotel, Frederic Henry engages an old Italian nobleman in a game of billiards. Count Greffi asks if Frederic Henry is a believer. "At night" is the facetious reply, to which Count Greffi says, "I had expected to become more devout as I grow older but somehow I haven't. It is a great pity." The two men continue their conversation, and just before they part Count Greffi repeats himself on the issue of faith, asking the narrator, "[I]f you ever become devout pray for me if I am dead. I am asking several of my friends to do that. I had expected to become devout myself but it has not come."

To this, Frederic Henry replies,

> "I might become very devout," I said. "Anyway, I will pray for you."
> "I had always expected to become devout. All my family died very devout. But somehow it does not come."
> "It's too early."
> "Maybe it is too late. Perhaps I have outlived my religious feeling."
> "My own comes only at night."
> "Then too you are in love. Do not forget that is a religious feeling."
> "You believe so?"
> "Of course."[15]

Here we have Hemingway's acknowledgment of faith in the only religion he now practised: romantic love. But Frederic Henry's love for Catherine Barkley is doomed by death: Their son is stillborn, strangled by the umbilical cord; later, the complications of her labor take her life. Anticipating her death, Frederic Henry muses on these losses:

> So that was it. The baby was dead. . . . I had no religion but I knew he ought to have been baptized.
> . . . Poor little kid. I wished the hell I'd been choked like that. No I didn't. Still there would not be all this dying to go through. Now Catherine would die.[16]

The unfairness of death—its impersonal, arbitrary, and complex rules never explained in advance—becomes the lament of the grieving lover and father.

> That was what you did. You died. You did not know what it was about. You never had time to learn. They threw you in and told you the rules and the first time they caught you off base they killed you. . . . You could count on that. Stay around and they would kill you.[17]

Through the narrator's bitter tone, Hemingway is preparing his reader for the final realization, that human existence is of no consequence to whatever supernatural power one has been gullible enough to believe in. Inevitably, human beings are on their own, and survival is in spite of—not because of—divine intervention.

Then Frederic Henry—or is it Nick Adams from *In Our Time*?—recalls an incident from his camping experience.

> Once in camp I put a log on top of the fire and it was full of ants. As it commenced to burn, the ants swarmed out and went first toward the centre where the fire was; then turned back and ran toward the end. When there were enough on the end they fell off into the fire. Some got out, their bodies burnt and flattened, and went off not knowing where they were going. But most of them went toward the fire and then back toward the end and swarmed on the cool end and finally fell off into the fire. I remember think-

ing at the time that it was the end of the world and a splendid chance to be a messiah and lift the log off the fire and throw it out where the ants could get off onto the ground. But I did not do anything but throw a tin cup of water on the log, so that I would have the cup empty to put whiskey in before I added water to it. I think the cup of water on the burning log only steamed the ants.[18]

From his Oak Park church attendance, Hemingway knew all about the Messiah and his mission to redeem humanity and all creation from the effects of sin. But neither he nor his fictitious narrator seems interested. The circumstances do not even call forth the rage of an angry son of a Methodist preacher—Stephen Crane—against an unjust deity or an impersonal and uncaring natural force. Yet Hemingway and his alter ego Frederic Henry are unable to dismiss God entirely as an impersonal force. When the bad news comes, that Catherine has suffered a hemorrhage, Frederic Henry resorts to prayer reminiscent of the vignette from *In Our Time:*

> Don't let her die. Oh, God, please don't let her die. I'll do anything for you if you won't let her die. Please, please, please, dear God, don't let her die. God, please make her not die. I'll do anything you say if you don't let her die. You took the baby but don't let her die. That was all right but don't let her die. Please, please, dear God, don't let her die.[19]

But she does die, and neither Frederic Henry nor his author is surprised when God does not answer this prayer.

From 1929 to 1952, Ernest Hemingway built his reputation upon carefree and careless living: big-game hunter, boxer, boozer, bull fight *afficianado,* battlefield correspondent, brawler, braggart. As his international fame increased, his personal insecurities also magnified, as evidenced by his four marriages, innumerable liaisons, public drunkenness, and the uneven quality of his work; he was clearly a writer surviving on his reputation. Then, in 1952, a breakthrough whose acclaim led to Hemingway's receiving the Nobel Prize for literature in 1954. For several years, Hemingway had lived in Cuba, where he had observed and respected the deep-sea fishermen and their customs. He took an account of one fisherman's encounter with a giant marlin and transposed it into his last great work, a one-hundred-page narrative called simply *The Old Man and the Sea.*

The reader meets Santiago on the eighty-fourth day of his fruitless fishing—an economic and moral disaster for someone whose livelihood and self-esteem depend on catching fish. Abandoned by other helpers because of his seeming bad luck, Santiago is encouraged only by a young boy. Together they talk of baseball. The year is 1950, and in the major leagues—some of whose players have competed in Cuba—Philadelphia and Brooklyn are battling, as are the New York Yankees, Detroit, and Cleveland. Santiago tells the boy, "Have faith in the Yankees, my son. Think of the great DiMaggio."[20] Santiago's faith runs deeper than mere sports fanaticism: Although he is no longer a devout Roman Catholic, he is able to recall and recite the Hail Mary and the Our Father, able to promise a pilgrimage to the shrine of the Virgin of Cobre if he lands a fish. But his real religion is awe in the presence of nature; his vocation is to be a man in the face of overwhelming disadvantage. For "man is not made for defeat," the Old Man says. "A man can be destroyed but not defeated."[21] Santiago's credo recalls the 1950 Nobel Prize speech of Hemingway's countryman and contemporary William Faulkner, who said,

> I decline to accept the end of man. I believe that man will not merely endure; he will prevail. He is immortal, not because he alone among creatures has an inexhaustible voice but because he has a soul, a spirit capable of compassion and sacrifice and endurance.[22]

The indomitable Santiago sets out once more and, on the eighty-fifth day, he hooks a gigantic marlin; thus begins an epic struggle beautifully told in Hemingway's best understated style. The line cuts into the Old Man's hand, which cramps under the strain of holding the fish. Then come the sharks. The old man encourages himself in the battle to save his fish from its predators by recalling that "San Pedro was a fisherman as was the father of the great DiMaggio."[23] But as the hours and days pass, Santiago becomes increasing aware "that a very bad time was coming," so bad that he compares his agony to "feeling the nail go through his hands and into the wood."[24] By the time Santiago has arrived back in port, the sharks have stripped the meat from his fish's body. But he bravely ties his boat, furls its sail, and removes the mast to climb the hill to his home.

> He started to climb again and at the top fell and lay for some time and lay for some time with the mast across his shoulder. He tried to get up. But it was too difficult and he sat there with the mast on his shoulder and looked at the road.[25]

Santiago's symbolic Via Dolorosa leads him not to crucifixion but to the fulfillment of his destiny as a man in conflict with the forces of nature that oppose him. The Old Man endures to face the sea and all it represents another day.

There is much about Santiago—as the final Hemingway hero—that is noble. He is without the same cynicism or arrogance that always marked earlier protagonists; instead, he is respectful of a power greater than himself, if only the nameless and inscrutable power that drives the sharks to eat his fish and rob him of both his livelihood and his trophy. But, like other Hemingway heroes, Santiago has also relegated religion to a corner of his life. Prayer is no more than a reflex from childhood, and the Christian symbolism of the cross only a convenient metaphor for suffering.

So too, one might argue, in the life of Ernest Hemingway. If others choose to rail against an unjust or even nonexistent deity, Hemingway is more composed. After all, the God of his childhood upbringing has simply become irrelevant to the man.

Perhaps a key to Hemingway's own personal irreligion lies in an obscure and irreverent fragment, published a quarter century earlier, in the spring of 1927, in a journal called *The Exile*. That same year, an Anglo-American poet named Thomas Stearns Eliot, author of *The Waste Land*, "The Love-Song of J. Alfred Prufrock," and other acclaimed verse, had made known his conversion to Christian faith and his confirmation as an Anglican. Throughout the English-speaking literary set there was not only skepticism but scoffing that such an urbane and secularistic voice as Eliot's should be tuned toward Christ and the church. For his part, Hemingway reacted with his smart-alecky humor, punning the title of his declaration as if Tom Eliot had become a disciple of Thomas Aquinas:

*Neo-Thomist Poem

The Lord is my shepherd, I shall not want him for long.

Then a footnote to explain the asterisk:

*The title "Neo-Thomist Poem" refers to temporary embracing of church by literary gents—E. H.

To satisfy a woman about to become his wife, Hemingway himself had once embraced the Church of Rome, but his devotion was short-lived. So, perhaps, his cynicism over Eliot's conversion is a reflection upon his own religious opportunism expressed as the snide disparaging of someone else's newfound faith. But there is no attack upon God himself, only on anyone seemingly *gauche* enough to announce one's religious persuasion to anyone else.

At the end, both Scott Fitzgerald and Ernest Hemingway knew regret. A few months before his death, in 1940, Fitzgerald wrote to his daughter, "I wish now I'd never relaxed or looked back— but said at the end of *The Great Gatsby:* 'I've found my line—from now on this comes first. This is my immediate duty—without this I'm nothing.'"[26] In his final published work, a series of essays called "The Crack-Up" appearing in *Esquire,* he admitted that he had always been "a moralist at heart," wanting "to preach at people in some acceptable form, rather than entertain them."[27] But, as Fitzgerald himself confessed, his life had lost its savor and he had no message of hope to deliver to anyone else. He died of a heart attack, his body weakened by years of alcoholic excess.

In 1935, Hemingway had sketched the fate of the American writer who, like Fitzgerald, had been cursed by making money. In *Green Hills of Africa,* the narrator sits in a safari camp musing on literature. "What are the things," he is asked, "the actual, concrete things that harm a writer?" The answer comes back like a lightning bolt: "Politics, women, drink, money, ambition. And the

lack of politics, women, drink, money, and ambition." His inter-
locutor replies, "But drink. I do not understand about that. That
has always seemed silly to me. I understand it as a weakness." "It
is a way of ending a day,"[28] Hemingway's persona responds.

Following the Nobel Prize, Hemingway declined as if, like
Alexander the Great, no other worlds existed to be conquered.
Always a careful editor of his own work—the entire manuscript
of *The Old Man and the Sea* had been rewritten by hand innum-
berably—he now labored over a collection of reminiscences of his
life in Paris, eventually issued posthumously as *A Moveable Feast*.
But by the spring of 1961, when asked to inscribe a set of books
to the new president, John F. Kennedy, Hemingway found himself incapable of writing anything at all that could please him. A
few months later, despairing of further physical and mental infir-
mity, he took his own life. He had found another way of ending
a day.

"You are all a lost generation," Gertrude Stein had once said of
these men in their youth. All too sadly, she was right.

"Our Nada Who Art in Nada"

The Nihilists

Well before the end of the nineteenth century, the philosophy fueling popular unbelief—even disbelief—was nihilism, the conviction that, having denied the existence of any transcendent spiritual realm and having looked at the material world and found it empty, all that remains is *nothing*. If *nothing*, then *nihil*, the Latin word for nothing. Nihilism is a worldview asserting the conundrum that the only reality is that nothing is real. Nihilism permits the enigma that claims the absence of everything, including the one who identfies that very absence. Nihilism thrives on such contradiction as this: that the only rational option is recognition of a universal irrationality. Thus, nihilism creates a canon of art whose theme is negativity, the literature of despair, the work of those who claim—with Ernest Hemingway—that the only valid form of prayer is a parody of the Paternoster: "Our nada who art in nada, nada be Thy name. Thy kingdom nada. Thy will be nada in nada as it is in nada."

Some of these writers would identify themselves under the banner of existentialism. Among those whose message seemed most shocking, the name of Friedrich Nietzsche ranks foremost.

Born in 1844 in Saxony, the son of a Lutheran pastor, he was the product of Prussian patriotism and discipline, against which he rebelled in his youth. Educated at Bonn and Leipzig, he rose to become professor of classical languages at Basel, where he met and formed a friendship with the composer Richard Wagner. A generation older than Nietzsche, Wagner had already developed his theory of the hero, for whom—in Wagner's vanity—he was himself the epitome. In the early period of their friendship, Nietzsche served almost as a public relations officer for Wagner and his work at Bayreuth. But as Wagner's reputation grew, so did his intolerance for ideas other than his own. Nietzsche began to find in Wagner both an anti-Semitism and mythologized Christianity that grew particularly distasteful, given Nietzsche's rejection of his upbringing. For instance, Nietzsche called Wagner's *Parsifal* "pure foolishness."

The break with Wagner, around 1878, was followed by Nietzsche's resignation from the University of Basel because of increasingly ill health. Over the next decade, in spite of debilitating headaches and near-blindness, Friedrich Nietzsche produced the canon of his work, including the single title for which he is best known: *Also Sprach Zarathustra,* or *Thus Spoke Zarathustra.*

Early in 1889, Nietzsche's fragile health broke; his death in the summer of 1900 followed a decade of insanity. Thereafter, his equally disturbed sister Elisabeth undertook the editing and publishing of his books; her purposes, however, were not to preserve or protect her brother's contribution to the realm of ideas but to aggrandize herself and her proto-Fascist sympathies. To this end, she rewrote passages from his manuscripts, altered letters he had written to others so that they appeared to have been intended for her, and in other unscrupulous ways confused scholars and general readers ever since. Furthermore, through her efforts, Adolf Hitler visited the Nietzsche library she had established at Weimar, where her brother had died some three decades earlier. The fact that Nazi propaganda included homage to Nietzsche did more to defame him than promote the Third Reich.

Thus the question arises, Is any text genuinely representative of Nietzsche, or is it his sister's corruption of his thought? Yet while considerable dispute exists over the authenticity of anything attributed to Friedrich Nietzsche, a single fact so pervades and colors his work that it cannot be ignored or misconstrued: His unmitigated hostility against the God represented by his natal Lutheran rearing, passed along from his two grandfathers—both of whom were also pastors—and his own autocratic father, then further rendered unappealing to Nietzsche by the conventions of civil religion and pious chauvinism by which he felt oppressed.

Of all religions, Nietzsche despised Christianity most for its appeal to weakness. To answer the question, "What is good?" he offered this definition: "Everything that heightens the feeling of power in man, the will to power, power itself." Its opposite he defined in these terms: "What is more harmful than any vice? Active pity for all the failures and all the weak: Christianity." Nietzsche blamed Christianity for having "sided with all that is weak and base, with all failures." He scorned Christianity for being "the religion of *pity*" and found this very pity to be the root cause of nihilism, since Christian pity "had inscribed the *negation of life* upon its shield. . . . Pity persuades men to nothingness!" Nietzsche equated this version of "nothingness" with Christian and other religious delusions about an afterlife: "Nirvana, salvation, blessedness." Thus, according to Nietzsche, Christianity was at fault for having deluded strong men such as Pascal into supposing "the corruption of his reason through original sin when it had in fact been corrupted only by his Christianity."[1]

To quell this oppression by pity, Nietzsche offered two solutions: First, he would lead a cadre of isolated philosophers—"Hyperboreans" he called them—in combat against Christianity.

> In our whole unhealthy modernity there is nothing more unhealthy than Christian pity. To be physicians *here*, to be inexorable *here*, to wield the scalpel *here*—that is *our* part, that is *our* love of man, that is how we are philosophers, we *Hyperboreans*.[2]

Second, he proposed the possibility of an *Ubermensch* or "superman" indwelling each individual. Since for Nietzsche, the desire for power was the central motivation among human beings—and the source of human conflict—the latent presence of the "superman" empowered a human being with the capacity to overcome the impotence most people feel, especially when confronted by orthodox religion's doctrine of a Creator and his creatures. Thus he wrote of the quest for "the will to power," even among the weak whose "will wants to be master over those weaker still; this delight alone it is unwilling to forgo."[3]

While he found all religions contemptible, Nietzsche's theory expressed itself with special contempt for the religion of his fathers, which he regarded as a specious rationale for enslaving humanity. In *Also Sprach Zarathustra* he argued that "the Christian scheme" and all other formalized morality insisted on teaching "hatred . . . of too much freedom." Religion "teaches the *narrowing of perspectives,* in other words, stupidity in a certain sense, as a necessary condition for life and growth."[4] To dispense with such slavery to narrowmindedness, Nietzsche posited his most notorious dogma, the death of God. In a tract published in 1895 as *The Antichrist,* Nietzsche wrote this famous passage:

> Have you not heard of that madman who lit a lantern in the bright morning hours, ran to the marketplace, and cried incessantly: "I am looking for God! I am looking for God!" As many of those who did not believe in God were standing together there, he excited considerable laughter. Have you lost him, then? said one. Did he lose his way like a child? said another. Or is he hiding? Is he afraid of us? Has he gone on a voyage? or emigrated? Thus they shouted and laughed. The madman sprang into their midst and pierced them with his glances.
>
> "Where has God gone?" he cried. "I shall tell you. *We have killed him—you and I.* We are all his murderers. . . . God is dead. God remains dead. And we have killed him."[5]

Often cited only to this point, the passage goes on with uncharacteristic eloquence and terrible beauty:

> "How shall we, the murderers of all murderers, console ourselves? That which was holiest and mightiest of all that the world has yet possessed has bled to death under our knives. Who will wipe this blood off us? With what water could we purify ourselves? What festivals of atonement, what sacred games shall we need to invent?

Is not the greatness of this deed too great for us? Must not we ourselves become gods simply to seem worthy of it? . . ."

Here the madman fell silent and again regarded his listeners;
and they too were silent and stared at him in astonishment. At last
he threw his lantern to the ground, and it broke and went out. "I
come too early," he said then; "my time has not come yet. This
tremendous event is still on its way, still travelling—it has not yet
reached the ears of men."[6]

Nietzsche's madman recognized belatedly that he was a man
ahead of his times; his audience was not yet prepared to hear his
message. In frustration, he broke his lantern and extinguished its
light. So too with Nietzsche himself. But threescore and ten years
after Friedrich Nietzsche first announced the death of God, a group
of academic theologians at universities in Great Britain and the
United States of America put forward their theories, popularized
by a *Time* magazine cover story. "The death of God" became the
slogan of the month, prompting bumper stickers to counter its
presumed blasphemy: "My God's not dead. Sorry about yours."

There is a sense in which Thomas J. J. Altizer—along with John
A. T. Robinson, Paul van Buren, William Hamilton, Harvey Cox
and others—were playfully toying with orthodoxy's reliance on
cliches to refer to God; another sense in which they were extir-
pating shallow, romanticized conceptions of God in order to create a new language, a new way of speaking about the mystery of
who God is. In this respect, perhaps, Altizer was doing nothing
more than did J. B. Phillips, paraphraser of the New Testament,
who entitled one of his other books *Your God Is Too Small*—another
yet different attempt at exploding an inadequate idea of God. Yet
for most Christians—less sophisticated, less accustomed to puzzling out the subtext of a catchy phrase—Altizer and the other
"death of God" theologians were simply indulging in blasphemy
rooted in their own sophisticated unbelief and in Nietzsche's hostility against the God known and worshiped by simple believers.

Thus, whether understood or misunderstood, Friedrich Nietzsche continued to affect the dialogue and discourse of serious-
minded people at the end of the twentieth century.

Nietzsche's lantern lay shattered for only a short while before other Europeans rekindled it. His aphorisms found eager disciples before and after World War I and during the crisis of the Bolshevik Revolution of 1917. His words brought comfort to persons already convinced that God was dead—or had never existed at all:

> Once you said "God" when you gazed upon distant seas; but now I have taught you to say "Superman."
>
> God is a supposition; but I want your supposing to reach no further than your creating will. . . .
>
> God is a thought that makes all that is straight crooked and all that stands giddy. What? Would time be gone and all that is transitory only a lie?
>
> To think this is giddiness and vertigo to the human frame, and vomiting to the stomach: truly, I call it the giddy sickness to suppose such a thing.[7]

Beyond aphorisms, one final passage to define Nietzsche's combat against the Christianity of his childhood:

> How can anyone today still submit to the simplicity of Christian theologians to the point of insisting with them that the development of the conception of . . . the Christian God, the quintessence of everything good, represents progress? . . . It may even represent the low-water mark in the descending development of divine types. God degenerated into the contradiction of life . . . God as the declaration of war against life . . . God—the deification of nothingness, the will to nothingness pronounced holy![8]

Thus, ironically, Friedrich Nietzsche blamed Christianity for contributing to the philosophy of nihilism. Among twentieth-century successors in Nietzsche's war against theistic religion were Martin Heidegger, a principal figure in German existentialism—although he rejected any application of that term to his thought—and Jean-Paul Sartre, the major French proponent. To them, nihilism meant "abandonment."

Martin Heidegger, born in 1889, studied at the University of Freiburg, then taught at Marburg before returning to Freiburg. His major work, *Sein und Zeit* or *Being and Time*, published in 1927, sought to explain both "the meaning of Being" or existence and why that human existence is so marked by denial. Eventually, Heidegger proposed "the oblivion of Being." The void thus created and through which most human beings wander Heidegger further refined as "dread" or "angst." This awareness exceeds mere anxiety, says Heidegger, which must always have a cause. Dread, on the other hand, carries with it "the indefiniteness of *what* we dread" and "the essential impossibility of defining the 'what.'" As a result, "Dread reveals Nothing," or *Nichtung*. "In dread," Heidegger continues, "we are 'in suspense' because it makes what-is-in-totality slip away from us." In short, the person conscious of dread must also be conscious of having no place to stand, nothing to support, no rockbottom on which to build. The reason—for Heidegger, as well as for Sartre—is that "God is no longer a living God."[9] So Heidegger declared in 1949, accepting at face value Nietzsche's *"Gott ist tot."*

If so, then no other recourse remains but to face up to and overcome our dread: "We must needs say that what we were afraid of was 'actually' Nothing. And indeed Nothing itself, Nothing as such, was there."[10] Obviously, Heidegger is playing with words; but one recalls the little boy named Ernest, in Oak Park, Illinois, who also professed to be "'fraid of nothing."

Jean-Paul Sartre was born in 1905, and as an orphan was brought up by his grandfather, an uncle of the famous missionary, theologian, and musician Albert Schweitzer. In *The Words*, Sartre's searing autobiography, published in 1964, Sartre acknowledges the pain of his childhood—he was almost grotesquely ugly—and the defenses he formed against human cruelty, which included conventional religious devotion. But the example of his humanitarian cousin appears to have had little philosophical influence upon Sartre, who seems never to have considered seriously his own quest for the historical Jesus.

Rather, he gravitated toward the thought of Heidegger, whose theories Sartre first studied in Berlin, then sought to develop through fiction and drama, modes of discourse which Sartre considered to be powerful vehicles by which to convey philosophical ideas. Early novels and plays included *Nausea, The Flies*, and Sartre's depiction of hell, *No Exit*. His major work, *Being and Noth-*

ingness, published in 1943, didactically expressed what these unpleasantly titled works of the imagination also spoke. The absence of moral authority in the universe means that "man is a useless passion." The only rule by which to govern one's life is indeterminism. Here Sartre parted from classical Marxism, to which he had earlier been drawn, and began to point toward a conception of human freedom, best achieved through action, which "makes man like a God."

Sartre's brand of existentialism is openly atheistic; he celebrated that certainty, acknowledging only human *existence,* followed by the essence of what it means. For Sartre, that essence is *freedom.* He wrote, in his 1946 tract *Existentialism and Humanism,*

> What do we mean by saying that existence precedes essence? We mean that man first of all exists, encounters himself, surges up in the world—and defines himself afterwards. . . . Thus, there is no human nature, because there is no God to have a conception of it. Man simply is. . . . Man is nothing else but that which he makes of himself. That is the first principle of existentialism.[11]

But the second principle is one over which many other atheistic humanists have stumbled. In a universe abandoned to Nothing, they would nonetheless strive to hold on to some concept of moral goodness, which they find innate within human experience. To do so, of course, requires extravagant departures from reality—the lead stories on most news broadcasts or most front pages, for instance. Sartre will have none of this equivocation; he is content not to try to have it both ways at once. He allows no idea of God to intrude itself upon his consciousness. "God does not exist," he states boldly, and so "it is necessary to draw the consequences of his absence right to the end."[12]

These consequences Sartre is willing to face head on; indeed, almost alone among antitheistic philosophers, Sartre shows no hesitation to confess that the nonexistence of God begs the question of finding moral values apart from "an intelligible heaven." In fact, says Sartre, "There can no longer be any good a priori, since there is no infinite and perfect consciousness to think it."[13] Nor can he acknowledge common grace as a beneficence. Thus, with no transcendent and immutable intelligence to set a standard for goodness, mere mortals are left without absolutes, without moral criteria, by which to judge themselves and others.

Then Sartre says,

> Dostoevsky once wrote, "If God did not exist, everything would be permitted"; and that, for existentialism, is the starting point. Everything is indeed permitted if God does not exist, and man is in consequence forlorn, for he cannot find anything to depend upon either within or outside himself. He discovers forthwith, that he is without excuse . . . ; in other words, there is no determinism—man is free, man is freedom. Nor. . . , if God does not exist, are we provided with any values or commands that could legitimize our behavior. Thus we have neither behind us, nor before us in a luminous realm of values, any means of justification or excuse. We are left alone, without excuse.[14]

Freedom and responsibility are the curse and challenge facing every human being. In Jean-Paul Sartre's universe, they must be faced alone. In fact, his play *No Exit* extols the state of loneliness when one of its characters declares that "Hell is other people." Sartre appears to have lived that philosophy, adopting a personal aloofness from and seeming contempt for much of the human race. He scorned such social conventions as marriage, defended the perverse life and art of Jean Genet, and rejected the Nobel Prize for literature offered him in 1964; furthermore, he appears to have reveled in his notorious social contrariness and political iconoclasm.

Sartre believed in the necessity of "the dignity of man" and opposed the dictates of dialectical materialism, which endeavored to "make man into an object . . . in no way different from the patterns of qualities and phenomena which constitute a table, or a chair, or a stone." This, for him, was the essence of "existential humanism," built upon the premise that, because God does not exist, "man is himself the heart and center of his transcendence."[15]

> This is humanism, because we remind man that there is no legislator but himself; that he himself, thus abandoned, must decide for himself; also because we show that it is not by turning back upon

himself, but always by seeking, beyond himself, an aim which is one of liberation or of some particular realization, that man can realize himself as truly human.[16]

Sartre's philosophy of existential humanism was inconsistent, contradictory, and problematic; but in the fiction and essays of Albert Camus, the nihilistic existentialism of the French radicals and its implications for human experience came alive. Albert Camus was born in 1913 into a nominally Roman Catholic family in Mondovi, Algeria; but before young manhood, he had already abandoned his religious upbringing. His father had died during World War I, he had contracted tuberculosis in his teenage years: reasons seemingly sufficient to undermine faith in a beneficent God. At the University of Algiers, Camus studied philosophy. His thesis topic was "Metaphysical Christianity and Neo-Platonism."

But—like many critics of a religion already rejected—Camus appears to have made his scholarly analysis of Christianity without benefit of firsthand knowledge of the Bible. His sources were almost exclusively secondhand; indeed, what little reference he made to Scripture seemed blurred by controversies and negative presuppositions from his prior reading of philosophy. The image of God projected by Camus was Søren Kierkegaard's tyrant who orders Abraham to kill Isaac as proof of faith or St. Augustine's sadist who damns unbaptized infants.

Illness prevented Camus from completing graduate studies, and he found employment in a series of unrelated jobs. Meanwhile, he read widely and wrote essays about North Africa. Reading Melville's *Moby-Dick*, Camus thought he had found a model to express "man's combat against evil and the irresistible logic that in the end pits the just man against creation and the creator to begin with, then against his fellowmen and against himself."[17] For Camus, such a combat was both logical and necessary to human survival.

At the outbreak of World War II, he joined the French Resistance, earning considerable respect for his underground journalism on the newspaper *Combat*; he also began to write fiction. His first novel, published in 1942, *The Outsider* in its English title—too literally, *The Stranger* in its American version—introduced readers to his dominant view of human experience: alienated by its absurdity from others, seared by suffering from compassion for others. The following year, still before his thirtieth birthday, Camus published *The Myth of Sisyphus*, perhaps the most readable and trenchant description of nihilism. A companion piece to his novel, Camus depicts modern man—similar to Meursault the Outsider— as someone damned like the victim of the Greek myth. To Camus, Sisyphus becomes "the absurd hero," forever condemned to push a gigantic rock up a hill, only to have the stone roll back to the bottom.

During the latter years of the War, Camus wrote several plays, but his production of novels increased following the defeat of the Axis: in 1947, *The Plague;* in 1951, *The Rebel.* By means of these narratives, Camus captured the imagination of the post–World War II generation weary of combat and disillusioned by empty promises of peace in a world now controlled by the fear of atomic catastrophe. In 1956, Camus published his last novel, *The Fall.* The following year, he received the Nobel Prize for Literature. In January 1960, while not yet forty-seven years old, he was killed in an automobile collision. The world of letters knew it had suffered a major loss.

Whereas *The Stranger* had shown the raw effect of a seared conscience upon an indifferent, alienated man—for whom it is enough if only he is true to his own convictions—*The Fall* reveals how the course of human experience leads from early slippage to precipitous collapse—like the very stone which Sisyphus cannot control. In *The Fall,* Camus introduces a new form and new tone to his fiction. Jean-Baptiste Clamence, a self-proclaimed libertine, engages the reader in a prolonged colloquy. The setting is a bar in one of Amsterdam's seamiest quarters; degeneracy dominates the atmosphere, and so the name the narrator gives himself is a pseudonym for self-protection. Clamence has a confession to make, and he has chosen his anonymous listener to be his confessor. Clamence has sinned, although the exact nature of his sin is a long time in coming forth from his tangled story. In seeking expiation, Clamence has discovered that the world he knows neither cares to condemn any sinner nor—in consequence—has the power to forgive. Clamence recalls a telling incident from his own experience. "Oh sir," cries an old beggar, "it's not just that I'm no good, but you lose track of the light." "I'm like that old beggar," Clamence realizes.[18]

No good and helplessly blind. How well Jean-Baptiste Clamence knows himself! Formerly a lawyer, he now identifies himself as "a judge-penitent." Thoroughly acquainted with the Bible, he fills his rambling speeches with allusions to Scripture. For instance, when he learns that his listener has not shared his possessions with the poor, Clamence accuses him of the same failure as the rich young ruler who was saddened by the exhortation of Jesus. Clamence sees the rings of Amsterdam's canals as representing the circles of hell, himself in the last circle.

Gradually, one learns what torments Clamence: His self-esteem, rooted in self-righteousness, has been shattered by an act of cowardice from which he has not been able to recover. "I, I, I is the refrain of my whole life. I could never talk without boasting," he admits. "For more than thirty years I had been in love exclusively with myself." Then, one evening, while crossing a bridge in Paris, he passed a young woman leaning over the railing. A few steps more, and he heard her body strike the river and her cries for help; but he did nothing. "The whole universe then began to laugh at me," says Clamence. He hears that laughter of scorn and condemnation wherever he goes, and in that laughter he begins to see himself for what he really is. Because of his exalted opinion of himself and his virtues, because of his need "to dominate," "to feel above," because he thought of himself as a *deus ex machina* in some cosmic drama, because he looked upon himself "as something of a superman," the extent of his moral collapse is all the more unbearable. Its only melioration comes from the knowledge that that he is no longer falsely innocent. "Otherwise," says Clamence, "everything would just be a joke."[19]

Here Camus reverts to his vision of Sisyphus, for in the mythic victim Camus found the central theme of his writings, the celebration of the manner in which the human race must wage its battle for survival. It would not be enough merely to rant against a God who isn't there; one must resist one's own inevitable annihilation with *style*—that most French of all human attributes—with dignity. Camus writes,

> The absurd man thus catches sight of a burning and frigid, transparent and limited universe in which nothing is possible but everything is given, and beyond which all is collapse and nothingness. He can then decide to accept such a universe and draw from it his strength, his refusal to hope, and the unyielding evidence of a life without consolation.[20]

So Camus imagines Sisyphus, "the absurd hero," after pushing his rock to the top of the hill and watching it tumble back to the bottom, descending that slope himself, "superior to his fate." In fact, says Camus, "One must imagine Sisyphus happy."[21] By the very attitude with which Sisyphus confronts his fate—not whimpering like T. S. Eliot's Hollow Men but triumphant—Camus can declare Sisyphus happy in his freedom to be indifferent to the future and thereby superior to it. Instead of despairing over life's lack of meaning—or, as seems so often the case, its *unfairness*—Camus advises man's acceptance of the void, even "on the brink of his dizzying fall." Only so can a human being achieve "absurd freedom," which Camus symbolizes as a sacrament of "the wine of the absurd and the bread of indifference on which he feeds his greatness."[22]

But, as a practical matter, Jean-Baptiste Clamence cannot claim to be a mythic hero; he is weak, guilt-ridden, in need of expiation, which he finds only by ensnaring someone else in his story in order to force his listener to confess his sins as well. "Please tell me what happened to you one night," he cries.

> You yourself utter the words that for years have never ceased echoing through my nights and that I shall at last say through your mouth: "O young woman, throw yourself into the water again so that I may a second time have the chance of saving both of us!"[23]

But such a second chance—were it to come—would always come too late. "Fortunately," Clamence concedes as the last word of his speeches.

Albert Camus knew exactly what his fictitious hypocrite meant by that enigmatic final word; he also knew the difference genuine faith might make to this world. As early as 1948, he had accepted an invitation from a group of Dominicans at the monastery of Latour-Maubourg. Camus had been asked to comment on the possibility of concord between unbelievers and Christians. From the outset, Camus expressed a gracious spirit toward his audience. Far from patronizing them intellectually, he acknowledged the essential nature of dialogue between believers and their opponents. But he also named as one of the handicaps to his own coming to faith "this universe in which children suffer and die."[24] He also accused then Pope Pius XII of silence during World War II and its atrocities. "What the world expects of Christians," said Camus, "is that Christians should speak out, loud and clear, . . . in such a way that never a doubt, never the slightest doubt, could rise in the heart of the simplest man."[25]

Peter DeVries never won the Nobel Prize for literature. If he had, he too—like Sartre—might well have rejected it. But no doubt, he would also have ridiculed it and all the prize signifies with a quip or an outrageous pun; for DeVries—privately, a gentle and gracious friend to those he trusted—could appear to be as much a misanthrope as anyone who ever lived.

Born in 1910, into a believing Christian Reformed family in the suburbs of Chicago, DeVries was brought up in an environment that mandated Christian elementary and secondary schooling, as well as faithful church attendance. In a 1983 interview in the *New York Times*, DeVries recalled,

> We went to church five times a week, three times on Sunday; I wasn't allowed to play ball on Sundays. We were force-fed a lot of doctrine. The two main beliefs were in the total depravity of man and the divine grace of God. I only believe in one of them now.[26]

DeVries's spiritual biography reached a turning point when his older sister died at age eighteen. DeVries remembered that his parents reacted to the tragedy in diametrically opposite ways.

My father became very, very religious, so that even prayers at the table and the school were not enough. We had to end the day by kneeling on the kitchen floor with our elbows on the chairs. My mother never sang in church again after my sister died.[27]

Nonetheless, DeVries followed his parochial schooling by enrolling at Calvin College, the citadel of the Christian Reformed Church's preparation for spiritual combat. He left the Grand Rapids campus, however, without a mature Christian faith to validate his denomination's theology of a covenant relationship through his parents' devotion. Invited to return for a reading in the 1980s, DeVries showed his contempt for the college by arriving drunk; then upon being introduced, he insulted his audience because they were "all too damned happy" and stumbled from the platform.

DeVries was a member of the same generation of Chicago Hollanders as refuse tycoon Harry Huizinga, who went on to found Waste Management, Inc. But while Huizinga and others turned trash into treasure and good works, Peter DeVries fled the garbage dumps of his youth for more alluring fields. Leaving Calvin College to pursue his career as a writer, DeVries met some of Chicago's literary set—Nelson Algren, among them—and began freelancing for such periodicals as *Esquire;* this led to an editor's post at *Poetry* magazine. Through this connection, he met James Thurber, who showed some of DeVries's work to Harold Ross at the *New Yorker.* In 1944, DeVries joined the writing corps at the *New Yorker,* where he continued as a mainstay, composing captions for the famous humorous drawings until his death in 1993.

But it was as a novelist—he wrote more than a score of these—that Peter DeVries most clearly shone. His mode was the comic narrative, a tale told tongue-in-cheek with characters adroitly named—or misnamed—in true Dickensian fashion: Doubtful pastors named Thrasher or Mackerel, a father named Joe Sandwich and his son Ham, a nymph called Bubbles Breedlove, a spiritual pilgrim named Wanderhope. His themes were never far removed from a satirical representation of his religious upbringing and often—as in the novels of John Updike—of the pastors who aided DeVries's parents in oppressing him.

One of his novels is entitled *The Tents of Wickedness,* a phrase DeVries explained in a note to the American Academy of Arts and Letters:

> A distasteful distaste for the milieu into which I was born, and in which I was repressively reared, bred the natural desire to flee it for a more congenial line of country, one regarded by the authors of my being as Sin itself. It would have been expected of me that I would say with the psalmist, "I would rather be a doorkeeper in the house of my God than dwell in the tents of wickedness." Having successfully opted for the latter scene, there was nothing for me to do but satirize it, and thus in some shaky accommodation propitiate the household gods being simultaneously flouted.[28]

The manner by which DeVries chose to mock the faith in which he had been "repressively reared" was never searing, never toxic; always humorous without being merely facetious. His humor is droll rather than slapstick or sarcastic, relying more on wit than on pratfall or prurience. DeVries is the master of the pun, the double entendre, the convoluted wisecrack, the carefully constructed malaprop that tickles the funny bone long after its context has been forgotten; but all these instances of wordplay are without meanness or antipathy. Rather, DeVries seems to cherish some remembered aspect of his religious upbringing, much the same way one recalls the once-amusing foibles of a beloved, aged, but semi-deranged aunt.

So—to take but one example—in *Slouching towards Kalamazoo,* his 1983 novel, DeVries tells the story of a preacher's kid, a precocious early teenager, whose teacher, Maggie Doubloon, first assigns for reading *The Scarlet Letter;* thereafter, with her student's intimate participation, she reenacts the novel's scandal. When he discovers that his teacher is pregnant, the narrator invents this witticism: "Teachers pet—and that's not all they do." In the course of the novel, the narrator's preacher-father loses his Christian faith; the narrator's mother takes up with an atheist dermatologist who converts and becomes an evangelist—and accuses the narrator of being the Antichrist. Meanwhile, the narrator drifts through this confusion, borne along by his abundance of literary, mostly biblical, allusions. For instance, to explain how popular psychology has invaded even the hinterlands of North Dakota, DeVries writes,

> In the beginning was the word. Once terms like identity doubts and midlife crisis become current, the reported cases of them increase by leaps and bounds, affecting people unaware there is anything wrong with them until they have got a load of the coinages. . . . The word was made flesh.[29]

The narrator amuses himself with one joke after another: "There was the riddle about what one strawberry said to the other. 'If we hadn't been in that bed together, we wouldn't be in this jam.'"[30] In another moment of wry awareness, Miss Doubloon quotes Nietzsche, to the effect that "man has invented laughter because he of all species needs it."[31] Thus, to meet his needs, DeVries gives his narrator improbable philosophical arguments to ponder, such as Emerson's distinction between sin and evil.

> The fact that one has committed a transgression does not necessarily link him with that eternal monolithic something we call Evil. Thus I might in the spirit of frail human rationalization justify my stopping short of true remorse over an act we had engaged in together, because it was Such Fun, feeling only a lower-grade type regret over its results: to wit, the mell of a hess we now found ourselves in.[32]

But while DeVries is hardly as caustic as other disbelievers, the world he depicts and human existence in such a world are no less absurd; in fact, it is this very absurdity that is the point of DeVries's mockery. An illustration occurs in *Slouching towards Kalamazoo* when two debaters—one, the narrator's presumably orthodox pastor-father, the other, the ardent atheist—having "locked horns energetically and sometimes savagely over such things as Darwin, the testimony of fossils, the pagan derivations of Christianity, the reliability of the Scriptures,"[33] end up convincing each other of their opposite positions. How could any serious-minded reader not recognize the essential insignificance of defending either belief or disbelief? These alternatives seem equally meaningless to

221

DeVries. He recognizes the arguments made by Pascal, C. S. Lewis, G. K. Chesterton, Graham Greene, François Mauriac, and T. S. Eliot; he fairly credits Malcolm Muggeridge—the onetime Marxist and arch-scoffer at Christianity—with having experienced a genuine conversion, after which he became a most articulate apologist for Jesus Christ. But DeVries is not to be convinced by any of them; nor will he accept the emptiness of sheer abandonment. Through the shallow talk of comic characters, he lampoons their "fashionable pessimism" or "this pessimistic intellectual outlook" as "existential godless despair" and scoffs at "a kind of pragmatic meliorism."[34] For DeVries, there appears to be ground for compromise: He looks for converts to what he calls "Christian atheism."

> Or turn it around and call them atheistic Christians, adherents of a faith and a religious discipline all the more necessary to a species sprung mysteriously into being in a universe devoid of any provable governance, or any evidence of meaning or purpose properly so called. Let, then, the Church serve in a Void: it was all the more essential for that. Voltaire was right. If there were no God, it would be necessary to invent one. And invent Him mankind jolly well had, to see him through this vale of tears.[35]

Late in *Slouching towards Kalamazoo*, DeVries explains further why Christian atheism seems to be the most tolerable accommodation of faith and reason to each other for our time, providing a discipline of belief and necessary ethical imperatives on the one hand, and intellectual realism on the other.

> We live as *though* life had meaning, and lo—it does! We live as though we are Christian soldiers following in our Captain's command, and lo—we are! Our best writers have told us this life is a flimflam, even some of the Old Testament prophets, but to the extent that we're wise to the scam, it isn't. Hemingway called life a dirty trick, Mark Twain a swindle, Fitzgerald a fraud, Shakespeare a tale told by an idiot, and on and on. . . .
>   The point I'm trying to make is that it takes more faith to live life without belief in the cozy self-delusions of what has tradition-

ally been called faith. That is our doctrineless doctrine, our creed-less creed.[36]

So goes this cockeyed novel of real and pseudo erudition, with even Sir Thomas Browne's *Religio Medici* making a cameo appearance. "The thing about Browne," the narrator tells a woman he is in the act of seducing, "what makes him appeal to the modern mind, over all those centuries, is his combination of faith and skepticism. Doubt is almost *a leaven in his belief.*"[37] But for DeVries, the bona fide saint of the First Church of Christian Atheists is Saint Bertrand Russell, "the great all-time infidel humanitarian of the twentieth century, claimable as a Christian atheist despite his pains to explain why he wasn't a Christian."[38]

Such was the earnestness of Peter DeVries, always in search of some amused resolution to the great mystery. But in one of his novels, all such preposterous humor found in the general run of Peter DeVries's work seems to disappear in a rush of rage against God. That book is *The Blood of the Lamb,* whose narrator is Don Wanderhope, a rebel against the Dutch Calvinism in which he has been reared. Like Peter DeVries himself, Wanderhope has a daughter stricken by leukemia. On her birthday, he goes to her hospital with a cake, only to learn that she will not survive the day. In spite of his rejection of religion, Don Wanderhope steps to the side of his daughter's bed to whisper a prayer: "The Lord bless thee, and keep thee: The Lord make his face shine upon thee, and be gracious unto thee: The Lord lift up his countenance upon thee, and give thee peace."[39]

Next door to the hospital stands a Roman Catholic church with a crucifix over the central entrance. The grieving father takes the cake and throws it in the face of the crucifix. It is an act of futile retaliation against the deity that has stolen his child. But a profoundly moving scene ensues:

Then through scalded eyes I seemed to see the hands free themselves of the nails and move slowly toward the soiled face. Very slowly, very deliberately, with infinite patience, the icing was wiped from the eyes and flung away. I could see it fall in clumps to the porch steps. Then the cheeks were wiped down with the same sense of grave and gentle ritual, with all the kind sobriety of one whose voice could be heard saying, "Suffer the little children to come unto me . . . for of such is the kingdom of heaven."[40]

The moment could have dissolved into sentimentality; instead, DeVries keeps it wrapped in ambivalence, for it is soon followed by Wanderhope's description of what it means to "learn to live without those consolations called religious."

> Philosophy can really give us nothing permanent to believe in either; it is too rich in answers, each canceling out the rest. The quest for Meaning is foredoomed. Human life "means" nothing. . . . Man has only his own two feet to stand on, his own human trinity to see him through: Reason, Courage, and Grace. And the first plus the second equals the third.[41]

In the end, writes Peter DeVries, "We are indeed saved by grace."[42] With what difficulty do the terms of one's youth—if not belief in the doctrines themselves—disappear.

"When Disbelief Has Gone"

After the Holocaust

This book set out to trace "the abdication of belief" from reluctant agnosticism and uncomfortable unbelief to the absorption of Christian doctrine into a melange of pagan shamanism, and thence to cold contempt for any suggestion that religion or religious concerns merit serious reflection. In this final chapter, we need to account briefly for another development: religion essentially ignored as irrelevant, religion regarded with condescension and contempt as if religion had never existed.

T. S. Eliot divided modern literature into three periods relative to their attitudes toward Christianity. The first period, he said, "took the Faith, in its contemporary version, for granted, and omitted it from its picture of life." This era may be said to have lasted until the middle of the nineteenth century, before the writers upon whom this book focuses; perhaps, to pin it down, until Darwin's *Origin of Species* was published in 1859. "In the second," Eliot continued, the age "doubted, worried about, or contested the Faith." Here we are talking about those writers with whom this book began: Arnold, Dickinson, Melville, Crane, Twain, Swinburne, Hardy, Yeats, and their contemporaries. Then Eliot offered a description of the third phase in which, he claimed, we are living: "It is the phase of those who have never heard the Christian Faith spoken of as anything but an anachronism." Eliot noted that, as a result, "the whole of modern literature is corrupted by what I call Secularism." To Eliot, secularism is "simply unaware of, simply cannot understand the meaning of, the primacy of the supernatural over the natural life."[1]

Using this framework and addressing ourselves to what the secular worldview represents, we do well to note Eliot's distinction between the present age and its immediate predecessor. That distinction lies not in secularism's rejection of any religious mentality but in secularism's ignoring and thereby dismissing the possibility of transcendence; indeed, secularism's stubborn refusal to grant even the most grudging acknowledgment that any dimension exists outside the boundaries of the natural world.

The late British poet Philip Larkin wrote a poem called "Church Going," in which he predicted the abandonment of churches to disuse. The speaker in Larkin's poem tells of his habit of stopping off to examine the interiors of old churches. He finds them uniformly the same:

> Another church: matting, seats, and stone
> And little books; sprawlings of flowers, cut
> For Sunday, brownish now; some brass and stuff
> Up at the holy end; the small, neat organ;
> And a tense, musty, unignorable silence,
> Brewed God knows how long.

On this occasion, however, the speaker is impelled to ask, what if any purpose will these buildings serve in the inevitable secularized future?

> When churches fall completely out of use
> What shall we turn them into . . . ?

He speculates for a few lines more before deciding that

226

> Power of some sort or other will go on
> In games, in riddles, seemingly at random;

but eventually, the narrator observes,

> . . . superstition, like belief, must die,
> And what remains when disbelief has gone?[2]

Larkin's answer, we may infer from the rest of the poem, is simply this: When even disbelief as distinct from mere unbelief has evaporated, nothing more remains of churches or the social institutions they sanction than the hollow shell of an anachronism.

But to counter the very existence of churches as a reminder, the secular mind must mount a strategic offensive, beginning with a denial of any dimension or description of Otherness: No other being, no other state-of-being, no other sempiternal sphere; most of all, no other hope beyond this existence. All that has energized the human imagination and motivated the human spirit with prospects of nirvana, the Elysian Fields, the happy hunting grounds, paradise, or heaven—all that is meant when the Book of Ecclesiastes declares that God "has set eternity in the hearts of men"—must be invalidated by counterclaims of atheism. But not mere philosophical atheism of the sort espoused by Baruch Spinoza—an intellectualized disputation with the concept of God; rather, the sort of atheism called for by secular man that acknowledges no common ground for debate, concedes no room for any discourse at all on a question as irrelevant and essentially futile as whether or not God exists. For the ardent disbeliever, the hypothesis and its given propositions are one and the same: *God does not exist.*

The secularist is most deeply offended—even scandalized—by Christianity's persistent claim that a sovereign deity has chosen to act in history, revealing himself through the mediation of his Son in human flesh. As Karl Heim has written, to the secularist "the transcendent Creator is no longer there. . . . The Creator has become an impossible thought, not framable by the mind."[3] In other words, secularism is far more than the absence of belief, which may be mere unbelief or skepticism; secularism is more than the diametric opposite of belief, which is disbelief. For while disbelief is an active adversary, inimical to faith's credibility, disbelief suffers this logical handicap: To *disbelieve* necessitates granting the possibility of a reasonable alternative, namely, to *believe*. So, "when disbelief has gone" means that the secular mind has passed even beyond this stage of contesting with Christian orthodoxy, no longer deigning to concern itself with the fantasies of faith. Denying what cannot be perceived by the physical senses, ignoring or explaining away as biochemical juices what stirs within a human being, the secularist sees only one power outside his or her control: time and its wringing out in history. And since to the secularist, history is itself a disarray of accidents and pratfalls, the human race has little better to do than watch the wheel turn or count the grains of sand sifting through the hourglass.

One observes this phenomenon of disbelief in four categories. The first consists of former believers who, for reasons of unresolved doubt and the quest for intellectual respectability, forsake their faith and turn aggressively against Christianity. In this century, a telling figure has been Charles B. Templeton, former colleague of Billy Graham in evangelism and pastor of a thriving church in Toronto. A high school dropout, Templeton had the natural flare and fluidity of a salesman. His Toronto "Youth for Christ" rallies in the late 1940s were sheer entertainment; his preaching at the Avenue Road Church, hellfire and brimstone. At the pinnacle of seeming ministerial success, Templeton shocked his following by announcing that he would resign to enroll at Princeton Theological Seminary to seek formal learning. Princeton after World War II was not a safe haven for shaky fundamentalists, and Templeton had many of his categories rocked by intellectual inquiry that dismissed simple biblical answers. As his doubts increased, he discovered only two options: Remain in the church as a hypocrite or demit his ministry. Eventually he chose the latter. From seminary, Templeton turned to ecumenical advocacy for the National Council of Churches, hosting a television program in Washington, D.C. This sojourn into broadcasting took him back to Toronto, where he became one of Canada's most listened-to radio personalities—and eventually a debunker of Christianity's claims.

Templeton's case resembles that of others who might belong to "Fundamentalists Anonymous"—who lash back at the religious upbringing or phase of life that they now deem to have been oppressive. James Balwin serves as an example: Brought up in Harlem's religious strictness, at age fourteen he was ordained to preach. But by eighteen he had left the church and his family to take up the homosexual life of Greenwich Village. His novel, *Go Tell It on the Mountain,* recounts his apostasizing. Another is Hugh Hefner, publisher of *Playboy* magazine, whose mother Grace had hoped that he would become a Christian missionary.

A second category of disbelief shows itself in public statements by popular science writers such as Carl Sagan and Stephen Jay Gould, who present their theories of cosmic beginnings as if already proven, while utterly dismissing—without need for rebuttal—the possibility of theistic origins. At his death in 1996, Carl Sagan was remembered as having declared his religion to be "respect for the universe," while rejecting any notion of a personal God who would hold him accountable for not having believed in any god's existence. Like Sagan, Stephen Jay Gould is as charming on television and in his popular essays about his atheism as he is about his love of baseball. Gould is almost jolly in his condescending remarks about religionists, patting such minor minds on the head with avuncular goodwill, as one might humor a foolish relative.

Third, pure rationalism also leads to earnest and militant disbelief. For many secularized intellectuals, for instance, theology of any stripe has always seemed patent folly, delusion, or fraud. Robert Gorham Davis, retired professor of English at Harvard University, spends his energies in writing letters to the editor of the *New York Times,* opposing any published reference to orthodox Christian doctrine. For instance, Davis wrote to refute a book reviewer's statement regarding the Bible's inspiration and authority:

> The God who "revealed Himself" in the Scriptures knew no more of the world and its future than those He presumably addressed. Jesus warned that the final days of tribulation were near: "Truly, I say to you, this generation will not pass away till all these things take place." But they did not take place, and have not yet.

229

On no clear evidence theologians and philosophers declare God to be omniscient and omnicompetent. Plainly if there were such a God who really wished to reveal Himself to mankind, He could do so in a way that left no doubt.[4]

Fourth are what might be called professional atheists, among whom Corliss Lamont and Madalyn Murray O'Hair stood apart even from each other in their manner of contending against religion in general, Christianity in particular. As president of the American Humanist Association, Lamont was civil toward his religious opponents—especially those of more liberal theology, whom he thought merely deluded by moral sentiment—and courteous in debate. Lamont published a revealing advertisement in 1988 in the *New York Times* and other newspapers, in which his reasonable tone set out to explain the fundamentals of his brand of atheistic dogma:

Humanism Is the Best Way of Life
Creating Joy and Beauty in the Here and Now[5]

Naturalistic or secular humanism is a philosophy of joyous service for the welfare, progress, and happiness of all humanity in this one and only life. There is no pie in the sky awaiting us. To achieve its goals, humanism relies primarily on the methods of reason and science, democracy and compassion. "The watchword of Humanism is compassionate concern for our fellow human beings."[6]

Humanism, with its nontheistic viewpoint, rejects all supernaturalism as poetic myth but embodies in its synthesis the sound principles of traditional philosophies starting with the ancient Greeks and including much of the Judeo-Christian ethic.

Lamont commends the Ten Commandments and the teachings of Jesus, whom he regards as a great and noble character, who spoke out repeatedly for social equality, the brotherhood of man, and peace on earth.

Humanists stress that Jesus was a courageous civil liberties victim. Humanists gladly cooperate with Christians and other religious groups on social, economic, and world peace issues. It is clear that humanism chiefly disagrees with Christianity in its theology.

Lamont then spells out his philosophical opposition "to all theories of universal determinism, fatalism or predestination and its belief that human beings, while conditioned by the past, possess genuine freedom of choice and creative action."

Rather, he maintains, "We are, within certain objective limits, masters of our own destiny."

The advertisement closes with this credo: "Above all, Humanism, with its faith in human intelligence and abilities, is a philosophy of hope and optimism."

Lamont's message is clear: There is no life beyond "the here and now." Each human being can look forward to "this one and only life," no more. Alluding to the familiar parody of the gospel song, "In the Sweet By-and-By," Lamont assures his reader that "there is no pie-in-the-sky awaiting us." Therefore, atheistic humanism urges each person to make the most of its "philosophy of hope and optimism."

Madalyn Murray O'Hair's message was even clearer—and also more crude. Her bumper stickers proclaimed:

> God Is Just Another Addiction
> Jesus Christ—Super Fraud
> Atheists Do It without Guilt
> Atheists Are Moral but Not Stupid

When we begin to speak of O'Hair and others like her, we turn directly into the face of aggressively militant *disbelief*. Here is no lady-like apologist, no grandmotherly disputant; for O'Hair, the cause is nothing short of all-out war. Notorious, first, for advocating the abolition of Bible reading in public schools, decided by the Supreme Court in its *Murray v. Curlett* ruling of 1963, O'Hair went on to campaign against the inscription "In God We Trust" on American coins and bills and also opposed any references to "Judeo-Christian morality" in the media. She reveled in calling herself "the most hated woman in America." The very style with which she carried on her attacks against those who believe in God hardly made her position appealing to the masses.

231

Ironically, her greatest setback occurred when the son on whose behalf she brought the Bible reading case, William J. Murray, became a believing Christian and an ardent opponent of his mother's influence. Furthermore, in 1995, O'Hair disappeared from her Austin, Texas, home and headquarters of American Atheists, Inc., taking with her corporate funds of more than $600,000. Some of her followers claim that she may have gone into hiding in order to die while avoiding her worst fear: That some "Christer"—her term of contempt for any believing Christian—or other religious person might offer a prayer over her corpse.

Beyond these four categories lies yet another class of antagonist against the God whose presumed nonexistence makes the thought of his existence too repulsive to consider. These are individuals who have suffered a great disappointment through some personal or universal incident representing a test of God's power or love. From their perspective, God failed the test. So is the experience of Samuel Langhorne Clemens, who became implacably embittered against God, after 1896, by the death of his favorite daughter, Susy.

In another case, the novelist W. Somerset Maugham recounts in his autobiography, *The Summing Up,* that as a boy afflicted with a desperate stammer he prayed earnestly to be delivered from his speech impediment. Upon waking, he was certain that God had answered his prayer—until his first encounter that day with someone and his need to speak. So profound was his disappointment, he never thereafter believed in God.

In the mid-1960s, another young man at the McCallie School in Chattanooga was devoutly religious, a spiritual model among his schoolmates, actively leading a prayer group and planning to serve as a foreign missionary. Then personal disaster overtook him: His sister died of leukemia, and his father committed suicide. The boy's Christian faith collapsed. His name is Ted Turner, founder of Cable News Network and other media innovations—and now an outspoken disbeliever.

Personal suffering may destroy one individual's belief in a God no longer perceived as sovereign and loving; an even more universal catastrophe might show such a God to be unjust and fundamentally cruel, therefore undeserving of worship, reverence, and obedience by an entire segment of human society. So seems to be the case of many Jews, now beyond disbelief after the Nazi atrocities of 1933 to 1945, known generally as the Holocaust. Among these are some of the premier writers of our time.

No one who lived through the plague called National Socialism—whether Christian, Gentile, Aryan, non-Jew, or whatever other catchword of Northern European ancestry one adopts—can begin to grasp the meaning of the Nazi outrage upon humanity in general, European Jewry in particular. Identity cards, a swastika's sacrilege upon a synagogue wall, the yellow star, a ban on certain artists and their work, the knock in the night, whole families vanishing without a trace, the cattle cars, the work camps, a number burned into the flesh; at last, the death camp and its invitation to a fatal shower. This madness, we must recall, was perpetrated in the name of purifying society.

To some readers, perhaps—especially to those too young to have been born at that time—the names of Dachau, Belsen, Buchenwald, Auschwitz, and the rest of those charnel houses seem foreign, the events distant in time. But to every Jew, the names themselves are as familiar as his own; the events—like the crusades, to many Muslims—are happening now! Some Christians find it relatively easy to rid their minds of the Jewish slaughter by blaming it solely on the aberration of Adolf Hitler's demonic hatred. But these Christians greatly oversimplify, ignoring other aspects of the shameful history of the times and, in particular, the collaboration in genocide by leading representatives of the church in Germany who, by their silence if nothing else, acquiesced to the extermination plot.

There were exceptions, of course, and their names are saintly; indeed, they are considered among "the Righteous Gentiles," recognized for their efforts to save Jews from death: Corrie ten Boom, who maintained a hiding place in her home; Martin Niemoller, the former submarine officer, then Lutheran pastor in a Berlin suburb, among the earliest clergymen to protest the Nazi terror against Jews; Dietrich Bonhoeffer, pastor and theologian who joined the conspiracy to overthrow Hitler and was hanged at

Flossenburg; Father Maximilian Kolbe, the Roman Catholic priest imprisoned at Auschwitz, who stepped forward to volunteer his own life in exchange for a Jew about to be condemned; Oskar Schindler, largely unknown until his story became famous through the making of an award-winning motion picture, *Schindler's List.*

Perhaps the most prominent of those who saved Jews from death was Raoul Wallenberg, a Swedish diplomat whose neutrality offered him unusual foreign access during the war. He is credited with saving thousands of Hungarian Jews; but following Germany's surrender in 1945, he is thought to have been arrested by the Soviet Union's Red Army and sent to one of the *gulag* camps. Less well known is the ambiguous Kurt Gerstein, whose story, told in Pierre Joffrey's biography, *A Spy for God*, may be the most transfixing account to come out of World War II. Known as the inventor of the deadly Zyclon B gas, Gerstein rose to high rank in the Gestapo. He regularly visited the camps where his invention was in use. But Gerstein—a believing Lutheran—found ways to delay or even abort a gassing, using such devices as his inventor's nose to detect leaks that others could not perceive. In these ways he hoped to prolong some lives of victims he could not otherwise rescue.

But for all the heroic efforts of these rescuers, surviving Jews know all too well that, among too many professing Christians, neither the German Evangelical Church, the official state ecclesiastical body, nor the Roman Catholic hierarchy, took a stand against Hitler on behalf of Jews. Instead, the prevailing attitude is what Friedrich Heer calls "the living lie of German Christendom."[7] Is it any wonder, therefore, that most Jews of that era and since despise whatever passes under the name of Christianity? Is it any wonder that their contempt is beyond disbelief?

Ever since Sethos and Ramses of Egypt, there had been tyrants who oppressed the children of Israel, villains like Haman who schemed, mobs of unreasoning men to carry out their foul business against the people of God. But always in the past there had also been a Moses or Esther to deliver. Where were these deliverers in 1933? More important, where was their God?

234

The question of God would seem to be the key to Jewish identity—although there are certainly self-proclaimed Jews who would protest that necessity. Joseph L. Blau has pointed out, "There is no criterion within Judaism for orthodoxy or heterodoxy. . . . The only way to answer the question 'What is Judaism?' is by enumerating and describing its current varieties."[8] In America today, one may find as many as eight different types of Jews in a population nearing six million. The first four of these classifications would define worshipers whose religious practices, in curious ways, parallel their Christian counterparts, whether as fundamentalist, mainstream, or liberal congregations.

At the extreme right end of the spectrum stand the zealously religious Zionists who base their geopolitical ideology firmly on the texts of Scripture, insisting on referring to territorial mandates by their Old Testament names of Judea and Samaria. Near them are the Orthodox of various persuasions, including the most visible of the several sects called Hasidim or "pious." In the middle of the spectrum are the third and fourth types of religious Judaism, Conservative and Reform, whose members comprise nearly 90 percent of American Jews and who, in 1997, were accused by some critics as betraying the very meaning of Judaism.

A fifth classification is the nonobservant Jew who is not a member of any congregation and makes no pretense of spirituality, whose Jewish identity is purely ethnic and cultural. If not more susceptible to cults than observant Jews, these are the Jews most likely to lapse into accommodation known as "assimilation," in which one's Jewish customs and beliefs are submerged, disguised, or overwhelmed by the still dominant Protestant culture. On the other side of nonobservance stands a sixth group consisting of those Jews who define themselves essentially as humanists, identifying with the movement known as the Ethical Culture Society or the Society for Humanistic Judaism, whose advertising promotes

The Humanist Haggadah

A Haggadah for Secular Jews who want to celebrate Passover with integrity.

> Passover does not need to celebrate supernatural events. It can celebrate human freedom, human courage, and the human ingenuity which leads slaves from despair to dignity. The great spring festival of the Hebrew calendar is a time to experience the creative renewal of the Jewish spirit.[9]

Like Gentiles who never attend church services but likewise never fail to exchange gifts around a decorated Christmas tree, these Jews celebrate Passover without its historic or symbolic meaning. So Rabbi Sherwin Wine, of Birmingham, Michigan, presents his views to the Alliance of Humanist, Atheist, and Ethical Culture Organizations of Los Angeles, an audience in which person after person identifies as a Holocaust survivor or a descendant who no longer believes in God.

The seventh classification of Jews is bound to the religion of psychotherapy founded by an archenemy of theism, Sigmund Freud. Born into a Jewish home, Freud never professed the traditions of Judaism, believing that religion—in particular, the concept of a loving heavenly Father—was a human concoction meant to account for the inadequacy of human fathers. He expected that, as the human race developed in sophistication, the need for religion would evaporate. While there are many non-Jews offering psychotherapeutic counsel—and many non-Jews on their couches—the profession is dominated by persons of Jewish upbringing and cultural values. How often does one find among them an observant Jew, a religious Jew, a God-fearing Jew? Instead, Freud's well-documented hatred of God has been transmitted through the decades until it becomes standard diagnosis for psychotherapists to regard any mention by a client of personal faith in a Supreme Being to be the first evidence of a disturbed mind. Instead of the covenant, Freudian psychotherapy preaches its dogma of the Oedipus complex, passive-aggressive behavior, anal retentive tendencies based on premature toilet training, and suppressed memory of alleged child abuse.

The last classification of Jew stands as the back-to-back opposite of the first group, as if the spectrum of 180 degrees had turned upon itself to become a circle; so, the eighth group finds itself closest in emotion to its first and most adamant opponents. Political

Zionists—as distinct from those Zionists who take the Scriptures seriously—stake their claim to *Eretz* Israel not on the covenant with Yahweh but on international mandates, treaties, and resolutions from the United Nations, as well as victories in warfare, by which possession becomes nine-tenths of the law. Few politicians in Israel speak of the covenant nor of the Torah; the State of Israel appears as secular as any other industrialized nation; yet, ironically, tourism by religious devotees who honor its history—indeed, its very geography—has become its primary source of foreign revenue.

Thus, when each band across the spectrum of Jewish experience has been accounted for, the only common bond that ties all Jews is neither their faith in the covenant nor their adherence to the law nor their hope in the coming Messiah. It is not even the Promised Land, the State of Israel itself. Rather, it is the Holocaust and its defiant promise, "Never Again!" The Holocaust connects even those at war with each other over dietary scruples or the validity of the Talmud in the modern era. It is the event that unites all Jews in sorrow, frustration, and rage. It also contributes to the enhanced faith of some and the chilling disbelief of others.

Facing a religious anomaly such as the varieties of Jewish belief, unbelief, and even disbelief, the question cannot be avoided: Without Yahweh—without the God of Israel—what is a Jew? If God did not call Abraham out of Ur of the Chaldees and set him in the land of Canaan, does not every Jew repudiate his patrimony, sell his birthright, and name Ishmael and Esau as his forebears? Must not a Jew believe this? Milton Himmelfarb specifies three choices facing modern Jews: "To be Jews, to be Christians, to be secularists." Many Jews, he writes, "cannot believe what Judaism requires them to believe."[10] Nor can a Jew who does not believe in God extend faith toward a revelation of that God in Jesus of Nazareth. The remaining choice, therefore, is secularism—or no belief whatsoever. For what is left to believe? To many contemporary Jews, therefore, God is—at best—a Jewish uncle who forgot to show up for the bar mitzvah; at worst, God is a faithless lover who fled for his own safety when the bullies and rapists approached.

After generations of growing apostasy, traditional belief in the God of Israel expired forever in the gas ovens of Europe. This loss of faith became particularly acute among American Jews. By 1963, sociologist Ernest van den Haag had published a survey of "The Political and Religious Attitudes of American College Students," which reported "Judaism in decay." The failure of God to deliver six million of his chosen people out of the hands of the Nazi butchers had disqualified God and his claims to a covenant relationship with the Jews. Thereafter, all that remained of a historic union between God and the Jews is tragic memory. The rest is silence.

Yet, since the end of World War II, Jewish writers have been anything but silent. In the second half of the twentieth century, Jewish novelists, playwrights, poets, and literary critics have commanded the spotlight of modern American literature. With only a few exceptions—Tennessee Williams, Robert Penn Warren, John Cheever, John Updike—centerstage has belonged to Jews: Saul Bellow, Bernard Malamud, Philip Roth, Isaac Bashevis Singer, Joseph Heller, Arthur Miller, Woody Allen, Delmore Schwartz, Karl Shapiro, Howard Nemerov, Allen Ginsberg, among many others. So too the arbiters of literary and cultural taste, the critics and professors whose essays and reviews shape opinion: For every Protestant Northrop Frye there are five Jews of the stature of Lionel Trilling, Philip Rahv, Leslie A. Fiedler, Cynthia Ozick, and Alfred Kazin.

One of the salient features of the Jewish literary canon has been its sense of hope-against-hope, whatever conditions would seem to prevail. Yet the very nature of this hope is tainted by irony and the lurking suspicion that another genocide could be in the offing. This time, however, there would be no dependence upon futile trust in a God who does not exist. Instead, the best one can do is to poke fun at one's own need to believe. "Not only is there no God," writes Woody Allen in one of his sketches, "but try getting a plumber on weekends."[11]

Playwright Arthur Miller is more serious in his analysis. Writing during the original Broadway run of *Death of a Salesman,* Miller attempted to offer a modern audience his version of Aristotle's definition of tragedy. He began by describing a circumstance: "When Mr. B., while walking down the street, is struck on the head by a falling piano, the newspapers call this a tragedy." To Miller, however, a man's being "struck on the head by a falling piano" is only *pathos* because "it merely arouses our feelings of sympathy, sadness, and possibly of identification"—not, however, "the tragic feeling." To achieve true tragedy, something more is needed: "Tragedy arises when we are in the presence of a man who has missed accomplishing his joy. But the joy must be there, the promise of the right way of life must be there."[12]

In the context of his Broadway play, Miller's thesis points toward the failure of Willy Loman, the Brooklyn salesman, husband, and father, to accomplish his joy because Willy and his sons have followed the myth of Willy's father and older brother, leading only to ruin. Willy has taught his sons the myth of an absconded father and a messianic older brother, but it is a myth whose values are based on irresponsibility, inflated ego, bullying, theft, and deceit. At the same time, the Loman family has lived next door to Charley—a decent skeptic and iconoclast—and his son, Bernard; yet the Lomans have never recognized that, by their behavior, these neighbors personify "the right way of life"—generosity, humility, honesty, integrity. As a consequence, Willy and his sons have all missed the joy that must be a testament of "the right way of life."

In 1949, when Miller wrote his essay for the *New York Herald-Tribune,* his readers and theatergoers were only four years removed from the awful disclosure of the death camps in Europe.

His definition of tragedy, therefore, took on meaning larger than any single family's drama; rather, it encompassed the whole scope of the human family's myth of Father and Elder Brother, of what it means to love one's neighbor as oneself. To be sure, what had occurred in Europe exceeded the limits of pathos; it had nothing whatever to do with a piano's accidentally falling on the head of Mr. B. These were circumstances far more deliberate than that.

Among those who could recall Jewish life prior to 1933, there had been much in which to find joy—in art, music, learning, research, trade, even the simple pleasures of home—for there was always "the promise of the right way of life," whether in or out of the *shtetl,* the ghetto, the Pale. But with the onslaught of "the final solution" and the treachery of much of Christendom's ignoring the Nazi slaughter of the Jews, all joy—all promise of joy—disappeared. With that disappearance arose contempt even for petty disbelief, rendered meaningless and unworthy of the effort by the enormity of God the Father's betrayal and the failure of the Elder Brother to rescue.

To the utterly secularized Jew, beyond disbelief in the Torah and the Holy Days, history is no longer a link with God; at its worst, history is a reminder of the oath taken in rashness: "His blood be upon us and upon our children." The curse of the Jew as Christ-killer is as indelible as the mark of Cain, as persistent as a schoolyard bully's threats. Its legacy creates the rupture between traditional faith and modern secularism that forms the theme of Karl Shapiro's poem, simply called "Jew."

> The name is immortal but only the name, for the rest
> Is a nose that can change in the weathers of time or persist
> Or die out in confusion or model itself on the best.
>
> But the name is a language itself that is whispered and hissed
> Through the houses of ages, and ever a language the same
> And ever and ever a blow on our heart like a fist.
>
> And this last of our dream in the desert, O curse of our name,
> Is immortal as Abraham's voice in our fragment of prayer
> Adonai, Adonai, for our bondage of murder and shame!
>
> And the word for the murder of God will cry out on the air
> Though the race is no more and the temples are closed of our
>   will
> And the peace is made fast on the earth and the earth is made
>   fair;
>
> Our name is impaled in the heart of the world on a hill
> Where we suffer to die by the hands of ourselves, and to kill.[13]

Thus, for the Jew—whether Orthodox or disbelieving—history becomes a hell to be lived through again and again—in the horrors of *Kristalnacht*, in the massacre of the Warsaw ghetto, at Munich's Olympic Village, at Entebbe airport, on the Golan Heights, in Crown

Heights. As Yakov Bok, in Bernard Malamud's novel *The Fixer,* comes to realize, "being born a Jew meant being vulnerable to history, including its worst errors." But Malamud has also said, "All men are Jews,"[14] meaning perhaps that no man knows the significance of his own existence apart from suffering.

Yet suffering without meaning is mere cruelty; suffering gains its meaning only when the sufferer knows that someone else cares. Belief in God carries with it an assumption that someone reaches out to the human race, created in his image, to validate the purpose of suffering. From the early narratives in Genesis—through God's provision of coverings for Adam and Eve after the fall, from Noah's ark to Abraham's bargaining with God for the deliverance of any remaining righteous souls in Sodom—to the story of the cross and the empty tomb, the divine message is the same: No human being suffers in vain, for in suffering lies the possibility of redemption.

But if, in order to be known, God demands suffering so meaningless as that inflicted by Nazi terror, then why does any Jew believe in such a deity? This is the question asked by the most famous of the death camp survivors, Elie Wiesel. In his searing narrative *Night,* he writes of the horror "which consumed my faith forever."

> Never shall I forget that night, the first night in camp, which has turned my life into one long night, seven times cursed and seven times sealed. Never shall I forget that smoke. Never shall I forget the little faces of the children, whose bodies I saw turned into wreaths of smoke beneath a silent blue sky. . . .
>
> Never shall I forget that nocturnal silence which deprived me, for all eternity, of the desire to live. Never shall I forget those moments which murdered my God and my soul and turned my dreams to dust. Never shall I forget these things, even if I am condemned to live as long as God Himself.
>
> Never.[15]

Yet even Wiesel cannot rid himself entirely of belief. He describes a victim in his final throes:

For more than half an hour he stayed there, struggling between life and death, dying in slow agony under our eyes. And we had to look him full in the face. He was still alive when I passed in front of him. His tongue was still red, his eyes were not yet glazed.

Behind me, I heard the same man asking: "Where is God now?" And I heard a voice within me answer him: "Where is He? Here He is—He is hanging here on this gallows. . . ."[16]

By attributing to God a comforting presence, even in such agony, Elie Wiesel allows for a spark of belief amid the dying embers of faith. Perhaps secularism's greatest hoax is its claim to have made God obsolete, for that can never be so long as there is human consciousness of the predicament called human existence. Moreover, Wiesel's narrative reminds us that we must allow for the possibility that some individuals, whatever their religious or philosophical bent, may possess unconsciously what they consciously reject. As John Baillie writes, in *Our Knowledge of God*, even those who "deny God with the top of their minds" may believe at the same time "from the bottom of their hearts."[17] Leslie A. Fiedler has also noted that

the belief of many atheists is closer to a true love of God and a true sense of his nature, than the kind of easy faith which, never having experienced God, hangs a label bearing his name on some childish fantasy.[18]

One of the most affecting accounts of such a spiritual journey is *A Walker in the City*, a personal narrative by Alfred Kazin, who elsewhere identifies himself as "this believing unbeliever." He tells his reader what it meant to be a Jew in this secular age. Recalling his boyhood, prior to World War II, in Brooklyn, Kazin speaks of his early struggle to believe.

I was a Jew. Yet it puzzled me that no one around me seemed to take God very seriously. We neither believed nor disbelieved. He was our oldest habit. . . . Yet I never really wanted to give Him up. In some way it would have been hopeless to justify to myself—I had feared Him so long—He fascinated me, He seemed to hold the solitary place I most often went back to.[19]

On the steps of the New York Public Library, the young Kazin accepted a copy of the New Testament and began reading eagerly.

> *. . . and the poor have the gospel preached to them. And blessed is he, whosoever shall not be offended in me.*
>
> Offended in him? I had known him instantly. Surely I had been waiting for him all my life—our own Yeshua, misunderstood by his own, like me, but the very embodiment of everything I had waited so long to hear from a Jew. . . . It was he, I thought, who would resolve for me at last the ambiguity and the long ache of being a Jew—Yeshua, our own long-lost Jesus, speaking straight to the mind and heart at once. . . . He was Yeshua, my own Reb Yeshua, of whose terrible death I could never read without bursting into tears—Yeshua, our own Yeshua.[20]

Much of Kazin's spiritual search has been to gain some understanding of how the God in whom he declines to believe could have permitted such atrocities. Once at a dinner table, Alfred Kazin asked me, "What do you Christians mean when you say that Jesus is Lord?" I must admit that I was overwhelmed by the question, tongue-tied and inarticulate, disappointing as I tried to express my own faith. At the end, one realizes that all one's own mental capacities are too limited to reason through the unreasonable. It becomes a matter of faith and trust in the character of God. So I come with hope to the words of a believer whose grasp of his own faith is more eloquent than mine. In his foreword to Wiesel's book *Night*, the Nobel Prize–winning novelist Francois Mauriac recalls the time when he too was asked to justify his faith in a God so seemingly cruel and unjust:

> And I, who believe that God is love, what answer could I give my young questioner . . . what did I say to him? Did I speak of that other Jew, his brother, who may have resembled him—the Crucified, whose Cross has conquered the world? Did I affirm that the stumbling block to his faith was the cornerstone of mine, and that the conformity between the Cross and the suffering of men was in my eyes the key to that impenetrable mystery whereon the faith of his childhood had perished? Zion, however, has risen up again from the crematories and the charnel houses. The Jewish nation

has been resurrected from among its thousands of dead. It is through them that it lives again. We do not know the worth of one single drop of blood, one single tear. All is grace. If the Eternal is the Eternal, the last word for each one of us belongs to Him. This is what I should have told this Jewish child. But I could only embrace him, weeping.[21]

This is the final challenge in a world shriveled by "the abdication of belief," atrophied by contempt beyond disbelief—the challenge to embrace and weep with those whose souls are devoid of faith. For while weakened by stammering tongues and the limits of one's own imagination, we who claim to believe nonetheless possess two certain gifts: not the power of rhetoric but the Word; not an *ignis fatuus* but the Light. In the words of my own favorite example in the Gospels, the father in Mark 9, we too can cry out in assurance, "I do believe; help me to overcome my unbelief!"

Afterword _____

For the church father Tertullian, it was sufficient to say, "I believe because it is impossible." For the modern "impossibility believer," another spokesman may be cited, the nineteenth-century Danish philosopher Søren Kierkegaard, who wrote, in his *Concluding Unscientific Postscript:*

> A believer is one who is infinitely interested in another's reality. This is a decisive criterion for faith, and the interest in question is not just a little curiosity, but an absolute dependence upon faith's object. . . .
>
> The object of faith is thus God's reality in existence as a particular individual, the fact that God has existed as an individual human being. . . . Christianity is therefore not a doctrine, but the fact that God has existed.
>
> The realm of faith is thus not a class for numbskulls in the sphere of the intellectual, or an asylum for the feeble-minded. Faith constitutes a sphere all by itself, and every misunderstanding of Christianity may at once be recognized by its transforming it into a doctrine, transferring it to the sphere of the intellectual.[1]

Then Kierkegaard states,

> The maximum of attainment within the sphere of faith is to become infinitely interested in the reality of the teacher.[2]

Whoever comes to God, the writer of the letter to the Hebrews declares, must first grant one premise in order to gain one benefit: The seeker "must believe that [God] exists and that he rewards those who earnestly seek him" (Heb. 11:6). And what is that reward? Confirmation that the search has not been in vain. In

Kierkegaard's terms, no one who by faith perceives "the reality of the teacher" can fail to have that faith confirmed.

For whatever reasons—personal disappointment, the bad example of parents or other adults, acute suffering unrelieved by prayer, colossal indifference on the part of supposedly religious persons, unanswered cosmic questions, or the perception that Christianity represents "a want of intellectual seriousness"—some men and women have chosen to resist and ultimately reject the notion of a personal and transcendent deity. For some, it has been a casual act of dismissal; for others—like Madalyn Murray O'Hair—the choice to disbelieve in God has made them become archenemies of the Christian gospel. So, they have battled against every manifestation of Christianity, whether positive or negative. They have scorned alike sincere and simple faith or magisterial dogma; they have debated propositional theology and doctrine; they have fought ritual and commemoration; they have gloried in every instance of ecclesiastical corruption and every other intellectual and spiritual misrepresentation of Christianity.

For in so doing, what they have missed is "the reality of the teacher"—the Christ of Christianity. In critiquing the broad landscape, they have failed to see the central person whose portrait the landscape surrounds; they have failed to recognize the dancer within the dance; they have missed the very essence of that which they attempted to grasp.

Can there be anything more ironic than to have given one's intellectual and moral energies to the extirpation of the only truth that matters?

Notes

Introduction

1. George Bernard Shaw, "Androcles and the Lion: A Fable Play with Preface on the Prospects of Christianity," *Collected Plays with Their Prefaces* (New York: Dodd, Mead, 1972), 515.

2. Robert Carlson, Letter to the Editor, *New York Times*, 14 January 1992.

Chapter 1

1. Matthew Arnold, "Dover Beach," *The Literature of England*, ed. George K. Anderson and Karl J. Holzknecht (Chicago: Scott, Foresman, 1953), 894–95.

2. T. S. Eliot, "Religion and Literature," *Religion and Modern Literature: Essays in Theory and Criticism*, ed. G. B. Tennyson and Edward E. Ericson Jr. (Grand Rapids: Eerdmans, 1975), 29.

3. Jacques Monod, *Chance and Necessity: An Essay on the Natural Philosophy of Modern Biology*, trans. Austryn Wainhouse (New York: Knopf, 1971), 172–73.

4. Eliot, "Religion and Literature," 29.

5. Matthew Arnold, "Hebraism and Hellenism," *Literature of England*, 898–903.

6. Matthew Arnold, "The Study of Poetry," *English Literature and Irish Politics*, vol. 9, ed. R. H. Super (Ann Arbor: University of Michigan Press, 1970), 161.

7. Ibid.

8. Matthew Arnold, *God and the Bible*, vol. 7, ed. R. H. Super (Ann Arbor: University of Michigan Press, 1970), 385–87.

9. Thomas Huxley, "Agnosticism and Christianity," *Science and Christian Tradition: Essays* (New York: D. Appleton, 1896), 310.

10. Matthew Arnold, "Literature and Science," *Philistinism in England and America*, vol. 10, ed. R. H. Super (Ann Arbor: University of Michigan Press, 1970), 61–62.

11. Matthew Arnold, "Science and Culture," *Essays: English and American*, ed. Charles W. Eliot (New York: P. F. Collier and Son, 1910), 221.

12. Matthew Arnold, "Sweetness and Light," *Culture and Anarchy*, vol. 5, ed. R. H. Super (Ann Arbor: University of Michigan Press, 1970), 96.

13. Matthew Arnold, "The Scholar-Gypsy," *Literature of England*, 891, lines 203–4.

14. Arnold, "Literature and Science," 72–73.

15. Arnold, *God and the Bible*, 392.

16. Matthew Arnold, "The True Greatness of Christianity," *Dissent and Dogma*, vol. 6, ed. R. H. Super (Ann Arbor: University of Michigan Press, 1970), 400.

17. Eliot, "Religion and Literature," 22.

18. Arnold, *God and the Bible*, 378.

19. Bernard Knox, *Oedipus at Thebes: Sophocles' Tragic Hero and His Time* (New Haven: Yale University Press, 1957), 166.

20. Ibid.

21. Sophocles, *Antigone*, trans. Dudley Fitts and Robert Fitzgerald (New York: Harcourt Brace Jovanovich, 1976), 209.

Chapter 2

1. Thomas H. Johnson, ed., *The Complete Poems of Emily Dickinson* (Boston: Little, Brown, 1960), #1551, 646. All poems cited are taken from this source and listed by poem #.

2. Richard Sewall, *The Life of Emily Dickinson*, vol. 2 (New York: Farrar, Strauss, and Giroux, 1974), 376.

3. Ibid., 325.

4. Thomas H. Johnson, ed., *The Letters of Emily Dickinson*, vol. 1 (Cambridge: Harvard University Press, 1958), 27 (letter dated 31 January 1846).

5. Johnson, *Letters*, vol. 1, 27–28 (letter dated 31 January 1846).

6. Johnson, *Letters*, vol. 2, 473–74 (letter dated 16 August 1870).

7. Johnson, *Letters*, vol. 1, 94 (letter dated 3 April 1850).

8. Ibid., 103 (letter dated late 1850).

9. Johnson, *Poems*, poem #501, "This World Is Not Conclusion," 243.

10. Johnson, *Letters*, vol. 1, 311.

11. Johnson, *Letters*, vol. 2, 502–3 (letter dated early 1873).

12. Johnson, *Poems*, poem #1207, 533.

13. Johnson, *Letters*, vol. 2, 31 (letter dated 28 March 1846).

14. Johnson, *Letters*, vol. 1, 37–38 (letter dated 8 September 1846).

15. Sewall, *Life of Emily Dickinson*, 360.

16. Johnson, *Letters*, vol. 1, 67 (letter dated 16 May 1848).

17. Ibid.

18. Ibid., 82 (letter dated 23 January 1850).

19. Sewall, *Life of Emily Dickinson*, 462.

20. David Lowe and Ronald Meyer, eds. and trans., *Fyodor Dostoevsky: Complete Letters*, vol. 1 (Ann Arbor: Ardis, 1988), 90, (letter to Mme. Natalya Fonvizina).

21. Johnson, *Letters*, vol. 2, 404 (letter dated 25 April 1862).

22. Johnson, *Letters*, vol. 3, 713 (letter dated October 1881).

23. Johnson, *Poems*, poem #338, 160.

24. Ibid., poem #555, 270.

25. Ibid., poem #324, 153–54; poem #376, 179–80; poem #502, 243–44.

26. Sewall, *Life of Emily Dickinson*, 664.

27. Johnson, *Poems*, poem #1492, 628–29.

28. Ibid., poem #964, 451.

Chapter 3

1. James E. Miller Jr., ed., *Complete Poetry and Selected Prose* (Boston: Houghton Mifflin, 1959), xxv.

2. Ibid., 198.

3. Ibid., 50.

4. Ibid., 382.

5. Ibid., 60.

6. Edmund Wilson, *The Shock of Recognition*, vol. 1 (New York: Farrar, Strauss and Cudahy, 1955), 269.

7. Stephen E. Whicher, ed., *Selections from Ralph Waldo Emerson* (Boston: Houghton Mifflin, 1957), 9–11.

8. Ibid., 67.

9. Ibid., 74.

10. Ibid., 80.

11. Ibid., 100.

12. Ibid., 147, 148, 149, 152–53.

13. Ibid., 222–41.

14. Ibid., 240.

15. Miller, *Complete Poetry*, 41.

16. Ibid., xxv.

17. Gay Wilson Allen, *The Solitary Singer: A Critical Biography of Walt Whitman* (New York: New York University Press, 1955), 43.

18. Van Wyck Brooks, *America's Coming-of-Age* (New York: Dutton, 1958), 60.

19. Allen, *Solitary Singer*, 364.

20. Miller, *Complete Poetry*, 68.

21. Ibid., 58.

22. Ibid., 363.

23. Ibid., 64.

24. Ibid., 60.

25. Ibid., 42.

26. Ibid., 35.

27. Ibid., 37.

28. Ibid., 394.

29. Ibid., 51.

30. Leslie A. Fiedler, *Whitman: A Dell Anthology* (New York: Dell, 1959), 183–84.

31. Miller, *Complete Poetry*, 56.
32. Ibid.
33. Ibid., 219.
34. Ibid., 288.
35. Ibid., 288–89, 290–91.
36. Whicher, *Selections from Emerson*, 224.
37. R. W. B. Lewis, *The American Adam* (Chicago: University of Chicago Press, 1955), 51.
38. Miller, *Complete Poetry*, 291.
39. Ibid.
40. Ibid., 293.
41. Ibid.
42. Ibid., 294.
43. Ibid.
44. Ibid., 63.

Chapter 4

1. Eleanor Melville Metcalf, ed., *Herman Melville: Cycle and Epicycle* (Cambridge: Harvard University Press, 1953), 83.
2. Ibid., 86.
3. Ibid., 87.
4. Ibid., 90.
5. Cotton Mather, "The Wonders of the Invisible World," *The Puritans*, ed. Michael L. Lasser (New York: Holt, Rinehart and Winston, 1969), 13.
6. "The Diary of Samuel Sewall," *Puritans*, 14–15.
7. Ibid., 14.
8. Ibid., 15.
9. Ibid., 15–16.
10. Ibid., 16.
11. Norman Holmes Pearson, ed., *The Complete Novels and Selected Tales of Nathaniel Hawthorne* (New York: The Modern Library, 1937), 89. All citations from *The Scarlet Letter* are taken from this source.
12. Hawthorne, *The Scarlet Letter*, 89.
13. Ibid., 187.
14. Ibid.
15. Metcalf, *Herman Melville*, 61.
16. Ibid., 57.
17. Ibid., 58.
18. Ibid., 70.
19. Ibid., 77.
20. Ibid., 111.
21. Herman Melville, "Hawthorne and His Mosses," *The Portable Melville*, ed. Jay Leyda (New York: Viking, 1959), 406.
22. Metcalf, *Herman Melville*, 129.
23. Herman Melville, *Moby-Dick, or The Whale*, ed. Luther S. Mansfield and Howard P. Vincent (New York: Hendricks House, 1962), 47.
24. Ibid., 47–48.
25. Ibid., 48.
26. Ibid., 73.
27. Ibid.
28. Ibid., 122.
29. Ibid., 181.
30. Ibid., 184.
31. Ibid., 161–62.
32. Ibid.
33. Ibid., 484.
34. Ibid., 536.
35. Ibid., 51.
36. Ibid., 308.
37. Ibid., 372.
38. Metcalf, *Herman Melville*, 161.
39. Ibid.
40. Melville, *Moby-Dick*, 486.
41. Cited by Bergen Evans, *Dictionary of Quotations* (New York: Delacorte Press, 1968), 75.
42. W. H. Auden, "Herman Melville," *The Oxford Book of American Verse*, ed. F. O. Matthiessen (New York: Oxford University Press, 1950), 1044.
43. Melville, *Moby-Dick*, 48.

Chapter 5

1. Robert Wooster Stallman, *Stephen Crane: A Biography* (New York: Braziller, 1968), 181.
2. Fredson Bowers, ed., *Stephen Crane: Prose and Poetry*, poem LIII (New York: The Library of America, 1984), 1318.
3. John Berryman, *Stephen Crane* (New York: William Sloane Associates, 1950), 14.
4. Bowers, *Prose and Poetry*, poem XII, 1302.
5. Stallman, *Stephen Crane*, 13.

6. Daniel G. Hoffman, *The Poetry of Stephen Crane* (New York: Columbia University Press, 1971), 45.

7. William Cullen Bryant, "Thanatopsis," *The Early Poems of William Cullen Bryant* (New York: Crowell, 1893), 32.

8. Hoffman, *Poetry of Stephen Crane*, 90.

9. Bowers, *Prose and Poetry*, poem VI, 1300.

10. Hoffman, *Poetry of Stephen Crane*, 91.

11. Lillian Gilkes, *Cora Crane: A Biography of Mrs. Stephen Crane* (Bloomington, Ind.: Indiana University Press, 1960), 257.

12. Bowers, *Prose and Poetry*, 901–2. All citations from "The Open Boat" are taken from this source.

13. Bowers, *Prose and Poetry*, poem XIX, 1304–5.

14. Danforth Ross, *The American Short Story* (Minneapolis: University of Minnesota Press, 1961), 32.

15. Bowers, *Prose and Poetry*, 902.

16. Hoffman, *Poetry of Stephen Crane*, 6.

17. Bowers, *Prose and Poetry*, 1335.

18. Hoffman, *Poetry of Stephen Crane*, 93–94.

19. Ibid.

20. Bowers, *Prose and Poetry*, 905.

21. Ibid., 905–6.

22. Ibid., 1348–49.

23. Hoffman, *Poetry of Stephen Crane*, 97.

24. Bowers, *Prose and Poetry*, 902.

25. Ibid.

26. Ibid., 908.

27. Berryman, *Stephen Crane*, 89.

Chapter 6

1. Van Wyck Brooks, *The Ordeal of Mark Twain* (New York: Dutton, 1933), 17.

2. Justin Kaplan, ed., *Great Short Works of Mark Twain* (New York: Harper and Row, 1967), 162.

3. Justin Kaplan, *Mark Twain: A Profile* (New York: Hill and Wang, 1967), 215.

4. Robert E. Spiller, et al., *Literary History of the United States* (London: Macmillan, 1969), 937.

5. Ibid., 936.

6. Ernest Hemingway, *Green Hills of Africa* (New York: Scribner's, 1935), 22.

7. Mark Twain, *Adventures of Huckleberry Finn* (New York: Norton, 1962), 7.

8. Ibid., 14.

9. Ibid.

10. Ibid., 72–73.

11. Ibid., 73.

12. Ibid.

13. Ibid., 8.

14. Ibid., 166.

15. Ibid.

16. William Shakespeare, *Hamlet* [III, 4, 97–98] (New Haven: Yale University Press, 1967), 107.

17. Twain, *Huckleberry Finn*, 167–68.

18. Ibid., 168.

19. Quoted in D. Bruce Lockerbie, ed., *Major American Authors* (New York: Holt, Rinehart and Winston, 1970), 129.

20. "The Man That Corrupted Hadleyburg," *Major American Authors*, 345.

21. Ibid., 354.

22. Ibid., 361.

23. Spiller, *Literary History*, 938.

24. Quoted in Henry Nash Smith, "Mark Twain," *Major Writers of America* (New York: Harcourt, Brace and World, 1966), 696.

25. *Major American Authors*, 325.

26. Quoted in ibid., 135.

Chapter 7

1. William Blake, "The Marriage of Heaven and Hell," *Anthology of Romanticism*, ed. Ernest Bernbaum (New York: Ronald Press, 1948), 122–23.

2. Ibid.

3. Ibid., 133.

4. Ibid., 132.

5. Ibid., 134.

6. William Wordsworth, "I Wandered Lonely as a Cloud," *Anthology of Romanticism*, 228.

7. Percy Bysshe Shelley, "A Defense of Poetry," *Anthology of Romanticism*, 975.

8. Ibid., 977.

9. Ibid., 988.

10. Ibid., 987.

11. John Keats, "Ode on a Grecian Urn," *Anthology of Romanticism,* 820.

12. *The Literature of England,* ed. George K. Anderson and Karl J. Holzknecht (Chicago: Scott, Foresman, 1953), 943.

13. Edward FitzGerald, *The Rubaiyat of Omar Khayyam* (Roslyn, N.Y.: Walter J. Black, 1942), 19–45.

14. William H. Marshall, ed., *The Major Victorian Poets* (New York: Washington Square Press, 1967), 685.

15. Ibid.

16. Anderson and Holzknecht, *Literature of England,* 1063–64.

17. Ibid., 1065.

18. Ibid., 1064.

19. C. S. Lewis, *The Great Divorce* (New York: Macmillan, 1955), 69.

20. Walter Pater, *The Renaissance* (New York: Modern Library, n.d.), 199.

21. Anderson and Holzknecht, *Literature of England,* 963.

22. Ibid., 964.

23. "From Greenland's Icy Mountains," *The Hymnal 1940* (New York: The Church Pension Fund, 1951), #254.

24. Denis Donoghue, *Walter Pater: Lover of Strange Souls* (New York: Knopf, 1997), quoted in a review by Valentine Cunningham, *The New York Times Book Review,* 14 May 1995, 15.

Chapter 8

1. Martin Seymour-Smith, *Hardy* (New York: St. Martin's Press, 1994), 400.

2. "John Keble," *The Hymnal 1940 Companion* (New York: Church Pension Fund, 1951), 479.

3. Robert Gittings, *Young Thomas Hardy* (Boston: Little, Brown, 1975), 48.

4. A. Alvarez, afterword to *Jude the Obscure* (New York: New American Library, 1961), 407.

5. "Candor in English Fiction," *New Review,* January 1890, quoted in Carl J. Weber's introduction to Thomas Hardy, *Tess of the d'Urbervilles* (New York: Modern Library, 1951), ix. All citations in the text are taken from this source.

6. William Shakespeare, *King Lear* [IV, 1, 36–37] (New Haven: Yale University Press, 1961), 103.

7. Hardy, *Tess of the d'Urbervilles,* 48–49.

8. Ibid., 90–91.

9. Ibid., 124.

10. Ibid., 508.

11. James Gibson, ed., *The Complete Poems of Thomas Hardy* (New York: Macmillan, 1976), 9.

12. Ibid., 120–21.

13. Ibid., 306–7.

14. Ibid., 66–67.

15. Herman Melville, *Moby-Dick, or The Whale,* ed. Luther S. Mansfield and Howard P. Vincent (New York: Hendricks House, 1962), 225.

16. Gibson, *Complete Poems,* 416–17.

17. Ibid., 468.

18. *The Collected Poems of W. B. Yeats* (New York: Macmillan, 1973), 213. All poems cited are taken from this source.

19. Austin Warren, *Rage for Order: Essays in Criticism* (Chicago: University of Chicago Press, 1948), 68.

20. J. I. M. Stewart, *Eight Modern Writers* (Oxford: Oxford University Press, 1963), 298.

21. Ibid., 304.

22. *Collected Poems,* 184–85.

23. Stewart, *Eight Modern Writers,* 356.

24. William Butler Yeats, *A Vision,* Book V (New York: Macmillan, 1956), 300.

25. *Collected Poems,* 226.

26. Ibid., 343.

Chapter 9

1. James Joyce, *A Portrait of the Artist as a Young Man* (New York: The Viking Press, 1968), 7.

2. J. I. M. Stewart, *Eight Modern Writers* (Oxford: Oxford University Press, 1963), 445.

3. Ibid., 426.

4. Joyce, *Portrait of the Artist,* 13.

5. Ibid., 18.

6. Ibid., 21.

7. Ibid., 24.

8. Ibid., 31–39.

9. Ibid., 33.

10. Ibid., 81.

11. Ibid., 99–100.

12. Ibid., 103–4.

13. Ibid., 145.

14. Ibid., 147.

15. Ibid., 172.

16. Ibid., 217.

17. Ibid., 223–24.

18. E. Michael Jones, *Degenerate Moderns* (San Francisco: Ignatius Press, 1993), 17.

19. Joyce, *Portrait of the Artist*, 240.

20. Ibid., 242.

21. Ibid., 243.

22. Ibid., 246–47.

23. John Milton, "Paradise Lost," I, 262–63, *Major British Writers*, ed. G. B. Harrison (New York: Harcourt, Brace and World, 1967), 227.

24. Jones, *Degenerate Moderns*, 18.

25. Diana Trilling, ed., *The Portable D. H. Lawrence* (New York: Penguin, 1955), 5.

26. D. H. Lawrence, "The Death of Pan," *The Modern Tradition: Backgrounds of Modern Literature*, ed. Richard Ellmann and Charles Feidelson Jr. (New York: Oxford University Press, 1965), 416–17.

27. Stewart, *Eight Modern Writers*, 548.

28. Ibid., 500.

29. D. H. Lawrence, "The Risen Lord," *Modern Tradition*, 921.

30. Ibid., 922.

31. Stewart, *Eight Modern Writers*, 580.

32. Ibid., 581.

33. D. H. Lawrence, "The Body of God," *Eight Modern Writers*, 591.

34. D. H. Lawrence, "Shadows," *Eight Modern Writers*, 592.

Chapter 10

1. Matthew J. Bruccoli, ed., *The Notebooks of F. Scott Fitzgerald* (New York: Harcourt Brace Jovanovich, 1972), 205.

2. F. Scott Fitzgerald, *The Crack-Up* (New York: New Directions, 1945), 141.

3. Carlos Baker, *Ernest Hemingway: A Life Story* (New York: Scribner's, 1969), 5.

4. F. Scott Fitzgerald, *This Side of Paradise* (New York: Scribner's, 1920), 282.

5. F. Scott Fitzgerald, *The Great Gatsby* (New York: Scribner's, 1925), 99.

6. Ibid., 43.

7. Ibid., 60.

8. Ibid., 99.

9. Ibid., 112.

10. Ernest Hemingway, *In Our Time* (New York: Scribner's, 1930), 87.

11. Ibid., 89.

12. Ibid., 93.

13. Ibid., 98.

14. Ibid., 100–101.

15. Ernest Hemingway, *A Farewell to Arms* (New York: Scribner's, 1929), 263.

16. Ibid., 327.

17. Ibid.

18. Ibid., 327–28.

19. Ibid., 330.

20. Ernest Hemingway, *The Old Man and the Sea* (New York: Scribner's, 1952), 17.

21. Ibid., 103.

22. William Faulkner, "Address upon Receiving the Nobel Prize for Literature," *The Portable Faulkner*, ed. Malcolm Cowley (New York: Viking, 1967), 409.

23. Hemingway, *Old Man and the Sea*, 105.

24. Ibid., 107.

25. Ibid., 121.

26. Andrew Turnbull, ed., *The Letters of F. Scott Fitzgerald* (New York: Scribner's, 1963), 79, (letter to Frances Scott Fitzgerald dated 12 June 1940).

27. Fitzgerald, *Crack-Up*, 305.

28. Ernest Hemingway, *Green Hills of Africa* (New York: Scribner's, 1935), 28.

Chapter 11

1. Friedrich Nietzsche, "The Death of God and the Antichrist," *The Modern Tradition: Backgrounds of Modern Literature*, ed. Richard Ellmann and Charles Feidelson Jr. (New York: Oxford University Press, 1965), 908–9.

2. Ibid., 910.

3. Friedrich Nietzsche, "Self-Overcoming," *Modern Tradition,* 771.

4. Ibid., 773.

5. Nietzsche, "The Death of God and the Antichrist," *Modern Tradition,* 905–6.

6. Ibid.

7. Ibid., 906–7.

8. Ibid., 911–12.

9. Martin Heidegger, "Dread Reveals Nothing," *Modern Tradition,* 838–39.

10. Ibid.

11. Jean-Paul Sartre, "Existence Precedes Essence," *Modern Tradition,* 828.

12. Jean-Paul Sartre, "Choice in a World without God," *Modern Tradition,* 837.

13. Ibid.

14. Ibid.

15. Jean-Paul Sartre, "The Common Condition of Man," *Modern Tradition,* 868.

16. Ibid., 870.

17. Oliver Todd, *Albert Camus: A Life,* trans. Benjamin Ivry (New York: Knopf, 1997), 168.

18. Albert Camus, *The Fall* (New York: Vintage Books, 1956), 145.

19. Ibid., 41.

20. Albert Camus, "Absurd Freedom," *Modern Tradition,* 848.

21. Ibid., 852.

22. Ibid., 845.

23. Camus, *The Fall,* 147.

24. Albert Camus, "The Unbeliever and Christians," *Resistance, Rebellion, and Death,* ed. Justin O'Brien (New York: Knopf, 1961), 71.

25. Ibid.

26. Ben Yagoda, "Peter DeVries: Being Seriously Funny," *The New York Times Magazine* (12 June 1983), 44.

27. Ibid.

28. Ibid., 46.

29. Peter DeVries, *Slouching towards Kalamazoo* (Boston: Little, Brown, 1983), 4.

30. Ibid., 71.

31. Ibid., 61.

32. Ibid., 62.

33. Ibid., 79.

34. Ibid., 102–3.

35. Ibid., 207.

36. Ibid., 235–36.

37. Ibid., 224.

38. Ibid., 237.

39. Peter DeVries, *The Blood of the Lamb* (Boston: Little, Brown, 1961), 234.

40. Ibid., 237.

41. Ibid., 241.

42. Ibid., 243.

Chapter 12

1. T. S. Eliot, "Religion and Literature," *Religion and Modern Literature: Essays in Theory and Criticism,* ed. G. B. Tennyson and Edward E. Ericson Jr. (Grand Rapids: Eerdmans, 1975), 24, 28.

2. *Philip Larkin: Collected Poems* (New York: Farrar, Strauss and Giroux, 1988), 97.

3. Cited by D. Bruce Lockerbie, "Laughter without Joy: The Burlesque of Our Secular Age," *Christianity Today,* 7 October 1977, 14.

4. Robert Gorham Davis, Letter to the Editor, *New York Times,* 5 July 1992.

5. *New York Times,* 14 February 1988.

6. Ibid.

7. Cited by Friedrich Meinecke, *The German Catastrophe: Reflections and Recollections,* trans. Sidney B. Fay (Boston: Beacon Press, 1972), 85–86.

8. Joseph L. Blau, "Alternatives within Contemporary American Judaism," *Religion in America,* ed. William G. McLoughlin and Robert N. Bellah (Boston: Houghton Mifflin, 1968), 300.

9. *The New York Times Book Review,* 11 March 1984.

10. Milton Himmelfarb, "Secular Society? A Jewish Perspective," *Religion in America,* 288.

11. Woody Allen, "My Philosophy," *The New Yorker,* 27 December 1969.

12. Arthur Miller, "The Nature of Tragedy," *The Theater Essays of Arthur Miller,* ed. Robert A. Martin (New York: Viking, 1978), 8–11.

13. Karl Shapiro, "Jew," *Karl Shapiro: Collected Poems 1940–1978* (New York: Random House, 1978), 78.

14. Bernard Malamud, *The Fixer* (New York: Farrar, Strauss and Giroux, 1966), 128.

15. Elie Wiesel, *Night* (New York: Bantam Books, 1982), 32.

16. Ibid., 62.

17. John Baillie, *Our Knowledge of God* (London: Oxford University Press, 1939), 5.

18. Lockerbie, "Laughter without Joy," 16.

19. Alfred Kazin, *A Walker in the City* (New York: Harcourt, Brace, 1951), 46–47.

20. Ibid., 161–62.

21. Wiesel, *Night,* x–xi.

Afterword

1. Søren Kierkegaard, "Concluding Unscientific Postscript," *The Modern Tradition: Backgrounds of Modern Literature,* ed. Richard Ellmann and Charles Feidelson Jr. (New York: Oxford University Press, 1965), 856.

2. Ibid., 857.

D. Bruce Lockerbie is author, coauthor, or editor of more than three dozen books whose topics range broadly: aesthetics, biography, literary and social criticism, history, education, family living, popular theology, and textbooks. Titles include *A Passion for Learning: A History of Christian Thought on Education, Take Heart, In Peril on the Sea, Thinking and Acting like a Christian, The Timeless Moment, The Cosmic Center, The Liberating Word, Fatherlove, Who Educates Your Child?* and *The Way They Should Go.*

After thirty-five years of teaching and administering, Lockerbie now serves as chairman of two consulting agencies: PAIDEIA, Inc., which works with schools and colleges as well as churches, helping agencies, and other public interest institutions and organizations, and The Olympvs Group, Inc., which plans, designs, and manages events and facilities for sport and entertainment.

A frequent lecturer at colleges, universities, and seminaries, Bruce Lockerbie and his wife, Lory, live on Long Island, New York.